# OFF THE BEATEN PATH®
# IOWA ➡

## Praise for previous editions

"Shift into second, pull out your Iowa map, and
discover these off-the-beaten-path destinations."
*—Chicago Herald*

"This [book] is for people who cherish
small towns and small town pleasures."
*—Pioneer Press* (St. Paul, Minn.)

## Help Us Keep This Guide Up to Date

We would love to hear from you concerning your experiences with this guide and how you feel it could be improved and kept up to date. Please send your comments and suggestions to:

editorial@GlobePequot.com

Thanks for your input, and happy travels!

NINTH EDITION

# OFF THE BEATEN PATH®
# IOWA  ➡

## A GUIDE TO UNIQUE PLACES

## LORI ERICKSON

## with TRACY STUHR

**gpp®**
travel

Guilford, Connecticut

All the information in this guidebook is subject to change. We recommend that you call ahead to obtain current information before traveling.

To buy books in quantity for corporate use or incentives, call **(800) 962-0973** or e-mail **premiums@GlobePequot.com**.

Editor: Kevin Sirois
Project Editor: Heather M. Santiago
Layout: Joanna Beyer
Text design: Linda R. Loiewski
Maps: Equator Graphics © Morris Book Publishing, LLC

ISSN 1540-1340
ISBN 978-0-7627-5042-9

Printed in the United States of America
10 9 8 7 6 5 4 3 2 1

# About the Author

Lori Erickson is a freelance writer who grew up on a farm near Decorah, Iowa. She holds degrees from Luther College and the University of Iowa, and her articles and essays have appeared in many regional and national magazines and newspapers. In addition to being the coauthor of *Iowa: Off the Beaten Path,* Lori has written the children's book *Sweet Corn and Sushi: The Story of Iowa and Yamanashi.* Lori lives in Iowa City with her husband, Bob Sessions, and sons, Owen and Carl.

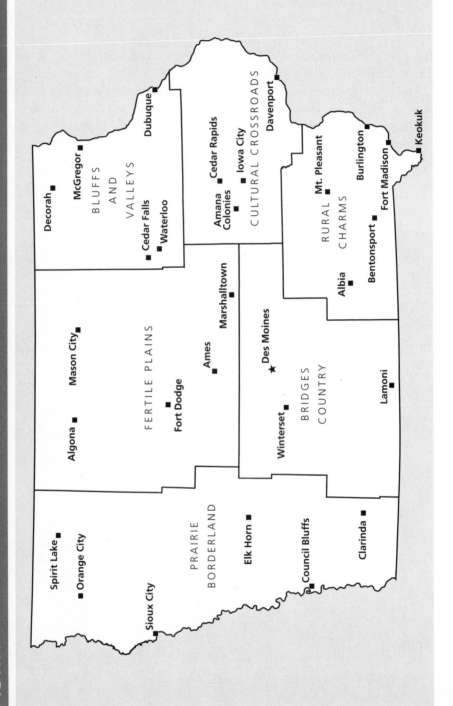

IOWA

Spirit Lake

Orange City

Sioux City

Decorah

McGregor

BLUFFS
AND
VALLEYS

Dubuque

Cedar Falls

Waterloo

Mason City

Algona

FERTILE PLAINS

Fort Dodge

Ames

Marshalltown

Amana
Colonies

Cedar Rapids

Iowa City

CULTURAL CROSSROADS

Davenport

Keokuk

Mt. Pleasant

RURAL

CHARMS

Burlington

Fort Madison

Bentonsport

Albia

Des Moines

BRIDGES
COUNTRY

Winterset

Lamoni

PRAIRIE
BORDERLAND

Elk Horn

Council Bluffs

Clarinda

# Contents

# Introduction

Nearly twenty years have passed since the first edition of *Iowa Off the Beaten Path* was published. During those years Iowa's tourism industry has blossomed, nurtured by the dedication and vision of countless citizens and civic leaders across the state.

Iowa isn't nearly as much of a well-kept secret as it was when the first edition of this book came out in 1991. While you can still find the occasional misguided person who mistakes Iowa for Idaho, you can also find many Americans who have come to view Iowa as a place that produces poets and writers as well as corn, a place of unexpected beauties, surprising strengths, and even (thanks to the movies *Field of Dreams* and *The Bridges of Madison County*) a touch of romance.

While Iowa's tourism industry has grown, what hasn't changed, thankfully, are the traits and values that have long defined the state. Here you'll still find generous and friendly people, wonderful small towns, dynamic cities, fascinating museums and historic sites, and beautiful nature areas. If this is your first visit, you're in for a treat. And if you've been here before, venture farther afield this time to discover even more of the state.

As with previous editions, this ninth edition has been revised and updated. This book represents a blending of the efforts of Lori Erickson, the original author of the book, and Tracy Stuhr, who became a coauthor beginning with the fourth edition.

On our travels through Iowa we have found many things to cherish and admire. Everywhere the land, its people, and its landmarks are bending and changing to find new ways to survive and prosper. Prairie is being replanted, historic buildings have been restored and rededicated to new uses, bicycle paths are being created from abandoned railroad tracks. We have been particularly impressed by the large number of heritage museums and historical restorations. No county and hardly a single town are without some remnant of the past that has been saved, in one shape or another, for the wandering traveler to explore.

Another major development in Iowa in the past decade has been the growth of farmers' markets and the sustainable agriculture movement. A quiet revolution is occurring in this agricultural state, mirroring the growing national interest in organic and locally grown foods. Iowa has some of the best soil in the world, and an increasing number of farmers, gardeners, cooks, and restaurateurs are using it to work culinary magic. You really haven't lived until you've tasted a freshly picked Iowa heirloom tomato, sampled a bit of Templeton Rye whiskey, or nibbled on a piece of Maytag Blue Cheese. If you're traveling through Iowa during the months between June and October, you simply must stop by a farmers' market on a Saturday morning. Iowa has more of them per capita than any other state in the nation, usually held in or near the town center. And at any time of year, you can patronize the growing number of restaurants that make use of seasonal, locally grown produce.

Although many new entries have been added to this edition, this book does not, by any means, provide a complete list of attractions in the state of Iowa. We believe, however, that it does provide a diverse sampling of the interesting sites and activities Iowa has to offer travelers. Much of the text has remained the same, updated to reflect current hours and prices. We have also added new sidebars to include some personal perspectives and reminiscences, as well as to highlight a selection of each area's attractions, events, and stories.

As you use this book you'll note that each section features a list of **New Deal murals** in the area. Grant Wood and his Stone City art colony received federal funds through President Franklin Roosevelt's New Deal program. The money was given to artists to paint murals depicting life "in their own backyard."

The work was commissioned to grace the public building projects that were being built as part of the effort to get Americans working again during

## Fun Facts about Iowa

- Iowa leads the country in pork, corn, and soybean production.
- Iowa averages thirty-four tornadoes annually.
- More than 25 percent of the nation's best crop soil is found in Iowa.
- Iowa is the only state name that starts with two vowels.
- One Iowa farm grows enough food to feed 279 people.
- Iowa boasts the highest literacy rate in the nation (99 percent).
- After the Civil War, Iowa was the first state to give the vote to African Americans.
- Iowa is home to the largest cereal company in the world (Quaker Oats in Cedar Rapids).
- Iowa is the only state whose east and west borders are formed by water (the Missouri and Mississippi Rivers).
- Iowa's weather ranges in temperature from below zero in winter (with wind chills dipping into negative double digits) to more than one hundred degrees in summer. Temperatures can fluctuate by as much as fifty degrees in one day.

## Famous Iowans

**President Herbert Hoover:** thirty-first president of the United States

**First Lady Mamie Doud Eisenhower:** wife of President Dwight D. Eisenhower

**Bix Beiderbecke:** jazz musician

**Johnny Carson:** comedian and television talk-show host

**Carrie Chapman Catt:** suffragist leader

**Buffalo Bill Cody:** Frontier scout and Wild West showman

**Norman Borlaug:** Nobel Peace Prize winner and father of the Green Revolution in agriculture

**Grant Wood:** regionalist painter

**John Wayne:** movie star

**Ashton Kutcher:** film and television actor

**Elijah Wood:** star of the *Lord of the Rings* film trilogy

**Glenn Miller:** big band musician

**Simon Estes:** opera singer

**Donna Reed:** star of the film *It's A Wonderful Life*

**James Van Allen:** space physicist

*Famous Fictional Iowans*

**Radar O'Reilly:** *M*A*S*H;* born in Ottumwa

**Captain James T. Kirk:** *Star Trek;* born in Riverside`

the Great Depression of the 1930s. More than fifty murals were painted in Iowa between 1934 and 1942, and many of these wonderful paintings can still be found across the state. While they vary in style and subject matter, most favor the Regionalist style of painting that Grant Wood had helped to popularize.

A few pointers on this guidebook: Keep a state map in your glove compartment as you travel because most of these attractions are off the interstates, and you may find yourself lost without a good map. We'd also recommend that you call ahead to verify hours and prices. Though all were correct at press time, they change frequently. Restaurants are described as inexpensive (entrees less than $12), moderate ($12 to $22), and expensive (more than $22). Lodgings have a similar rating system: inexpensive (less than $90 per night), moderate ($90 to $120), and expensive (more than $120).

We would like to thank the many family members, friends, and strangers who have given us suggestions and recommendations. In particular we'd like to acknowledge the help we've received from convention bureaus, visitor centers, and chambers of commerce across the state. Both of us have many fond memories of our encounters with volunteers, employees, and helpful citizens who went out of their way to show us the best of their communities.

## FOR MORE INFORMATION

For more information on the state of Iowa, contact the following:

**Iowa Tourism Office**
200 E. Grand Ave.
Des Moines, IA 50309
(515) 725-3083
(888) 472-6035
www.traveliowa.com

**Eastern Iowa Tourism Association**
P.O. Box 189
Dyersville, IA 52040
(563) 875-7269
(800) 891-3482
www.easterniowatourism.org

**Central Iowa Tourism Region**
P.O. Box 454
Webster City, IA 50595
(515) 832-4808
(800) 285-5842
www.iowatourism.com

**Western Iowa Tourism Region**
103 N. Third St.
Red Oak, IA 51566
(712) 623-4232
(888) 623-4232
www.visitwesterniowa.com

**Iowa Department of Natural Resources**
Wallace State Office Building
Des Moines, IA 50319-0034
(515) 281-5918
(877) IA-PARKS
www.iowadnr.gov

**Iowa Department of Transportation**
800 Lincoln Way
Ames, IA 50010
(515) 233-7964
www.iowadot.gov

**Historical Society of Iowa**
State Historical Building
600 E. Locust St.
Des Moines, IA 50319
(515) 281-6412
www.iowahistory.org

**Iowa Lodging Association/Iowa Bed & Breakfast Guild**
9001 Hickman Rd., Suite 220
Des Moines, IA 50322
(515) 278-8700
(800) 743-IOWA
www.ia-bednbreakfast-inns.com

**Iowa Bed & Breakfast Innkeepers Association**
P.O. Box 171
Spencer, IA 51301
(712) 580-4242
(800) 888-4667
www.iabedandbreakfast.com

**Road Condition Hotline**
Dial 511 (toll-free)

In closing, we'd like to suggest a few ways that we can all give back to this rich and beautiful state. It's important to patronize our small and independent businesses; they stand as reminders of where we have come from and where we are going. We need to keep everything as beautiful as we find it and make donations where and when we are able. Remember to talk to the folks you meet along the way—everything and everyone has a story. In other words, please be generous with your words and time. Listen to the many voices of Iowa, to the farmers, the meat packers, the teachers, the factory workers, the businesspeople, the artists, the children, and the retired. Listen to the farms, to the steely roar and prowl of farm machinery, to the eloquence of a faded barn, to the snort and snuffle of pigs. Listen to the voices of the cities and towns, to the sounds of demolition, construction, and renewal. Listen to the voices of the parades, the festivals, the celebrations; to the museums, the cemeteries, and the long-quiet Native American mounds. Listen to the low-throated rumble of advancing thunder and to the lush stillness of snow; to the reedy tune of crickets on a summer night; to meadowlarks, robins, and the quarrel of jays. Listen, deeply, to the whispering silence of corn.

No, Iowa is not boring, but it does demand a fresh and almost child-like imagination to truly appreciate it. Curiosity and imagination are the most important things you should pack for your travels across Iowa.

From the limestone bluffs bordering the Mississippi River to the Loess Hills flanking the Missouri, from the picturesque lakes in the north and across the rolling central plains to the southern border, Iowa is, above all, a place to savor, to enjoy, to visit, and to revisit. Welcome—and happy exploring!

—Lori Erickson and Tracy Stuhr

# BLUFFS AND VALLEYS

Northeast Iowa is a land of thickly wooded hills, steep bluffs, secluded valleys, and scenic vistas—countryside that in many places seems more like that of New England than the Midwest. From river towns rich in history to immigrant enclaves where old-world traditions remain strong, northeast Iowa offers a host of unique treasures.

## River Region

Begin your tour of northeast Iowa in **Dubuque,** one of our favorite destinations in the state. Much of what makes the city so appealing relates to its long and colorful history as a Mississippi River town. The city is named after Julien Dubuque, a French-Canadian fur trader who received permission in 1788 from the Fox Indians to work the lead mines in the area. The territory was opened to white settlement in 1833, and soon hundreds of new residents—many of them immigrants—were pouring into the new town. The next century saw a decline in mining and the growth of the lumbering, boatbuilding, shipping, and meatpacking industries. As the city grew rich, its citizens filled its streets with

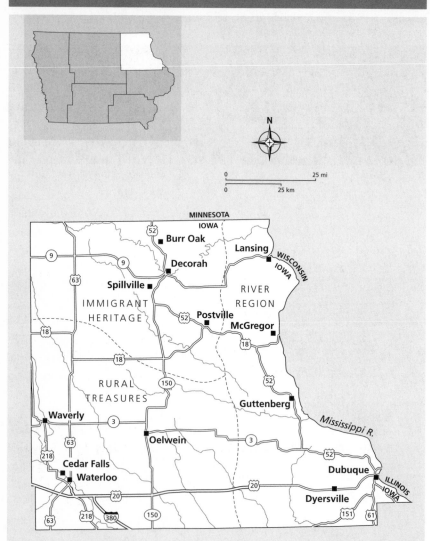

magnificent homes and buildings, structures that stand today as eloquent reminders of the city's past.

Within the past decade Dubuque's tourism industry has undergone a rebirth, thanks to a major redevelopment project on its waterfront. More than $400 million has been spent on the city's harbor area to create a complex of sites celebrating the historical, environmental, educational, and recreational majesty of the mighty Mississippi.

The centerpiece of the riverfront project is the *National Mississippi River Museum & Aquarium.* An affiliate of the Smithsonian Institution, the museum is the best place in the nation to explore the cultural and natural history of the Mississippi River.

Begin your tour at the *William Woodward Discovery Center,* which contains large freshwater aquariums, live animals (including alligators, otters, turtles, fish, and snakes), touch pools, stream tables, living-history demonstrations, and the National Rivers Hall of Fame. Here you can "pilot" a steamboat, touch stingrays from the Gulf of Mexico, see a simulated flood, and marvel at massive catfish and peculiar longnose gar (fish with long, rodlike noses).

The adjacent *Fred W. Woodward Riverboat Museum* is the city's original museum, located on the site of a boat works that once manufactured some of the largest boats and paddle wheelers in the nation. Inside are displays that bring to life the history of the river, including exhibits on Native Americans, river explorers, the lumber industry, and recreation on the river.

Outside you'll find more attractions, including the **William M. Black.** The *Black* is a large dredge boat (almost the size of a football field) that once roamed the waters of the Missouri River digging up tons of mud and muck in order to make the channel safe for navigation. Today visitors can tour the boat and even (for an additional fee) stay overnight in the crew's quarters.

## AUTHORS' FAVORITES

| | |
|---|---|
| Effigy Mounds National Monument | Fenelon Place Elevator |
| Seed Savers Heritage Farm | Waverly Midwest Horse Sale |
| Hayden Prairie | Breitbach's Country Dining |
| Bily Clocks | River Junction Trade Company |
| World's Smallest Church | Backbone State Park |

## thegreat mississippi

The *Mississippi River* is the longest river in North America, passing through ten states as it winds 2,552 miles from its headwaters in northern Minnesota to the Gulf of Mexico in Louisiana. The river serves as a water source for more than four million people and drains 40 percent of the continental United States. It is also a major flyway for migratory birds.

The harbor area outside the museum also features a wetlands walk with a Native American wickiup home and a boatyard area featuring steamboat artifacts, boatbuilding demonstrations, and a children's play area. *The Depot Café,* located in the restored Chicago Burlington Northern Railway Depot, sells inexpensive snacks, sandwiches, and refreshments.

The National Mississippi River Museum & Aquarium is located in the port area of downtown Dubuque. It's open daily from 10 a.m. to 6 p.m. (during the winter months it closes at 5 p.m.). Admission is $10.50 for adults; $8 for youth. Call (800) 226-3369 or visit www.mississippirivermuseum.com for more information.

The *Grand Harbor Resort and Waterpark,* located adjacent to the museum, offers fun of a different type. The resort overlooks the river and features 193 guest rooms, and its 25,000-square-foot indoor water park has enough slides, tubes, water spouts, rope ladders, water cannons, and wading pools to keep children entertained for hours. You can visit the water park even if you're not staying at the hotel. For more information, visit www.grandharbor resort.com or call (866) 690-4006.

Other parts of the waterfront complex include the *Alliant Energy Amphitheater,* which features special events and live entertainment, the *Mississippi Riverwalk,* and the *River's Edge Plaza.* The Riverwalk is part of a 44-mile trail connecting the Mississippi River to the Field of Dreams in Dyersville, another popular Iowa attraction that is described later in this section. The River's Edge Plaza serves as a docking site for the Delta Queen Company riverboats and other large excursion vessels.

Two more riverfront attractions are the *Diamond Jo Casino* (which offers gaming year-round) and the **Celebration Belle,** an 800-passenger, four-deck non-gaming riverboat that cruises between Dubuque and the Quad Cities. The boat is the largest luxury excursion boat on the Upper Mississippi. For information on its cruises, call (800) 297-0034 or visit www.celebrationbelle.com.

Thanks in part to the rebirth of the riverfront, downtown Dubuque also has undergone a renaissance. The area known as *Lower Main* includes new restaurants, galleries, coffee shops, and stores, attracting locals and visitors alike.

For a delicious meal head to **Pepper Sprout,** which specializes in seasonal, locally raised ingredients prepared in creative ways. It's one of eastern Iowa's finest restaurants and well worth every penny. You'll find it at 378 Main St. For information call (563) 556-2167 or see www.peppersprout.com.

Another popular place in downtown Dubuque is the **Café Manna Java** (563-588-3105), a cozy coffee shop at 269 Main St. where you can sample freshly baked pastries and pizza and artisan breads baked in a wood-fired oven.

A good way to sample the history of the city—and some delicious food as well—is on a **Victorian House Tour and Progressive Dinner** held at four of Dubuque's loveliest old mansions. Courses are served at the **Mathias Ham House,** a home built in the Italian-villa style by a man who grew rich off the area's lead mines; the **Redstone Inn,** an 1894 mansion; the **Ryan House,** a restaurant that once was the home of Civil War general "Hog" Ryan; and the **Mandolin Inn,** which gets its name from a window overlooking its grand staircase, which features Saint Cecelia (the patron of musicians) holding a mandolin.

## TOP ANNUAL EVENTS

### JUNE

**My Waterloo Days**
Waterloo, weekend after Memorial Day
(319) 233-8431
www.mywaterloodays.org

**Strawberry Days**
Strawberry Point, second weekend
in June
(563) 933-4417

**Sturgis Falls Celebration**
Cedar Falls, last full weekend in June
www.sturgisfalls.org

**America's River Festival**
Dubuque, second weekend in June
(800) 798-8844

### JULY

**Nordic Fest**
Decorah, last full weekend in July
(800) 382-FEST
www.nordicfest.com

### SEPTEMBER

**German Fest**
Guttenberg, fourth Sat in Sept
(800) 252-2323
www.germanfestinguttenberg.com

### OCTOBER

**Fall Arts & Crafts Festival**
McGregor, first weekend in Oct
(800) 896-0910

### NOVEMBER

**National Farm Toy Show**
Dyersville, first weekend in Nov
(800) 533-8293

The Victorian House Tour and Progressive Dinner is available by reservation. The cost is $48 per person. Call (800) 226-3369, ext. 214, for information.

Once you've had a peek at the Redstone Inn, you may want to return to stay the night. The wine-colored mansion is built in a gloriously Victorian style, complete with towers, turrets, and cupids frolicking across the ceiling in the front parlor. Fourteen rooms are open to guests, and rates are moderate to expensive. You'll find the Redstone Inn at 504 Bluff St.; call (563) 582-1894 or visit www.theredstoneinn.com for more information.

Another lovely place to stay in Dubuque is the **Hancock House,** a magnificent Queen Anne mansion with a spectacular view of Dubuque and the Mississippi River valley. The house, which is listed on the National Register of Historic Places, features nine guest rooms, some with whirlpools and fireplaces. A full breakfast is served each morning. The Hancock House (563-557-8989; www.thehancockhouse.com) is at 1105 Grove Terrace. Rates are moderate to expensive.

A pleasant place to stop while you're in Dubuque—at any time of the year—is the **Dubuque Arboretum and Botanical Gardens.** The gardens showcase many different plant and tree collections, including a formal herb

## "Going Up?"

Not far from the Redstone Inn is one of the city's most unusual attractions, the **Fenelon Place Elevator.** Described as the "world's steepest, shortest railway," the elevator connects downtown Dubuque with the residential neighborhoods on top of a steep bluff. It was built in 1882 by J. K. Graves, a businessman who worked downtown but liked to return home each day for lunch and a nap. The problem was that it took him a good hour to drive his horse and buggy there and back again. To solve the problem, he commissioned a small cable car modeled after those he had seen on trips to Europe and had it installed on the bluff near his home. Now he could easily fit in both lunch and a nap, and he returned to work each day a happy man.

Then Graves's neighbors started asking permission to use the elevator, and soon it had become a fixture of the city. In the intervening years, the cars and support structure have been rebuilt several times, so even if it seems like you're going to tumble to the ground as you're riding it, rest assured, the cars are safe. The elevator is even listed on the National Register of Historic Places—quite an honor for a machine designed to give a businessman time enough for a nap.

The Fenelon Place Elevator is located at 512 Fenelon Place. It is open Apr 1 through Nov 30, from 8 a.m. to 10 p.m. Round-trip rates are $2 for adults and $1 for children. (And while you're in the area, browse through the Cable Car Square shopping district at the foot of the elevator, an area of renovated homes and buildings that now house gift shops, antiques stores, and boutiques.)

garden, woodland wildflowers, lily ponds, and one of the largest public hosta gardens in the United States, with over 13,000 hosta plants of more than 700 varieties. You will be accompanied by the sound of trickling waterfalls and on Sunday by musical concerts. All of this was developed by volunteers from the community, and the admission is free. The gardens are open daily during the growing season and are located at 3800 Arboretum Dr. Call (563) 556-2100 or see www.dubuquearboretum.com for more information.

For evening entertainment in Dubuque, two performance centers in the downtown area offer a variety of shows in elegant settings. The *Five Flags Theater* was built in 1910 and was modeled after the great music halls of Paris. Today it has undergone a plush restoration that will make you think you've gone back a century in time. A few blocks away is the *Grand Opera House,* a hundred-year-old stage where Ethel Barrymore, George M. Cohan, and Sarah Bernhardt once performed. After years of service as a movie house, it is once again home to live community theater. And according to its resident acting company, the venerable old building is haunted—literally—by the spirits of actors who once performed here. "Where else would old actors go once they died?" asks one performer who's heard the ghostly voices. "It seems logical they'd go back to the place they'd loved best."

Regardless of whether ghosts make an appearance during a performance, you're likely to enjoy a show at either one of the stately old theaters. Five Flags Theater is located at Fourth and Main Streets; (563) 589-4254. The Grand Opera House is at 135 Eighth St.; call (563) 588-1305 for more information.

There are a number of other attractions in the Dubuque area that are well worth a visit, including many fine bed-and-breakfasts, the Dubuque Museum of Art, the Dubuque County Courthouse, trolley tours, and several beautiful parks and nature areas. For more information on what to see and do in the city, call the Dubuque Convention and Visitors Bureau's Welcome Center at (800) 798-4748 or see www.traveldubuque.com.

Five miles south of Dubuque on US 52 is the *Crystal Lake Cave,* which is open from May 1 to Nov 1. The cave was discovered accidentally in 1868 when some miners, drilling for lead, happened upon this incredible natural cave. In 1932 one of these miners christened it and opened it to the public. Tours through the cave wind along a ¾-mile track, and the temperature hovers around fifty degrees so you will want to dress accordingly. You will see anthrodites—otherwise known as cave flowers—a rare form of aragonite crystals, as well as large formations of brown onyx, which only take about a million years or so to form. There are delicate hollow "soda straw" stalactites through which water flows and a crystal "chandelier" formed of still-growing, active stalactites. The cave is open from 9 a.m. to 6 p.m. daily from Memorial

Day to Labor Day; the rest of the year the hours vary. Call (563) 556-6451 or see www.crystallakecave.com for more information.

Ten miles northwest of Dubuque on CR C9Y is an Iowa dining landmark that you shouldn't miss: **Breitbach's Country Dining** in the small town of **Balltown** (563 Balltown Rd.). Breitbach's likes to boast that it's the only restaurant in the world to be visited by both the outlaw Jesse James and the actress Brooke Shields, but that's not the restaurant's only claim to fame. Breitbach's has been refreshing the palates of weary travelers since 1852, making this the oldest bar and restaurant in continuous operation in Iowa history.

During the past few years, Breitbach's has endured more than its fair share of hardship. On Christmas Eve 2007, its historic building was totally destroyed in a fire, after which the local community rallied to help fifth-generation owner Mike Breitbach and his family rebuild. Just four months later another fire destroyed the new building. Mike wasn't certain he had the strength to rebuild yet again, but once more loyal patrons and friends came to his aid.

# didyouknow?

One dairy cow produces seventy-two glasses of milk a day.

One cow hide provides enough leather for twelve basketballs.

The restaurant was rebuilt, and today it draws patrons from a wide region. The key to Breitbach's longevity is simple: homemade, delicious food, reasonable prices, and a welcoming and cozy atmosphere. In 2009 the restaurant won an America's Classics Award from the James Beard Foundation, which is given to only a handful of restaurants each year—a well-deserved accolade for an Iowa treasure. Breitbach's is open for breakfast, lunch, and dinner (closed Mon from Nov 2 through Mar 14). For information call (563) 552-2220.

Before heading north along the Mississippi, you may want to take a short detour east to the small town of **Dyersville.** One of its attractions is the **National Farm Toy Museum,** a facility housing more than 30,000 rare and antique farm toys as well as newer items, all designed to reflect the agricultural heritage of the nation. There are also interactive displays describing the lives of farm families from the post–Civil War era to the present.

The National Farm Toy Museum is located near the junction of IA 136 and US 20 at 1110 Sixth Ave. Court Southeast; (877) 475-2727. Hours are 8 a.m. to 6 p.m. every day. Admission is $5 for adults and $3 for children (under six free). For more information see www.nationalfarmtoymuseum.com.

Dyersville has become known as the Farm Toy Capital of the World not only because of the museum but also because of the fact that three of the world's major farm toy manufacturers are located here: RC2, Scale Models, and

SpecCast. Each November the town hosts the ***National Farm Toy Show,*** an event that attracts thousands of toy collectors and exhibitors. There are also a half dozen stores here that sell farm toys.

Another attraction in Dyersville is the ***Basilica of St. Francis Xavier,*** one of the finest examples of Gothic architecture in the Midwest. The church has a main altar of Italian marble and Mexican onyx, a pulpit of butternut, and twin towers that rise to a height of 212 feet. It was given the title of basilica in 1956 in recognition of its outstanding architecture and spiritual significance and is one of only forty-one basilicas in the United States. Thanks to the generosity of a local family, in 2000–01 the basilica underwent a $1 million restoration.

Visitors are welcome to visit the church at 104 Third St. Southwest. Information packets are available at the main entrance for self-guided tours. The basilica is open daily from sunrise to sunset.

Doll lovers won't want to miss the ***Dyer-Botsford Doll Museum,*** home to a collection of more than 1,200 dolls plus rare Christmas ornaments. The Victorian-era structure was once the home of Dyersville's founder and is open daily from May through Nov. The museum (563-875-2414) is at 331 First Ave. East in Dyersville.

Three miles northeast of Dyersville is the **Field of Dreams** *Movie Site.* *Field of Dreams,* filmed here in 1988, tells the story of an Iowa farmer who plows up his field to build a baseball diamond so that "Shoeless" Joe Jackson and his fellow players can return to play (the men were banned from baseball

## Toys 'R' Dyersville

Dyersville's first toy factory was founded after World War II by Fred Ertl Sr. During the war all metal toy production had stopped, and after the conflict ended there was a tremendous demand for toys (think of all those newly hatched baby boomers). Ertl started making toy tractors in his basement to earn some extra money, and soon it became his full-time business.

Over the next four decades, the *Ertl Company* grew to become the world's leading farm toy manufacturer. In 1999 it merged with Racing Champions, a maker of die-cast collectibles, to become *RC2*. While the company now makes its toys overseas, its Dyersville plant continues to serve as a sales and distribution center, employing 160 people.

Fred's son, Joe Ertl, meanwhile, carries on the family toy-making tradition at *Scale Models*, a Dyersville company he founded in 1971. The company's 140 employees make farm toys in a wide variety of designs, tiny models of the huge machines made by companies like John Deere, Massey Ferguson, and Allis-Chalmers.

for allegedly throwing the 1919 World Series). Since then, thousands of fans from as far away as Japan have visited the diamond, which still remains among the cornfields. Visitors can sit and dream on the bleachers, walk the bases, and toss a few baseballs. The baseball diamond is open free of charge Apr through Nov, 9 a.m. to 6 p.m. From Dyersville take IA 136 to the north edge of town and follow the signs to the farm. The address is 28995 Lansing Rd. Check out its Web site at www.fodmoviesite.com or call (888) 875-8404 for more information.

From Dyersville head north for 25 miles on IA 136 and US 52 to the Mississippi River port of **Guttenberg.** Lovely scenic overlooks are on both the north and south ends of town on US 52. While you're here, you can enjoy Guttenberg's 1-mile river walk or visit its charming historic district. For more information about the mighty Mississippi that flows by the town, tour the **Guttenberg Aquarium and Hatchery,** which is operated by the Iowa Department of Natural Resources. Inside its tanks are many of the species that inhabit the river, from northern pike and catfish to turtles. You'll find the aquarium (which is open daily May through Sept) at 331 S. River Park Dr., south of Lock and Dam 10. Call (563) 252-1156 for information.

From Guttenberg head north on CR X56 to the small river port of **Clayton,** where you'll find the **Claytonian Bed and Breakfast** (100 S. Front St.; 563-964-2776; www.claytonianinn.com). Its owners are Don and Eileen Christensen. The rooms are individually and tastefully decorated with antique furniture, and guests also have the use of a comfortable "gathering room." Each of the three suites enjoys a panoramic view of the Mississippi and surrounding bluffs. Rates are moderate.

Just east of Clayton, visit the charming town of **Elkader,** at the junction of IA 13, IA 56, and IA 128. Take a stroll on the river walk along the bank of the Turkey River. The walk connects the downtown area with the city park. Take in the view of the **Keystone Bridge,** one of the prettiest bridges in the state, built more than one hundred years ago and still holding its own. If you want a more active river visit, one of the town's canoeing outfitters will be happy to provide everything you need for some time on the Turkey—not a bad way to spend a beautiful summer or fall afternoon!

Spend a delightful (and informative) hour or two at the **Osborne Nature Center,** 5 miles south of Elkader on IA

## it's all in the name

The town of Elkader derives its name from an Algerian emir, Abdel Kader. He was admired for his revolutionary spirit by one of Elkader's original city founders, Timothy Davis. Elkader has a "sister city" relationship with Mascara, Algeria, Kader's hometown.

# What is a Famous Gunderburger?

Visit the community of **Gunder** (population thirty-two), northwest of Elkader on Gunder Road, and find out! Gunderburgers make their home at **The Irish Shanti,** a restaurant owned by Kevin and Elsie Walsh. Bring your appetite with you—or better yet, a friend (or two or three) to help you eat one. Please believe me when I tell you that this burger is one full pound of specially seasoned ground beef—that's right, one full pound—that comes smothered with Swiss cheese, sautéed mushrooms, green peppers, and fried onions. At least, that's one variation; you can pick and choose your toppings. This is not a fast-food place. Each Gunderburger is shaped and made by hand, and a burger this size needs about twenty minutes to cook.

Oh yes, I should add that a Gunderburger does come with a bun. The bun is obviously here for decorative, not practical, purposes. You couldn't lift this burger if you tried! Most diners never make it to the bottom half of the bun but are amused by the way the top half perches on this gigantic burger like a beanie on an elephant. How much will you pay for this behemoth of a burger? $8. For a little over $2 more you can also get a small mountain of hash browns or American fries. There are plenty of other choices on the menu as well, but really, someone in your party is going to have to order this monster of a meal.

For more information call The Irish Shanti at (563) 864-9289. The address is 17455 Gunder Rd., Gunder.

13. This place is one of Iowa's best-kept secrets. Set on 300 acres of diverse and well-maintained grounds along the Volga River, the Osborne is an educational treasure. The center itself houses natural exhibits galore. On the grounds is one of Iowa's largest wildlife farms, with more than fifty species of animals and birds, even a couple of (not native) peacocks! In addition, there are a variety of trails for hiking and cross-country skiing. Still not tired? Take a look around the pioneer village. Call (563) 245-1516 for more information.

North of Clayton is **McGregor,** a river town that's one of the loveliest in the state. The explorers Marquette and Joliet passed through here in 1673, followed by Zebulon Pike in 1805. Pike lent his name to the 500-foot bluff that towers above the town (though the peak he later climbed in Colorado would gain greater fame). The scenic spot—one of the most beautiful along the entire Mississippi River—is part of **Pike's Peak State Park,** located 2 miles southeast of McGregor on IA 340. Nearby are hiking trails and picnic and camping facilities.

In 1837 an enterprising fellow named Alexander MacGregor came to settle here. The son of Scottish immigrants, MacGregor established a ferry business that transported furs and other goods between the new settlement of

# A Haven for Wildlife

The Mississippi River and surrounding shoreline near McGregor are part of one of the nation's ecological treasures: the *Upper Mississippi River National Wildlife and Fish Refuge.* Established in 1924, the refuge stretches from Wabasha, Minnesota, to the Quad Cities and is the longest wildlife refuge in the lower forty-eight states. It encompasses more than 200,000 acres of water, wetlands, wooded islands, forest, and prairie along 261 river miles.

Hundreds of species of birds, mammals, reptiles, amphibians, and fish make their home here. The refuge is critically important because of the reduction of habitat elsewhere throughout the Midwest. Natural lakes are increasingly scarce, bottomland forests are vanishing, and more than half of the wetlands have been lost.

More than one hundred bald eagle nests are present in the refuge, which also each year provides a vital migratory bird corridor for thousands of waterfowl, songbirds, and raptors. You can also see muskrat, mink, beaver, otter, weasel, fox, raccoon, and jackrabbits.

The best way to see the refuge is by canoeing its secluded backwaters. For more information on this national treasure, stop by the visitor center on US 18 North just outside of McGregor.

MacGregor's Landing on the west bank of the river and Prairie du Chien on the east bank. The town bustled with steamboat traffic and commerce, and by 1865 the town's population had grown to more than 5,500.

The nineteenth century saw a number of memorable characters pass through the town. The best-known of early residents was the Ringling family of circus fame. The five Ringling brothers spent part of their childhood in McGregor (the "a" having been dropped from its original name) and staged their earliest shows here before leaving for larger venues. Diamond Jo Reynolds was another larger-than-life resident. He operated a thriving riverboat business from a building that still stands at 123 A St.

The decline of the steamboat era brought a decline in the town's fortunes as well, with the population eventually dwindling down to a few hundred people. But through the next century McGregor attracted a faithful cadre of residents who treasured the slow pace of life along the river. Visitors came to the area as well, people drawn to the beauty of the Mississippi and also to the town's many antiques stores.

The most recent chapter in the town's history began about a decade ago, when a new generation of residents began to revitalize McGregor's fortunes. The area's beautiful scenery is still the primary draw, especially in the fall when the surrounding hills are full of color. McGregor's fall festival on the first two weekends in October draws between 10,000 and 15,000 visitors. But increasingly it's a year-round destination as well, with a number of fine new stores and restaurants.

The **Old Man River Brewery and Restaurant** is one of the new businesses fueling the economic rebirth. The thriving microbrewery and restaurant is located in the 1880s building once owned by Diamond Jo Reynolds at 123 A St. Quench your thirst with a dunkel lager; then try the Sleepy Old Man burger with the ale-battered onion rings. Call (563) 873-1999 or see www.oldmanriver brewery.com for information.

Another bright spot in the downtown is **Paper Moon**, a bookstore and gift shop owned by the mother-and-daughter team of Jennifer and Louise White. The store's resident cats draw nearly as much attention as their whimsical range of merchandise. Paper Moon (866-496-8480) is at 206 A St.

## Sandhill Cranes

Sandhill cranes migrate to and from their winter campground in Florida over a large portion of the upper Midwest in the spring and fall. Spring is a more popular time to watch for them because their fall migration is much more relaxed and leisurely than the businesslike one they make in the spring. This is because they have to make accommodations for their young that cannot fly either as fast or as far. (I'm sure at least a few of you know what I'm talking about!) They may fly as much as 300 miles a day at an altitude below 5,000 feet. You can recognize them by their appearance during flight—long necks stretched out in front, longer legs trailing behind—and their bugling calls can be heard for miles. During migration the birds "paint" themselves, preening mud into their gray feathers for camouflage. When you see them in the Midwest, they will appear to be brown.

Younger birds form "bachelor flocks," feeding and nesting together until they settle down. Males and females mate for life at about four years of age. Their nests are adequate yet plain (just a bunch of marsh plants piled on the ground), but they seem content. Sandhill cranes are most active just before sunrise and just after sunset.

Listen for their unison calls during these times, the one-noted male and the two-noted female singing together. The female usually lays two eggs in April or early May, and incubation takes about a month. When one bird leaves the nest to forage, the other takes over incubation duties. Unison calls, I am told, are particularly loud at this time. Cranes, like people, have difficulty deciding what to have for dinner.

The International Crane Foundation sponsors the **Midwest Sandhill Crane Count** every year. Volunteers take to the fields on a designated morning in April to count cranes. If you are interested in participating, contact the foundation at (608) 356-9462. What a great way to learn about some fly-by-night neighbors. (Just kidding. These cranes almost always travel by day—no "red-eye flights" here!)

Just up the street from the Paper Moon is the ***River Junction Trade Company,*** a store that has a most unusual niche. Located in an 1880s-era storefront, the company was founded in 1973 by Jim Boeke, a man who has been fascinated by the Old West since he was a boy. The store sells reproductions of nineteenth-century dry goods ranging from bib-front shirts and ladies' corsets to frock coats. In addition to serving local customers, the store does a thriving business with reenactors and Hollywood movie sets, including the recent films *Public Enemies* and *The Assassination of Jesse James by the Coward Robert Ford.* The store (866-259-9172) is at 312 Main St. For more information see www.riverjunction.com.

Next head to ***Spook Cave,*** 7 miles west of McGregor near the junction of US 52 and US 18. Here you can take what's billed as "America's longest underground boat tour." Bring your sweater (the temperature is usually forty-seven degrees) and take a half-hour guided cruise. The tour is the perfect activity for a hot Iowa summer afternoon.

Spook Cave tours are $10 for adults and $7 for children. The cave is open from 9 a.m. to 5:30 p.m. daily from Memorial Day through Labor Day

## The Mysteries of the Mounds

High on the bluffs above the Mississippi River in northeast Iowa, a chain of mysterious mounds stand as mute reminders of a civilization that flourished here more than a thousand years ago.

The first animal-shaped mounds were built around 650 A.D. Each was constructed by digging up soil from the forest floor and clay from the riverbank and then depositing it inside an outline drawn on the ground, a laborious process that likely took hundreds of trips.

While conical-shaped mounds were usually used as burial places, most of the effigy mounds appear to have been used solely for ceremonial purposes. Perhaps they acted as territorial markers or totems for the people who built them, visible symbols of a spiritual tie to the land. Burnt residue indicates that fires were set on the head, flank, or heart regions of the animal effigies.

Effigy mound building ended here around 1300, for reasons unknown. As American settlers began moving into this region in the early 1800s, many of the mounds were destroyed by farming, road building, and logging. Others were plundered for grave offerings such as stone tools and pottery. Out of an estimated 10,000 mounds that likely once existed in the region, fewer than 1,000 remain today.

Fortunately, local groups recognized the priceless value of these northeastern Iowa mounds and worked to protect the site. Their efforts resulted in the establishment of ***Effigy Mounds National Monument*** in 1949.

and on weekends in May and Sept. Call (563) 873-2144 for more information or see www.spookcave.com. Camping and swimming are available nearby.

Five miles north of McGregor you'll find one of northeast Iowa's premier attractions, **Effigy Mounds National Monument.** This 1,500-acre area preserves outstanding examples of more than 2,000 years of prehistoric Indian mound building. Within its borders are nearly 200 known burial mounds, twenty-nine of which are in the shape of bears or birds (most of the rest are conical or linear in form). The Great Bear Effigy is one of the most impressive mounds, stretching 70 feet across the shoulders and forelegs, 137 feet long, and more than 3 feet high. The mounds are all the more impressive when you realize that their builders didn't have the ability to see the giant shapes from the air but instead worked out all the shapes from ground level.

The visitor center at the monument has exhibits explaining the mounds and the artifacts found within them, plus a film on the culture of the Indians who lived here. The center is open daily and admission is $3. Call (563) 873-3491 for information.

From Effigy Mounds continue north on the river road (IA 76 and IA 364) through the towns of **Waukon Junction** and **Harpers Ferry.** A few miles north of Harpers Ferry, the scenic river road takes you to one of the loveliest spots in the state, the tiny **Wexford Immaculate Conception Church.** Inside the exquisite stone building covered with ivy are simple wooden pews, a floor of colored mosaic tile, and an altar of lovely murals and statues. The church was built in the 1860s by a group of immigrants who journeyed here from County Wexford, Ireland. On the back wall of the church is a framed photocopy of the passenger list from the boat that brought the Wexford immigrants over the ocean, their names written in a beautiful flowing script. A peaceful cemetery surrounds the building, and just north of the church there's a shrine with a statue of Mary surrounded by blooming flowers.

Continue north on CR X52 to the town of **Lansing,** where you can enjoy a lovely view of the Mississippi from Mount Hosmer, a city park perched atop a high bluff.

Six miles north of Lansing off IA 26 are the **Fish Farm Mounds,** a smaller cousin of Effigy Mounds to the south. The site includes at least twenty-eight mounds overlooking the Mississippi River. The mound group is one of the few sites that remain of the many that once dotted bluffs and terraces along the Mississippi River.

# Immigrant Heritage

From Lansing drive 37 miles southwest on IA 9 and IA 51 to **Postville,** one of Iowa's most unusual small towns. Thanks to a kosher slaughterhouse that has been operating in town for more than a decade, Postville has a sizable population of Orthodox Jews, many of them immigrants from countries that were once part of the Soviet Union. The town has also attracted immigrants from Mexico, Guatemala, and many other nations—making Postville the most ethnically diverse small town in the state.

To sample local flavors, stop by **S & F Grocery** (121 W. Green St.; 563-864-7087), a grocery store and restaurant specializing in kosher items. The market has the feel of a Jewish deli in the middle of Brooklyn, with its shelves full of corned beef, pastrami, salami, lox, herring, bagels, and challah. At the adjoining restaurant, you can enjoy delicious kosher meals that include *schwarma* (turkey seasoned with herbs on a pita) and deli sandwiches.

## postville's most famous son

In 1946 former Postville resident **Dr. John Mott** received the Nobel Peace Prize for founding the World Council of Churches. Dr. Mott lived in Postville as a boy, and his father was the town's first mayor. Hailed as an international religious leader, Mott was particularly respected for his tireless humanitarian efforts. His boyhood home at 225 Williams St. is identified with a bronze plaque.

Downtown Postville is also home to **Sabor Latino** (142 Lawler St.), which caters to the Hispanic community in the area. The restaurant serves inexpensive, hearty Mexican entrees, and the adjacent grocery store is a great place to stock up on south-of-the-border food items.

From Postville take US 52 north for 28 miles to **Decorah,** a picturesque community that was the first Norwegian settlement beyond the Mississippi. About half of the residents are of Norwegian ancestry, and most of the half that aren't pretend that they are. Throughout the town you'll see evidence of Decorah's ethnic past, from the Norwegian *nisse* (gnomes) peeking out of windows to shops decorated with rosemaling, a type of Norwegian flower painting. Each year on the last full weekend in July, the town celebrates its heritage with **Nordic Fest,** a three-day festival featuring parades, ethnic foods and music, historical displays, arts and crafts demonstrations, and antiques shows.

To learn more about Decorah's past, visit **Vesterheim Norwegian-American Museum,** which tells the story of Norwegian immigrants from their lives in Norway to their assimilation as Americans. The name means "home in the west," and throughout the facility you'll see the clothes, tools, household

## Nordic Fest Memories

As a native of Decorah and a full-blooded Norwegian, I must admit to growing up with a somewhat skeptical view of the whole proceedings. My friends and I called the summer festival "Nordic Fester" and used to amuse ourselves by wandering the crowded streets talking gibberish in a singsong voice to make people think we were speaking Norwegian. Today, however, I can't help but admire the immigrants who ventured from the old country to make a new life in Iowa. Even though they did afflict their descendants with such culinary abominations as lutefisk (cod soaked in lye), they also left a rich heritage that's well worth celebrating.

—L. E.

objects, and everyday items used by the immigrants, as well as replicas of homes and displays on the arduous sea crossing the settlers endured. There are also many examples of Norwegian folk crafts on display, as well as a gallery of paintings by Norwegian American artists and an extensive outdoor exhibit area. This is regarded as the largest and most comprehensive museum in the United States devoted to a single immigrant group, so plan to spend several hours touring the entire sixteen-building complex.

Vesterheim is located at 502 W. Water St., Decorah (563-382-9681). From May through Oct, hours are 9 a.m. to 5 p.m. daily; Nov through Apr, hours are 10 a.m. to 4 p.m. Tues through Sun. Admission is $7 for adults, with reduced rates for children and senior citizens. For more information visit www.vesterheim.org.

Another Decorah attraction is the ***Porter House Museum*** (401 W. Broadway St.; 563-382-8465), a Tuscan villa built of native brick in 1867. Inside you'll find an impressive collection of rare butterflies, moths, and insects as well as artifacts from around the world. The Porter House is open daily from June through Aug, and a small admission is charged. After touring the museum, take a stroll through the nearby Broadway-Phelps Park Historic District, an area of lovely homes and stately trees.

While you're in Decorah you might want to take a stroll around the lovely campus of ***Luther College,*** which is one of the most scenic in the Midwest. The Decorah area also has many fine parks, including Dunning's Spring, which has a beautiful waterfall, and Phelps Park, which offers hiking along a network of trails. The Upper Iowa River, which runs through the center of town, is popular with canoeing enthusiasts. *National Geographic Explorer* magazine named it one of the "world's top 100 adventures." The area also has many well-stocked trout streams.

## Decorah's Showplace

In 1999 Decorah's *Hotel Winneshiek* reopened its doors as a lodging establishment for the first time in twenty-five years. Built in 1904–5, the three-story brick hotel had been the busy social hub of Decorah's downtown for seven decades until its conversion into apartments and gradual decline into shabbiness. Then in 1997 the neglected landmark found a fairy godmother in the form of Helen Basler, a Chicago philanthropist who had grown up in Decorah and who still cherished many ties to the community.

Basler's $4.5 million renovation of the hotel stands as a testament both to her commitment to her hometown and to the craftsmanship of the many local artisans and contractors who labored for two years to restore the building. A three-story, octagonal lobby with a stained-glass skylight serves as the hotel's focal point, a stunning hub for thirty-one luxurious guest rooms and suites. Each is individually decorated with antiques, plush furnishings, and the latest in guest amenities.

The reborn hotel also features *Albert's,* a casual restaurant well-known for its barbecued ribs, and Rifresh Day Spa.

Though Basler sold her interests in the hotel in 2002, her gift to the town of her birth will continue to benefit Decorah for many decades.

The Hotel Winneshiek is at 104 E. Water St. (800-998-4164; www.hotelwinncom). Rates are in the expensive category.

Decorah has a number of fine restaurants, including the **Dayton House** (next to Vesterheim at 516 W. Water St.), where you can sample Norwegian specialties like *lefse* and *rummogrot*. Call (563) 382-9683 for information. And one of my favorites is **T-Bock's Sports Bar & Grill** (563-382-5970) at 206 W. Water St. The inexpensive, down-home eatery is the perfect place for a brew and a sandwich (and their potato salad is legendary in Decorah).

If you're spending the night in Decorah, try the **B & B on Broadway** at 305 W. Broadway St. The turreted Victorian home was built in 1910 and offers five guest rooms. Rates are moderate to expensive. For information call (563) 382-1420 or visit www.bandbonbroadway.com.

From Decorah take US 52 north for 6 miles to **Seed Savers Heritage Farm** at 3076 N. Winn Rd. (also known as CR W34). The farm is the headquarters of the Seed Savers Exchange. This unique 890-acre farm is a living museum of historic varieties of endangered fruits and vegetables and is the largest nongovernmental seed bank in the United States. The farm is set beside limestone bluffs and century-old stands of white pine woods. Seeds—for example, 500 varieties of tomatoes, 330 of beans, 125 of peppers—are multiplied and gathered from the organic gardens and offered for sale in the barn's cathedral-like loft, which was built by Amish carpenters. Seed Savers preserves 25,000 rare vegetable varieties, including 4,000 traditional varieties from eastern Europe and Russia. About 10 percent of the varieties are grown each summer, on a ten-year rotation, to ensure fresh seeds for the collection. The Cultural History Garden displays culturally rich vintage flowers and vegetables.

The Seed Savers Exchange has also developed the most diverse public orchard in the United States—700 varieties of apples are grown there. And don't miss the ancient White Park cattle! They're from the British Isles and are distinguished by their white coats, black-tipped lyre-shaped horns, and black noses, ears, and hooves. There are only 800 in the world today, and eighty of them reside at the Heritage Farm. The gardens and gift shop in the barn are open from Apr to Oct from 9 a.m. to 5 p.m. daily. For more information call (563) 382-5990 or visit www.seedsavers.org.

Ten miles north of Seed Savers, just off US 52, you will find **Willowglen Nursery** at 3512 Lost Mile Rd., Decorah. Owners Lee Zieke and Lindsay Lee have created a little bit of paradise in this corner of northeast Iowa. You can view all the perennial plants offered for sale in their own incomparable gardens—no more guessing about what a plant will look like at maturity or how it grows and blooms. The selection of plants is large and varied and offers many hard-to-find varieties as well as those you've come to know and love. There is always someone on hand to help, whether you're just curious about a primrose or have several acres to landscape. Willowglen is open Tues through Sun from 10 a.m. to 6 p.m. from May 1 to Sept 30. Call (563) 735-5570 for more specific schedule information or to set up an appointment for the off-season.

## Uff da!

One expression you're likely to hear in Decorah is the all-purpose, ever-useful "Uff da!" Brought to the New World by immigrants, Uff da is the Norwegian-American equivalent of "Oy vey"; just the thing to say when you put too much butter on your *lefse* or lost your chewing gum on the chicken coop floor.

Norwegian jokes are also popular in Decorah. It's a testimony to the good nature of Decorah residents that they love to tell these jokes on themselves. Have you heard the one about the Norwegians and Germans who went ice fishing together? They're all casting away like mad, but while the Germans are catching lots of fish, the Norwegians aren't catching anything at all. Finally one of the Norwegians tells his friend to go over to the other group to see why they're catching all those fish. Off the man goes and comes back a few minutes later to report, "Well, it looks like the first thing they do is cut a hole in the ice."

North of Decorah you'll also find **Winneshiek Wildberry Winery.** Owners Ken and Yvonne Barnes worked for decades as dairy farmers until their two daughters helped them launch a wine-making business in 2005. In addition to 3.5 acres of grapes, they grow 750 rhubarb plants, a tart plant that makes a surprisingly good wine.

The farm's former dairy barn houses the winery, its interior refurbished by Amish carpenters into an airy tasting room and gift shop with a cathedral ceiling and oak floor. In the basement, fermentation tanks, pressing machines, and other wine-making paraphernalia stand where once the Barnes milked cows. You can find the winery at 1966 337th St. For information call (563) 735-5809 or see www.wwwinery.com.

For more information on the Decorah area, call (800) 463-4692 or visit www.decoraharea.com.

Continue north on US 52 to the site of the **Laura Ingalls Wilder Museum,** located at 3603 236th Ave. in Burr Oak. This National Historic Landmark was once home to the author of the famous *Little House* series of children's books. In the fall of 1876, the Ingalls family moved to **Burr Oak** following disastrous grasshopper plagues in Minnesota. Laura's father managed the hotel that is now the museum, while Laura, her mother, and her sister waited tables, cooked, and cleaned. The Ingalls family lived here for one year before moving back to Walnut Grove, Minnesota.

Local Ingalls fans borrowed $1,500 to purchase the hotel in 1973 and launched a campaign to raise money for its restoration. With public dances, benefit auctions, book sales, donations, and a "Pennies for Laura" campaign, enough funds were raised to open the old hotel as a museum. This building is the only childhood home of Laura Ingalls Wilder that remains on its original site. It's open daily; call for hours. Admission is $7 for adults and $5 for children. Call (563) 735-5916 for information or see www.lauraingallswilder.us.

Prairie lovers will want to take a detour east of Burr Oak to see one of the state's largest remaining sections of native grasslands, **Hayden Prairie.** The 240-acre tract is located 3 miles south of Chester on CR V26 and shows what much of Iowa looked like before it was broken by the plow. Owned and managed by the state of Iowa, Hayden Prairie contains more than a hundred species of wildflowers and attracts quite a variety of birds and wildlife.

Southwest of Decorah on IA 325 lies the ethnic enclave of **Spillville.** While Decorah is known for its Norwegian heritage, Spillville was settled by Czech immigrants. The little town takes great pride in one of its former residents, the famed Czech composer Antonin Dvořák, who spent a summer here in 1893. Homesick for the companionship of his countrymen after a year's work as director of the New York Conservatory of Music, Dvořák came to Spillville

# The Secrets of Midwestern Prairies

When it comes to loving prairies, I was a late bloomer. Raised on an Iowa farm, I had a farmer's disdain for wasted land that didn't produce crops or feed livestock. A wild meadow or stand of woods could be pretty, but in the end it wasn't worth as much as a well-plowed field.

And then I discovered **Hayden Prairie**. A stretch of grassland marked only by a modest sign, it is easy to miss as you drive north to the Minnesota border. A botanist friend took me there, and spent an hour introducing me to the life within its boundaries. I was interested, but it took something more to begin the love affair.

I came back on my own one day, looking for a place to stretch my legs on a trip north. I parked the car and began to wander through the grasses, and eventually found a spot away from the road, where I lay down on a soft mat of last year's vegetation. I breathed in the freshness of the air, felt the prickle of plants against my skin, listened to the restless whisper of the wind, and slowly, ever so slowly, the prairie began to weave me into its web.

Since then I've returned often to Hayden Prairie, and any other prairie I can find. If you're looking hard you can discover them scattered throughout the Midwest, hidden treasures tucked away in parks, along gravel roads, and scattered in patches on the occasional farm—a small section the farmer "just can't bear to plow because it's so pretty in the summer." These are the paltry remnants of an expanse of grassland that once extended from Pennsylvania and Ohio to the Rocky Mountains, and from southern Canada to the Gulf of Mexico.

At a distance these may seem to be just another stand of pasture, but come closer and they have a wild, ragged appearance. Come closer still, spend an afternoon, a season, or a lifetime, and the prairie will begin to reveal its secrets to you.

—L. E.

and spent the summer completing his most famous work, the *New World Symphony.*

The building where Dvořák lived that summer is now the home of **Bily Clocks,** a museum filled with the hand-carved clocks of brothers Frank and Joseph Bily. The two were local farmers who whiled away long winter days and evenings by carving. In thirty-five years they created twenty-five intricately carved clocks ranging in height from a few inches to 10 feet, using woods from various foreign countries as well as butternut, maple, walnut, and oak from America. Among the outstanding clocks on display are an apostle clock from which the twelve apostles parade every hour, an American pioneer clock showing important historical events, and a clock built to commemorate Lindbergh's crossing of the Atlantic in 1928.

Bily Clocks is located at 323 Main St. It is open daily May through Oct, with shortened hours in Apr and Nov. Call (563) 562-3569 for more information or to arrange a visit during the winter months. A small admission is charged.

Before you leave Spillville, pay a visit to the lovely St. Wenceslaus Church, where Antonin Dvořák played the organ for daily Mass during his stay in the village. St. Wenceslaus is the oldest Czech Catholic church in the United States.

South of Spillville on IA 24 is the town of **Fort Atkinson,** site of the **Fort Atkinson State Preserve.** Here you'll find a partial reconstruction of the only fort in the country built to protect one Indian tribe from another. It was constructed in 1840–42 to keep the Winnebago Indians on Neutral Ground (a 40-mile-wide strip of land established by the Treaty of 1830) and to protect them from the hostile Sioux, Sac, and Fox tribes. The state of Iowa acquired the property in 1921, and reconstruction of the old fort was started in 1958. Part of the original barracks is now a museum housing documents relating to the history of the fort.

A good time to visit Fort Atkinson is during its annual **Rendezvous,** held on the last full weekend in Sept. The event draws buckskinners from several states who re-create the days of the frontier. Events include cannon drills, skillet- and tomahawk-throwing contests, anvil shooting, and melodrama performances—and when you get hungry you can sample such frontier treats as venison stew and Indian fried bread.

Fort Atkinson is open on weekends from noon to 5 p.m. from Memorial Day through Labor Day. Admission to the fort and its annual Rendezvous is free (563-425-4161).

On a country road near the town of **Festina,** east of Fort Atkinson, is the **St. Anthony of Padua Chapel,** better known as the **World's Smallest Church.** The stone chapel is only 14 by 20 feet and holds four tiny pews. It was constructed to fulfill a vow made by Johann Gaertner's mother, who promised God she would build him a chapel if her soldier son survived Napoleon's Russian campaign. The son did indeed return home unharmed, and the chapel was built of locally quarried stone in 1885. A small, peaceful graveyard filled with old cedar trees is located in back of the little church and includes the grave of Johann Gaertner (who died a natural death, one hopes).

To reach the chapel, follow the signs from Festina. The building is open during daylight hours and has no admission charge.

Twenty miles east of Festina you'll find **Green's Sugar Bush** at 1126 Maple Valley Rd., **Castalia.** This is one of Iowa's longest continually operating and unique industries: maple syrup production the old-fashioned way. They just tap it! Since 1851, when current owner Dale Green's great-grandfather started his maple sugar and syrup business, the Greens have remained in business, weathering fads and fashions. On the last Sunday in March and the first Sunday in April (dates move up a day if Easter falls on one of the two Sundays), they host a Maple Fest, featuring horse-drawn wagon rides through the timber, followed by a pancake and sausage breakfast for a minimal charge. Dale says, "People call and ask me if it's muddy. I tell them if they want to eat pancakes in a church basement they should go there instead!" In other words, be prepared. People begin to gather at "the Bush" around 10 a.m. Call Dale at (563) 567-8472 for more information. The Greens also sell maple syrup out of their home year-round.

Take US 18 south of Frankville to *Clermont,* where you'll find *Montauk,* a lovely mansion that was home to Iowa's twelfth governor, William Larrabee. Larrabee built the Italianate house in 1874 high on a hill overlooking the Turkey River valley, and his wife, Anna, named it after the lighthouse on Long Island that guided her sea-captain father home from his whaling voyages.

## didyouknow?

It takes forty gallons of sap to make one gallon of maple syrup.

The fourteen-room home is built of native limestone and local brick kilned in Clermont, and it is surrounded by forty-six acres of flower gardens and trees. Inside are the home's original furnishings, including Tiffany lamps, Wedgwood china, statues from Italy, onyx tables from Mexico, a large collection of paintings, and thousands of books. The elegant and cultured mansion reflects the character of its owner, a man of boundless energy and ambition as well as great intelligence and charisma. He ran for governor on a platform that called for tighter control of the railroads, women's suffrage, and strict enforcement of Prohibition (his campaign slogan was "a schoolhouse on every hill and no saloons in the valley").

Montauk is located 1 mile north of Clermont on US 18. Hours are noon to 4 p.m. daily from Memorial Day through Oct 31. A small admission is charged. Call (563) 423-7173 for more information.

In nearby Clermont you can visit the Union Sunday School, which houses a rare pipe organ donated by William Larrabee, and also the Clermont Museum in the former Clermont State Bank building on Mill Street. On display in the museum are collections of china, crystal, coins, fossils, and seashells, as well as antique furnishings and Native American artifacts.

From Clermont head 3 miles south to *Elgin,* where you'll find the *Gilbertson Nature Center* (563-426-5740). Run by the Fayette County Conservation Board, the park features a variety of attractions each summer, including a petting zoo, a corn maze, a nature center, a campground with displays on local wildlife, and a complex of historic buildings.

## Rural Treasures

Southeast of Montauk at the junction of IA 3 and IA 13 lies the town of ***Strawberry Point.*** Though the town has only 1,500 residents, it's difficult to miss, for a huge strawberry has been erected at its city hall. The name was given to the town by soldiers, traders, and railroad workers who enjoyed the bountiful wild strawberries once found along the area's trails and hillsides. Each year in June the town holds ***Strawberry Days,*** a community celebration that culminates with the serving of free strawberries and ice cream on the last day of the festival.

Strawberry Point is also home to the ***Wilder Memorial Museum,*** 123 W. Mission St. The museum is best known for its collections of dolls and of Victorian glass, porcelain, lamps, and furniture. Much of its collection was donated by Marcey Alderson, a local music teacher and avid antiques collector who spent his lifetime acquiring exquisite pieces. Dresden, Limoges, and Haviland porcelains, beautiful glassware and lamps, and ornately carved furniture are all on display here. (A favorite with many visitors is a lamp once used on the set of *Gone With the Wind.*) The Wilder Museum is located on IA 3 and is open daily, Memorial Day through Labor Day, and on weekends only in May, Sept, and Oct. Admission is $4 for adults and $2 for students. For more information call (563) 933-4615 or see www.wildermuseum.org.

Just south of Strawberry Point on IA 410 is one of Iowa's loveliest nature preserves, ***Backbone State Park.*** The park's most prominent feature is an unusual spinelike rock formation that is known in local lore as the "devil's backbone." Legend has it that the devil lost his nerve one day and left his backbone behind as he slithered east to the Mississippi River. The park has campsites, cabins, hiking trails, and wonderful views of the Maquoketa River and surrounding countryside.

From Strawberry Point travel south to the small town of ***Quasqueton,*** where you can visit one of the state's most significant architectural landmarks. ***Cedar Rock*** (2611 Quasqueton Diagonal Blvd.) was designed by famed architect Frank Lloyd Wright and was built between 1948 and 1950. The house was commissioned by wealthy businessman Lowell Walter and his wife, Agnes, who later bequeathed their home to the Iowa Conservation Commission and the people of Iowa.

Nearly every item in the Walter house bears the imprint of the famous architect. The overall design is strongly horizontal, lines that Wright felt reflected prairie landforms. The long, low structure is skillfully integrated into the landscape and sits on a limestone bluff overlooking the Wapsipinicon River. Wright designed the furniture, selected the carpets and draperies, and

## How to Play Pony Express

First you must have some great cousins who live on a farm (mine lived between Postville and Luana). They must have ponies! A saddle and bridle are not necessary, but at the very least you must have a halter. Your headquarters should be in a culvert under the gravel road that leads to town, and you should have a network of stops where the ponies can eat. (Ponies don't like to hang out in culverts even if you have oats.)

These stops can be anywhere you choose: a neighbor's barn or an old oak tree, anywhere you can pick up mail and check out the WANTED posters. The posters are important, otherwise you would have no occasion to gallop (or trot, if that's all your pony will do—some of them are very fat). WANTED posters must have at least three things: a face (either an eye patch or a mask is obligatory), a name (Deadeye is always popular and never goes out of style), and, of course, a reward (you may want to print up some money for this). The general rule is simple: The more desperate the desperado, the higher the reward. The posters should be taped to the culvert walls and delivered to your outposts at specified times. It is always important to keep things moving.

There will be times when these desperadoes may look suspiciously like a grown-up, say a mother or father, aunt or uncle. It is vital to outrun them—remember, they are probably in disguise! Keep this up at least until dinnertime or until they reveal, usually by a particular tone of voice you will soon come to recognize, that they really are who they say they are. It's just as well at this time—no earlier!—to return to the farmhouse, stable your pony, and sit down and eat as much sweet corn and pie as you possibly can, because tomorrow will be another very long day, and the mail must get through.

—T. S.

even helped pick out the china, silverware, and cooking utensils. In addition to the house, the wooded eleven-acre site has a river pavilion, a fire circle, and an entrance gate that were all designed by Wright. The Walter house is one of the most complete designs Wright had the opportunity to create in his long and productive career.

The house is open May through Oct, Tues through Sun from 11 a.m. to 5 p.m. Admission is free. Call (319) 934-3572 for more information.

From Quasqueton go west on US 20 to the adjoining cities of **Waterloo** and **Cedar Falls.**

Cedar Falls is best known as the home of the **University of Northern Iowa,** a school founded in 1876 to fill the need for qualified public school teachers in the state. Today it enrolls about 13,000 students in a wide variety of undergraduate and graduate degree programs. One of the most prominent landmarks on campus is the UNI Campanile, a 100-foot-tall structure built to commemorate the school's fiftieth anniversary. The UNI-Dome is the other most recognizable landmark on campus. The bubble-topped building houses various sports facilities and also hosts many nonathletic events. The university is also home to the Gallagher-Bluedorn Performing Arts Center. Call (877) 549-7469 for an events schedule.

Also in Cedar Falls is the *Ice House Museum,* a structure containing artifacts of the ice-cutting industry as well as other historic items. In the days before mechanical refrigeration, natural ice was cut from the Cedar River and stored year-round in this unusual circular building constructed in 1921. Each year some six to eight thousand tons of ice were stacked within its 100-foot diameter (the circular shape allowed only one wall to touch the stacked blocks rather than two, thus slowing the melting process). In 1934 the icehouse owner lost his business, and the structure was used for a variety of purposes in the following years. In 1975 it escaped demolition when a group of local citizens raised money to restore it and open it as a museum. Today you can see the array of equipment once used in ice cutting plus photographs of the entire process, from harvesting to selling. A visit here is certain to make you appreciate your refrigerator and freezer at home.

The Ice House Museum is located at First and Franklin Streets. Hours are from 2 to 4:30 p.m. on Wed, Sat, and Sun, May 1 through Sept. Call (319) 266-5149 for more information.

Another unusual museum to visit is the *Iowa Band Museum* at 203 Main St. This historic band hall houses the memorabilia and history of the Cedar Falls Municipal Band, which has been entertaining this area since 1891. It is open Wed and Sun from 2 to 4 p.m. during June and July, or you can call (319) 266-4308 for an appointment.

Two other museums operated by the Cedar Falls Historical Society are the *Victorian Home and Carriage House Museum,* a historic Civil War–era home, and the 1907 *George Wyth House,* once the family home of the founder of the Viking Pump Company. Visit the Victorian Home and Carriage House Museum at 308 W. Third St. The George Wyth House is located at 303 Franklin St. The society also preserves the *Little Red School,* an early twentieth-century country school moved in 1988 to a location near the Ice House Museum. For more information call (319) 266-5149 or (319) 277-8817.

In the neighboring city of *Waterloo*, visit the Grout Museum District near Washington Park, which includes four sites of interest to visitors. Begin your tour with a visit to the *Rensselaer Russell House Museum*, which is considered to be the best example of Italianate architecture in Iowa. The lovely brick structure is one of the oldest homes in the county. It was built by Rensselaer

Russell, a Waterloo businessman who completed the house in 1861 at the then-princely cost of $6,000. Today it has been restored to its original Victorian splendor and is open to the public for tours.

The Rensselaer Russell House is located at 520 W. Third St. A small admission is charged. It is open Tues through Sun. Call (319) 233-8708 for more information.

Not far from the Russell House is the **Grout Museum of History and Science** on the corner of West Park Avenue and South Street. Here you can wander through an impressive variety of exhibits describing local history and the natural environment. On the lower level are five full-scale dioramas depicting a log cabin, a toolshed, a blacksmith shop, a carpenter shop, and a general store. On the upper level are displays that will inform you about the geology of Iowa, its first inhabitants, and the plant and animal life of the state. There's also a gallery for changing exhibitions and an impressive exhibit, "Engine of the Heartland," that traces the evolution of Waterloo from a small town into an industrial center.

A highlight of the museum is its planetarium. The facility features a 17-foot dome and a star projector that dramatically displays the stars, the moon, and the planets seen in an Iowa night sky. Topics range from the seasonal constellations to the chemical composition of space.

The Grout Museum (319-234-6357) is open Tues through Sat. Admission is $10; $5 for children.

The Grout Museum District also includes the **Bluedorn Science Imaginarium,** a hands-on science museum, and the **Sullivan Brothers Iowa Veterans Museum,** which honors Iowans who have served in the military. The site is named in honor of the five Sullivan Brothers, Waterloo natives who during World War II died while serving together on the USS *Juneau*. For more information call (319) 234-6357 or see www.groutmuseumdistrict.org.

A Waterloo attraction that attracts children like flies to honey is the **Lost Island Water Park.** It's not hard to see why: This place is a kid's paradise. Eight waterslides, a wave pool, a slow-moving "river," and a tree house with waterspouts make this the perfect place to spend a hot summer day. I promise that by the end of the afternoon everyone in the family will be pleasantly soaked and exhausted. Lost Island is near the intersection of US 218 and US 20. Admission is $23. For more information call (319) 233-8414 or visit www.thelostisland.com.

Other attractions in the area include the award-winning **Black Hawk Children's Theatre,** which holds performances at the Waterloo Center for the Arts, and the **Dan Gable International Wrestling Institute and Museum,** which honors the Waterloo native who was an Olympic gold medalist and

## newdealmurals

During the Depression, the Works Progress Adminstration commissioned artists to paint murals across the state. You can see these WPA murals in towns that include:

**Cresco:** Post Office

**New Hampton:** Post Office

**Waverly:** Post Office

**Waterloo:** Public Library

**Independence:** Post Office

**Manchester:** Post Office

**Dubuque:** Post Office

legendary wrestling coach at the University of Iowa. One of the area's largest employers, the John Deere Company, provides free two-hour tours of its tractor assembly division each weekday. Call (319) 292-7668 for information. For more information on any of these attractions, contact the Waterloo Convention and Visitors Bureau at (800) 728-8431 or visit www.waterloocvb.org.

South of Waterloo you'll find the *Heritage Farm and Coach Company,* located 3 miles south of *Hudson* on CR D35 at 7731 Zaneta Rd. At Dick and Marie Brown's eighty-acre working farm, you can pile into a horse-drawn wagon or sleigh and enjoy a trip down to their cabin in the woods, where you can either be served a meal or eat one you've brought in with you. The Browns' twenty-five Percheron draft horses pull you in the right direction. They were all raised on the farm and, as Marie says, "they are like part of the family." There are special events throughout the year, including a Fall Fest, a Bunny Brunch before Easter, and a "Breakfast with Santa" (the three Saturdays before Christmas). Call (319) 988-3734 for more information or to make reservations.

## Silos & Smokestacks

If you're eager to deepen your understanding of agriculture, the network of attractions known as *Silos & Smokestacks* is the perfect vacation alternative. Clustered in the northeastern quadrant of Iowa, the sites bring to life the complex story of how American agriculture has helped feed the world. Formed in 1991, Silos & Smokestacks is a private, nonprofit partnership that is one of forty-nine federally designated National Heritage Areas. It includes more than eighty communities, attractions, and events relating to agriculture, agribusiness, and the rural way of life.

The headquarters of Silos & Smokestacks is located in Waterloo, an area once known as the "land of 100 smokestacks." Here is where the machinery used to work the land was manufactured and the factories needed to process farm products were built. Other sites are scattered throughout the region. For a complete listing, contact Silos & Smokestacks, P.O. Box 2845, Waterloo, IA 50704-2845; (319) 234-4567; www.silosandsmokestacks.org.

# The Church in the Wildwood

The story behind Iowa's *Little Brown Church in the Vale* begins in 1857 when William Pitts, a young music teacher, was traveling west from Wisconsin to visit his fiancée, who lived in Iowa. On the way he stopped to take a stroll along the Little Cedar River and came across a place that he thought would make a lovely location for a church. On his return home he sat down to write a hymn describing what he had imagined, a song with a refrain of *"Oh, come to the church in the wildwood, Oh, come to the church in the vale."*

The years passed, and eventually Pitts returned to the area to teach music at a local academy. He was stunned by what he found, for a small church was being built at the very spot he had visualized in his hymn. On dedication day in 1864, Pitts's vocal class sang the song in public for the first time, and the church and the hymn became inseparable. The song later gained wider fame when it became the theme of a popular gospel group that toured the country in the early twentieth century.

From **Waterloo** and Cedar Falls head north on US 218 for 15 miles to **Waverly,** the site of the **Waverly Midwest Horse Sale.** Twice a year this event draws buyers and sellers from around the country and the world. With a sale bill that includes more than a thousand horses and mules, plus hundreds of harnesses, saddles, wagons, carriages, cutters, and sleighs, the sale is the largest event of its kind in the country. The majority of the horses sold here are draft horses—the massive Percherons, Shires, Belgians, and Clydesdales, breeds that once farmed the country. Today they're bought and sold by a varied clientele—Amish farmers, lumber companies that use them in areas inaccessible to machines, ranchers who buy them to haul hay, and places like Disney World that use horses in parades and to pull trolleys. Even if you're not in the market for a Belgian or a Clydesdale, the sale is a fascinating slice of rural life. The sales are held each year in Mar and Oct on the grounds of the Waverly Sales Company on US 218 on the northwest side of Waverly. For more information call (319) 352-2804 or visit www.waverly sales.com.

From Waverly head north on US 218 for 17 miles to **Nashua,** home to perhaps the most famous church in Iowa, the **Little Brown Church in the Vale.** The church was immortalized in the hymn "The Church in the Wildwood" and has become a popular spot for weddings. More than 72,000 couples have been married in this simple Congregational church, and on the first Sunday in August, many of them return for the chapel's annual Wedding Reunion. The Little Brown Church is located 2 miles east of Nashua on IA 346, at 2730 Cheyenne Ave. The church is open for weekday tours, and worship services are held on Sun at 10:15 a.m. For more information (or to arrange a wedding) call (641) 435-2027. Visit its Web site at www.littlebrownchurch.org.

Adjacent to the Little Brown Church is the ***Old Bradford Pioneer Village,*** a reconstruction of what was once a thriving village in the area. The fourteen-building complex includes log cabins, a railroad depot, a country school, and the building where William Pitts had his office. The village (641-435-2567) is open daily May through Oct and is located at 2729 Cheyenne Ave. in Nashua.

## Places to Stay in Bluffs and Valleys

### CEDAR FALLS

**Carriage House Inn**
3030 Grand Blvd.
(319) 277-6724
expensive

### DECORAH

**Dee Dee's Bed and Breakfast**
201 Riverside Ave.
(563) 382-2778
moderate

**Dug Road Inn**
601 W. Main St.
(563) 382-9355
www.dugroadinn.com
expensive

### DUBUQUE

**Mandolin Inn**
199 Loras Blvd.
(800) 524-7996
www.mandolininn.com
moderate to expensive

**The Richards House**
1492 Locust St.
(563) 557-1492
www.therichardshouse.com
inexpensive to expensive

### GUTTENBERG

**The Court House Inn**
618 S. River Park Dr.
(563) 252-1870
www.thecourthouseinn.biz
moderate

### LANSING

**McGarrity's Inn on Main**
203 Main St.
(866) 538-9262
www.mcgarritysinn.com
moderate

### MCGREGOR

**Little Switzerland Inn**
126 Main St.
(563) 873-2057
http://littleswitzerlandinn.certainbuddies.com
expensive

**McGregor Manor**
320 Fourth St.
(563) 873-2600
www.mcgregorinn.com
moderate

### VINTON

**The Lion & The Lamb Bed & Breakfast**
913 Second Ave.
(888) 390-5262
www.lionlamb.com
expensive

## Places to Eat in Bluffs and Valleys

### CEDAR FALLS

**Montage**
222 Main St.
(319) 268-7222
www.montage-cf.com
moderate

**My Verona**
419 Main St.
(319) 266-9920
www.my-verona.com
moderate

### DECORAH

**Mabe's Pizza**
110 E. Water St.
(563) 382-4297
inexpensive

**Rubaiyat**
117 W. Water St.
(563) 382-9463
www.rubaiyatrestaurant
.com
moderate

**DUBUQUE**

**Catfish Charlie's**
1630 E. 16th St.
(563) 582-8600
www.catfishcharlies
dubuque.com
inexpensive

**180 Main Pub &
Restaurant**
180 Main St.
(563) 584-1702
www.180main.com
moderate to expensive

**DYERSVILLE**

**Country Junction
Restaurant**
US 20 and IA 136
(800) 598-9466
www.countryjunction
restaurant.com
inexpensive

**WATERLOO**

**Cu Restaurant**
320 E. Fourth St.
(319) 274-8888
www.curestaurant.com
moderate

**Galleria de Paco**
622 Commercial St.
(319) 833-7226
www.paco-rosic.com
expensive

# CULTURAL CROSSROADS

East central Iowa is truly a cultural crossroads. Here you'll find two of Iowa's largest metropolitan areas, the Quad Cities and Cedar Rapids, as well as the cosmopolitan charms of Iowa City, home of the University of Iowa. This region also includes the state's most popular tourism attraction, the Amana Colonies, which were founded as a religious communal society and where German traditions still remain strong. Here in east central Iowa you can also explore the legacies of two of Iowa's most famous native sons, President Herbert Hoover and artist Grant Wood.

## Village Charm and City Sophistication

If I had to name my favorite destinations in Iowa, the *Amana Colonies* would certainly be near the top of my list. Part of the reason is sheer gluttony: The restaurants in these seven picturesque villages are among the best in the state, each serving bounteous portions of hearty German food. If I ever get to heaven, I hope the cafeteria there is staffed by Amana natives.

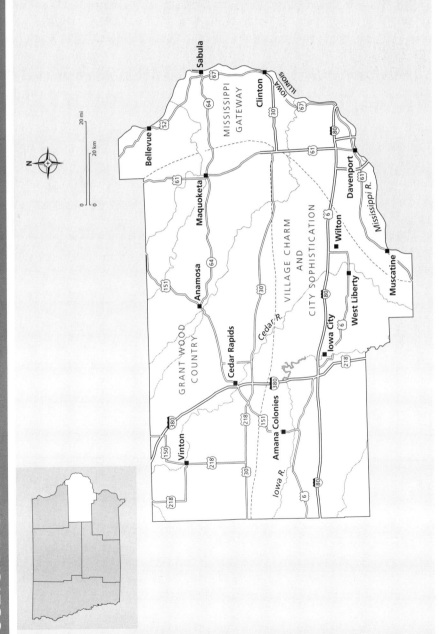

But the food is not the only reason to visit this community, located 20 miles southwest of Cedar Rapids on US 151. Its rich history alone makes it a fascinating stop. The villages were settled by a group of German immigrants, bound together by a common religious belief that has its roots in the Pietist and Mystic movements that flourished in Germany during the early 1700s. The group fled religious persecution in Germany in 1842 and settled in New York State, but eventually they sought a larger and more isolated location for their community.

They came to Iowa in 1855 and built their new home on 26,000 acres of timber and farmland in the rolling countryside of eastern Iowa. Soon they had established a nearly self-sufficient communal society, sharing work, meals, and all worldly goods. This system continued until 1932, when the pressures of the modern world and the Depression combined to convince the villagers that changes were needed. A profit-sharing corporation was formed to manage the farmland and businesses, and the community kitchens served their last meal. So ended one of America's longest-lived and most successful experiments in utopian living.

Visit the Amanas today, however, and all around you'll see reminders of the past. These tidy brick villages look more European than midwestern, with their houses clustered in the center and weathered barns on the periphery. For a better understanding of their history, visit the *Amana Heritage Museum* (4310 220th Trail), housed in three nineteenth-century buildings set on spacious grounds. There you can view exhibits about the history of the Amana Colonies, their culture and religious life, and the various crafts and industries of the society. The museum also operates five other museum sites in the Amana Colonies: the Communal Kitchen and Cooper Shop in Middle Amana, the Community Church Museum in *Homestead,* the Homestead Store Museum, the Homestead Blacksmith Shop, and the Communal Agriculture Museum in South

## AUTHORS' FAVORITES

| | |
|---|---|
| The Amana Colonies | Rochester Cemetery |
| Garden Sanctuary for Butterflies | Tabor Home Vineyards and Winery |
| The Black Angel | The Tug |
| Maquoketa Caves | Wildcat Den State Park |
| Prairie Lights Books | Wilton Candy Kitchen |

Amana. Each gives additional insights into the world of the Amanas before the Great Change of 1932. In High Amana, you can also visit an old-fashioned general store operated by the museum.

The Amana Heritage Museum is open from Apr through Oct, Mon through Sat from 10 a.m. to 5 p.m., Sun from noon to 4 p.m. It is open only on Sat in Mar, Nov, and Dec. Call for the hours of the other museum sites. A ticket that is good for admission to all the sites is $8 for adults, $15 for families. Call (319) 622-3567 for more information or log onto www.amanaheritage.org.

While you're in the village of Amana, take the time to stroll through its streets and browse in the many shops filled with the handcrafted items that have made the Amanas famous. The *Amana Furniture Shop* sells beautiful walnut, cherry, and oak furniture and has a room devoted entirely to grandfather clocks, which create a delightful cacophony of ticks and chimes. Another popular spot is the *Amana Woolen Mill Salesroom,* an outlet that carries blankets, sweaters, jackets, mittens, and other items. Free factory tours are available from Mon through Fri. Across the road is the *Millstream Brewing Company,* where premium local beers are brewed. Elsewhere in the village are wineries, gift shops, bakeries, and enough specialty shops to keep you occupied for several hours.

Though Amana has the most shops and visitor attractions, don't confine yourself to just one village. A leisurely drive through the countryside will take you on a tour of the other villages, most of which have their own shops, restaurants, wineries, and historical sites. In *Middle Amana* you'll drive past the villages' best-known industry, Amana Refrigeration Products. The business was founded by Amana native George Foerstner and is the largest employer in Iowa County. (It is currently owned by the Whirlpool Company.)

From any of the seven Amana villages—Amana, East, Middle, High, West, South, and Homestead—it is easy to get on the Amana Colonies Trail, the roads that link the seven villages. Each village has its own unique flavor, and a pleasant day or two can be spent exploring them. Take your time admiring the houses and buildings of brick, stone, or wood. If you are planning a picnic during the summer months, make sure you stop at the *Lily Lake,* located on IA 220 on the outskirts of Middle Amana. This small lake is literally covered with water lilies during mid- to late summer and offers a luxuriant display of green, gold, and creamy white foliage and flowers.

And before you leave the Amanas, enjoy a meal in one of the village restaurants, known for such German specialties as sauerbraten, Wiener schnitzel, smoked pork chops, and pickled ham. Most serve their meals family style, with overflowing bowls of salads, potatoes, and vegetables, plus delicious homemade pies and desserts. In the words of one Amana native, "If you leave here hungry, it's your own fault."

## TOP ANNUAL EVENTS

**MAY**

**Maifest**
Amana, first weekend in May
(800) 579-2294
www.festivalsinamana.com

**Houby Days**
Cedar Rapids Czech Village,
third weekend in May
(800) 735-5557

**JUNE**

**Grant Wood Art Festival**
Stone City, second weekend in June
(319) 462-4879

**JULY**

**Jazz Festival**
Iowa City, July 4
(319) 337-7944
www.summerofthearts.org

**Riverboat Days**
Clinton, July 4
(563) 242-5702
www.riverboatdays.org

**Bix Beiderbecke Memorial Jazz Festival**
Davenport, July
888-BIX-LIVS
www.bixsociety.org

**AUGUST**

**Hoover Fest**
West Branch, first weekend in Aug
(319) 643-5327

**The Tug**
Le Claire, mid-Aug
(563) 289-3946
www.tugfest.com

**OCTOBER**

**Oktoberfest**
Amana, first weekend in Oct
(800) 579-2294
www.festivalsinamana.com

Several other attractions in the villages may also strike your fancy. One is the *Amana Colonies Nature Trail,* located at the junction of US 151 and US6 near Homestead. The trail winds for more than 3 miles through hardwoods and along the Iowa River, reaching its turnaround point on a scenic bluff overlooking an Indian dam built some 250 years ago.

Another fine trail is the *Amana Kolonieweg,* a 3.1-mile route that connects the villages of Amana and Middle Amana. The trail circles Lily Lake, and it is especially lovely when the water is abloom with lilies in mid-July and early Aug. You can also watch for geese, pelicans, herons, and bald eagles.

The *Amana Colonies Golf Course* is set in 300 acres of forest and was named by *Golf Digest* as one of the top new courses in the country. Care has been taken to preserve the natural features of the land, and each hole is unique. For information call (319) 622-6222.

Overnight guests to the Amanas can choose from a variety of accommodations, from motels and campsites to intimate bed-and-breakfasts. *Die Heimat Country Inn* (4434 V St., Homestead; 319-622-3937 or 888-613-5463) offers eighteen rooms with private baths and is furnished with Amana antiques. In the late 1850s, Die Heimat (which is German for "The Home Place") was an inn for travelers, and later the building became a communal kitchen. Today it is a gracious small hotel offering a mixture of old-fashioned style and modern amenities. See www.dheimat.com for more information.

Another delightful spot is the *Dusk to Dawn Bed and Breakfast* (2616 K St., Middle Amana; 319-622-3029 or 800-669-5773). Here you'll also find a pleasing mixture of traditional Amana furnishings and modern conveniences, including an outdoor Jacuzzi. Seven bedrooms are available for guests, each with a private bath. See www.amanadusktodawn.com for more information.

In South Amana, visit *Fern Hill,* a charming emporium that sells quilts, both new and old, and quilting supplies, as well as antiques and gift items. You can find Fern Hill at 103 220th Trail. For more information call (319) 622-3627 or check out their Web site at www.fernhill.net.

The Amana Colonies Visitors Center, 622 Forty-Sixth Ave. in Amana, will give you a complete listing of attractions as well as hotel accommodations in the area. The center, which is open daily, also has an informational video presentation on the Amanas and a gift shop. Call (319) 622-7622 or (800) 579-2294 for information about the Amana Colonies or visit www.amanacolonies.com.

If you like to shop, one more destination should be on your itinerary before you leave this part of the state: the *Tanger Outlet Center* near the town of *Williamsburg* off I-80 (exit 220). Here you'll find more than fifty shops selling merchandise from nationally known manufacturers at savings up to 70 percent off retail prices. From Liz Claiborne dresses to Mikasa dinnerware, this is the place to find bargains. Call (319) 668-2885 for information.

Next head east on I-80 for 20 miles to *Iowa City,* a lovely university town that we're delighted to call home. Iowa City is also home to the *University of Iowa,* a Big 10 school with nearly 30,000 students. Most Iowans have at one time or another attended a Hawkeye football or basketball game or visited the other major draw in Iowa City: the University of Iowa Hospitals and Clinics, where more than a half-million patients are seen each year. Thanks to the hospital complex, Iowa City has the second-highest concentration of physicians per capita of any place in the country—which means that Iowa City is a great place to get sick.

But there are other, more enjoyable things to do in this tranquil college town. Aside from the Saturdays when the football team has a home game, the pace here is as relaxed as the leisurely current of the Iowa River,

## Literary Haven

Walk the downtown streets of Iowa City and you don't have to look far for evidence of the town's love for literature: The sidewalks on Iowa Avenue feature bronze panels bearing quotations from writers ranging from Flannery O'Connor and Tennessee Williams to W. P. Kinsella and Gail Godwin. The **Literary Walk** honors forty-nine authors who have a connection to Iowa City and is a testimony as well to how the people of Iowa City treasure the writers in their midst.

Iowa City is a literary mecca because of the **Iowa Writers' Workshop,** the nation's oldest and most respected program for creative writing. Based in an 1857 Victorian-style house overlooking the Iowa River, the workshop is a two-year graduate program at the University of Iowa that nurtures the next generation of fiction writers and poets.

The workshop was founded in 1936 as the first creative writing degree program in the United States, pioneering a model that other universities would later follow. Its graduates include four U.S. Poet Laureates, a dozen Pulitzer Prize winners, and a host of writers who have won National Book Awards and other major literary prizes. The contributions that the workshop has made to the nation's cultural life were honored in 2003 when it was awarded a National Humanities Medal from the National Endowment for the Humanities, the first medal ever given to a university.

Iowa City received another major honor in 2008, when it was named one of the world's three Literary Cities by the United Nations' UNESCO organization (along with Edinburgh, Scotland, and Melbourne, Australia).

The Writers' Workshop is just one of several highly regarded writing programs at the University of Iowa. The campus is also home to the **International Writing Program** (a residency program that attracts authors from around the world), the Iowa Playwrights Workshop, and a writing program in literary nonfiction.

which flows through the center of town. The university sits in the heart of Iowa City and is the focus of much of its life, but stroll just a few blocks from downtown and you'll find yourself on tree-lined, peaceful residential streets. (One neighborhood you shouldn't miss is Summit Street, a stately parade of Victorian homes and beautifully kept lawns about ¼ mile east of the downtown area.)

Iowa City's nickname is the Athens of the Midwest, and though the title may seem a bit exalted, there are an extraordinary number of cultural attractions here for a town of its size.

The best way to see the University of Iowa is to take a stroll along the river walk that runs through its center. If you're an animal lover, be sure to bring along some bread crumbs, for you're likely to encounter the determined ducks that waddle down the sidewalks here with all the swagger of frontier

cowboys. Frequent feedings have made them bold and sassy, and their rau-
cous conversations are a steady accompaniment to the bustle of university life.

Just up the hill from the river is the **Old Capitol,** a lovingly restored Greek
Revival structure that served as the state's first capitol from 1842 until 1857. Its
golden dome can be seen throughout Iowa City; thus, if you're given directions
by local residents they're likely to begin, "From the Old Capitol it's about . . ."

Designed by John Francis Rague, the building served as the first permanent seat of Iowa's territorial and state governments until 1857, when the capitol was moved to Des Moines. For the next 113 years, the building was used
for various university purposes until a restoration effort was begun in 1970.
Today the centerpiece of the Old Capitol is a magnificent self-supporting spiral
staircase that leads to the restored legislative chambers upstairs. This National
Historic Landmark (319-335-0548) is open daily except for Mon. Admission and
guided tours are free.

Next door to the Old Capitol is the venerable Macbride Hall, home for
many years to the **University of Iowa Museum of Natural History.** In
1985 **Iowa Hall** was opened, offering a comprehensive look at Iowa's geology, archaeology, and ecology. As you move through the gallery's three inter-
related exhibits, you'll witness the passage of five billion years. One of the
most impressive exhibits is a diorama depicting the arrival of Europeans into
the state in 1673, seen from the perspective of two Ioway Indians looking out
over the Mississippi River from tall bluffs on the Iowa shore. Another highlight is a life-size re-creation of a giant ground sloth, a sight that never fails
to draw a gasp from young children. Two other galleries at the museum will
intrigue those with a scientific bent. Hageboeck Hall features more than 1,000
birds, including nearly every species recorded as residents or seasonal visitors
to Iowa. Mammal Hall displays animals ranging from aardvarks to zebras. Its
specimens represent nearly every order and family of mammals, including a
giant panda from China and an orangutan from the Borneo jungle. The museum's lobby features a small gift shop, plus displays on the pioneering work of
Iowa's early naturalists. The Museum of Natural History is open daily except
for Mon. Admission is free. Call (319) 335-0480 for more details.

Though the University of Iowa tends to overshadow the rest of Iowa City,
there are many other attractions to explore here. The walking mall downtown
is the perfect place to people-watch, and during the summer months various
food vendors peddle their wares. Stop by any of the food carts on the pedestrian mall or at any of the downtown area's numerous restaurants.

Theater buffs should book tickets at **Riverside Theatre,** Iowa City's very
own professional company at 213 N. Gilbert St. It's been entertaining audiences
since 1981 with provocative, thought-provoking performances of classics and

contemporary works. During the summer months, Riverside presents an outdoor Summer Shakespeare Festival in City Park, with three plays performed in repertory. For more information, call (319) 338-7672 or see www.riversidetheatre.org.

Don't leave Iowa City without spending an hour (or two or three) at **Prairie Lights Books,** Iowa's largest independent bookstore. The downtown landmark offers readings by nationally touring authors throughout the year, but it's also a great place to visit if you just want to have a good cup of coffee or a glass of wine, or browse through a book or newspaper. Prairie Lights is open daily and is located at 15 S. Dubuque St. in Iowa City. Call (319) 337-2681 or see www.prairielights.com for information.

There are a number of fine restaurants in Iowa City, but one of the best—both for food and atmosphere—is **Devotay.** Located at 117 N. Linn St. Devotay specializes in Mediterranean cuisine. It has a wide variety of tapas, both hot and cold, as well as distinguished entrees, which change seasonally (except for the chicken salad—I have been told there would be a riot if the chef took that off the menu!). Owned by chef Kurt Friese and his wife, Kim McWane Friese (who is a potter and makes all of the cups, bowls, and plates), Devotay offers a casual and delightful eating experience. With its high ceilings and huge paned windows, there are few more wonderful places to sit and eat and watch the world go by. For more information or to make reservations (always a good idea), call (319) 354-1001 or click on www.devotay.net.

Another popular place is **The Sanctuary** at 405 S. Gilbert St. The Sanctuary serves some of the best pizza in town (as well as a good variety of other choices) and has a huge selection of international beers, in addition to offering entertainment on the weekends—usually a folk singer or a small band. The ambience is delightfully bohemian and the Pizza Fontina (a pizza covered with broccoli, tomatoes, mushrooms, and fontina cheese) is a personal favorite. The Sanctuary (319-351-5692) opens Mon through Sat at 4 p.m. and serves dinner until midnight.

## didyouknow?

The fur of the giant sloth located in the Iowa Hall on the University of Iowa campus was made out of 500 cow tails.

Don't pass up a visit to **Plum Grove** at 1030 Carroll St. in Iowa City. The Greek Revival structure was once the home of Robert Lucas, Iowa's first territorial governor from 1838 until 1841. Called Plum Grove after a thicket of plum trees on the property, the home was a showplace in frontier Iowa. In the late 1930s the state of Iowa agreed to purchase it, thanks to a local preservation effort led by a grandson of Lucas. Today it's fully restored and furnished with period antiques.

Interesting for those who garden, and even for those who don't, are the heritage garden plots on the grounds of Plum Grove. Planted with only the flowers, vegetables, and herbs that would have been used before the 1850s, these plots re-create a different, growing kind of history. On Sunday a master gardener is available to answer questions. You may also, during part of the year, watch archaeologists at work on active digs. Finds have ranged from arrowheads to a 1950s Iowa Football Homecoming pin. Plum Grove is open from Memorial Day weekend through Oct, Wed through Sun from 1 to 5 p.m. Admission is free. Call (319) 337-6846 for more details.

A newer attraction in the Iowa City area owes its existence to a natural disaster. During the Flood of 1993, massive amounts of water surged over the emergency spillway at Coralville Lake and eroded a 15-foot-deep channel. When the waters receded, a geologic treasure emerged: an ancient seabed filled with thousands of fossils. The ***Devonian Fossil Gorge*** has become a popular spot for anyone interested in geology—and a good spot to see first-hand the awesome power of a flood. The gorge is located 3.4 miles north of I-80 on Dubuque Street (turn right at West Overlook Road).

## The Black Angel

No sojourn to Iowa City is complete without a visit to the enigmatic *Black Angel,* a grave marker that is a source of local tradition and speculation. Dozens of legends cling to the marker: One of the most popular says that a grieving husband spent his savings to place a white angel over the grave of his wife, only to have it turn black overnight because of her unrevealed infidelity to him.

Another cheery story says that anyone who touches the angel will die within the year. There's a happier bit of folklore associated with it as well—college students say that you're not a true University of Iowa coed until you've been kissed in the shadow of its wings.

The real story behind the angel is a bit more prosaic, though it has its share of intrigue as well. The statue was commissioned in 1911 by a Bohemian immigrant named Teresa Feldevert for the graves of her son and her second husband. When the statue arrived in Iowa City, however, Teresa refused to pay for it, saying that it wasn't what she had ordered. The dispute ended up in court, and the woman was ordered to pay the Chicago sculptor $5,000. The disgruntled Teresa decided to have the statue erected in spite of her dislike of it—and ever since it's been a source of fascination for Iowa City residents.

This hauntingly beautiful grave marker, located in the Oakland Cemetery (1000 Brown St.), stands 9 feet tall and really has to be seen to be appreciated—I can promise you she is not what you will expect. Does her posture admonish or beckon, forbid or entreat? I leave it for you to decide.

The visitor center, run by the Army Corps of Engineers, provides a brief but interesting video of the Flood of 1993, which describes the uncovering of the gorge and includes some incredible footage of the flood itself. Also available are maps and guides to the numerous campgrounds and hiking, biking, and cross-country ski trails in the Coralville Reservoir/Lake Macbride area. One recommended trail is the Veterans' Trail, a wonderful barrier-free raised walkway with interpretive signs. Close to the visitor center, it is about ¼ mile long and is accessible to everyone.

Iowa City's neighboring city is *Coralville,* a town named after the coral formations left behind by the same sea that created the Devonian Fossil Gorge. Coralville's *Heritage Museum of Johnson County* is housed in an 1876 former school and features exhibits that bring to life the history of the area, including an early twentieth-century schoolroom. The Heritage Museum (319-351-5738) is open Wed through Sun afternoons. It is located at 310 Fifth St.

Another attraction in Coralville is the *Iowa Firefighters Memorial.* The monument recognizes the sacrifices of those who have lost their lives while fighting fires. The larger-than-life bronze statue depicts a firefighter rescuing a child, and the memorial wall at the end of the plaza lists the names of Iowa firefighters killed while rescuing others. The memorial is located at exit 242 off I-80.

Those wishing to stay overnight in the area should book a room at *The Golden Haug Bed and Breakfast* at 517 E. Washington St. It is run by Nila and Dennis Haug and features guest rooms with names that include "Swine and Roses" and "Sir Francis Bacon." The 1920s Arts and Crafts–style home has been whimsically decorated and offers cozy accommodations close to Iowa City's downtown. Their Web site is www.goldenhaug.com. Rates are in the expensive category; call (319) 354-4284 for reservations.

For more information about attractions in the Iowa City and Coralville area, call (800) 283-6592 or visit www.iowacitycoralville.org.

Eight miles east of Iowa City lies the historic small town of *West Branch,* birthplace of President Herbert Hoover and the location of the *Herbert Hoover National Historic Site* (Parkside Drive). Here you'll find his official presidential library, a museum detailing his life, the cottage where he was born, a blacksmith shop, an 1853 schoolhouse, and the Quaker meetinghouse where the devout Hoover family attended services. All are set on expansive, beautifully kept grounds, making this a favorite picnic spot for many visitors.

If you're like me, the thought of visiting the Hoover site might not fill you with excitement. My only memory of Hoover before I visited was a vague knowledge of "Hooverville" shantytowns and the grim man who plunged the country into the Great Depression. After I spent a fascinating afternoon in West

Branch, however, I came away surprised and impressed. The much-maligned Hoover, I learned, was a complex man of extraordinary abilities.

Tour the library and museum and you'll learn the history of his life. The son of an Iowa blacksmith, Hoover was orphaned at the age of ten and went on to become a noted mining engineer and businessman. He made his entry into public life during World War I as the director of food relief programs that fed an estimated 318 million victims of war and drought in Europe and the Soviet Union (take special note of the display of embroidered flour sacks sent to Hoover by grateful children). Later he became secretary of commerce and in 1928 was elected the thirty-first president of the United States—a position for which he refused to accept a salary. Defeated for reelection during the depths of the Depression, the indomitable Hoover continued his work as an active public servant until his death at age ninety. By the end of his life he had once again regained the respect of his fellow citizens, and his passing was marked by tributes from around the country and the world.

Be sure to visit the various buildings on the Hoover site, and don't miss the large statue near the library that was given to Hoover as a gift from the people of Belgium. The figure is a larger-than-life woman wearing a veil, a depiction of the Egyptian goddess Isis. Her air of mystery is irresistible.

The Hoover Library-Museum complex is open from 9 a.m. to 5 p.m. daily, and admission is $6 for adults. A particularly fun time to visit is during "Hooverfest," held the first weekend in Aug. Call (319) 643-5301 for more information or visit www.hoover.archives.gov.

Before you leave West Branch, take the time to tour its charming downtown, an area that has been named a National Historic District. A number of antiques and craft shops line the streets, and one that you shouldn't miss is **Main Street Antiques and Art,** located at 110 W. Main St. Not only will you find an eclectic and unique assortment of antiques, but in the back of the shop is a gallery of paintings by proprietor Lou Picek. Noted for their colorful and "primitive" style, they offer a unique depiction of the artist's experiences or, as Lou says, his "everyday life with a touch of humor and fantasy." Main Street Antiques (319-643-2065) is open Mon through Sat from 10 a.m. to 5 p.m. and from noon to 5 p.m. on Sun. See www.msantiquesandart.com for more information.

You might want to take a road trip along the historic **Herbert Hoover Highway,** which runs from the Old Capitol in Iowa City (see page 39) and ends where it meets the old Lincoln Highway in Lowden. This 42-mile route, designated as the Hoover Highway in 1923, was once heralded as a "short-cut"—first between Iowa City and Lowden (which was the supply station stopping point for the Chicago, Iowa, and Nebraska Railroad) and later between

Des Moines and Chicago. This route will take you through the heart of Cedar County and is well marked by the distinctive "three H" signs, some of which are still attached to the utility poles, as they were in 1923.

From West Branch head southeast to the small town of **West Liberty,** where a vibrant Hispanic community flourishes in rural Iowa. Walk its streets and you'll find several Mexican restaurants, a Mexican bakery, and a *tortilleria* where homemade tortillas by the hundreds roll off the grill each day. If you're looking for a piñata for your birthday or an order of chiles rellenos washed down with a margarita, West Liberty is the place to visit.

About 50 percent of the town's residents are Hispanic, hailing from Mexico, Guatemala, Colombia, Honduras, and other Latin American nations. The best way to sample the flavor of West Liberty is to pull up a chair in one of its Mexican restaurants. All are informal, inexpensive, and unpretentious, with menus that feature such traditional favorites as enchiladas as well as meat-for-the-more-adventurous (brain or tripe tacos, anyone?). Many consider El Patio (214 N. Columbus St.; 319-627-7334) to be the best, but you won't go wrong at any of these eateries.

West Liberty is also home to the **Eulenspiegel Puppet Theatre,** a nonprofit company that has entertained both children and adults for more than thirty years. The theater has experimented with almost every type of puppet,

## Wildflowers and Gravestones

If you're traveling the Herbert Hoover Highway, make sure you plan a stop at the **Rochester Cemetery,** located just southeast of the Cedar River bridge in Rochester. Particularly during the spring and summer months, this remarkable cemetery, set as it is on thirteen acres of natural prairie, comes alive with wildflowers and prairie grasses. Around Mother's Day the cemetery is filled with swirling galaxies of shooting stars and mayapples. Later, false dandelion predominates, punctuated by prairie phlox and golden alexanders. In late June and July, there are beautiful patches of black-eyed Susans sprinkled among the other flowers, and in August the prairie grasses glow with their subtle inflorescence. All told, more than fifty species of wildflowers have been counted here.

Don't miss the grave of Mary King in the southwest portion of the cemetery. This grave is the source of a Cedar County legend that claims that Mary King was the mother of the great actress Sarah Bernhardt. Once, immediately before Miss Bernhardt took the stage in Iowa City in 1904, a gigantic bouquet of red roses was placed on the grave. The rumor has it that the Divine Miss Sarah was in reality little Sarah King who had run away earlier with an acting troupe and was never heard of—at least under her own name—again.

often collaborating with other artists in witty productions featuring handmade puppets and live music. Most performances are held at the New Strand Theatre in the downtown, which was built in 1910 as an opera house. For information call (888) 879-6519 or see www.puppetspuppets.com.

East of West Liberty you'll find another Iowa treasure: the **Wilton Candy Kitchen**, which may be the oldest continuously operating ice-cream parlor in the nation. This old-fashioned soda shop and ice-cream parlor was built in the small town of **Wilton** in 1856 and has been owned by the Nopoulos family since 1910.

George Nopoulos began working in his family's business in 1926 at the age of six, when he was given the job of winding the record player. Today he and his vivacious wife, Thelma, continue the establishment's long tradition of serving scrumptious homemade ice cream and soda treats, as well as a selection of sandwiches. Among the dignitaries who have visited the Wilton Candy Kitchen are actors Gregory Peck (who made himself a cherry Coke behind the counter) and Brooke Shields. In the back of the building, you'll find a museum of Wilton history. The Wilton Candy Kitchen is at 310 Cedar St. For hours and more information call (563) 732-2278.

## Mississippi Gateway

Begin your tour along east central Iowa's portion of the Mississippi River in **Muscatine.** Life in this river port has always been dominated by the Mississippi River. In 1835 an influx of white settlers came to the area, and two years later James Casey started a trading post here to service the flourishing riverboat industry. Soon people began calling the area "Casey's wood pile"—though by 1850 the growing town had adopted the more elegant name of Muscatine. The word was taken (depending on whom you believe) either from the Mascoutin Indians who lived here or from an Indian word meaning "burning island." (It's interesting, however, to speculate on what the town's sports teams would have been called had the original name been kept. Casey's Wood Pile Termites, perhaps?)

You can find out more about Muscatine's history at the **Muscatine History & Industry Museum** at 117 W. Second St. The site includes exhibits on several of Muscatine's most important industries, including pearl-button manufacturing. Here you can see the complete button-making procedure, from collecting shells from the bottom of the Mississippi River through processing, cutting, and dyeing. The museum is open Tues through Sat, and a small admission fee is charged. Call (563) 263-1052 or see www.muscatinehistory.org for information.

The **Muscatine Art Center,** a combination museum and art gallery, is located at 1314 Mulberry Ave. The museum is housed in a 1908 mansion donated to the city by the Laura Musser family. The first floor is furnished in the fashion of the Edwardian era, and upstairs is gallery space for various exhibits and an art library. Connected to the elegant mansion is a modern three-level facility with gallery space for the art center's collections, which include works by Grant Wood, Georgia O'Keeffe, and Mauricio Lasansky, as well as a Great River collection of works featuring the Mississippi River. Outside is a small but nicely landscaped area featuring a Japanese garden and native Iowa wildflowers.

The Muscatine Art Center is open Tues through Sun. Call (563) 263-8282 or visit www.muscatineartcenter.org for details. Admission is free.

While you're in the Muscatine area, plan a stay at the **Strawberry Farm Bed and Breakfast,** 3402 Tipton Rd. This charming redbrick residence is owned by Karl and Linda Reichert and offers pleasant and hospitable accommodations for visitors. Karl is the great-grandson of Henry Smith, who moved west from New York in 1868 to pursue horticultural interests and built this fine house. Call (563) 262-8688 for reservations or visit www.strawberryfarmbandb .com. This is a great place to kick off your shoes and enjoy yourself. Prices are moderate.

If you visit Muscatine during the summer months, don't leave without buying one of the region's renowned melons. I've yet to taste any watermelons or cantaloupes that can compare with those grown here. Open-air markets are held on Muscatine Island from mid-July through Oct.

If you're headed to the **Quad Cities,** take IA 22 east to the small community of **Fairport.** On the riverbank next to the Fairport Landing .Marina, there is a wonderful restaurant and bar with fine river views. The **Lighthouse Restaurant,** best known for unbreaded tenderloin sandwiches, offers a casual but varied menu. There is nothing more delightful than sitting on the wide screened-in porch watching the Mississippi slide by and chatting with people at the adjoining tables. The Lighthouse is a fun-filled place, noisy with the laughter of boaters, especially during the evening hours when the porch twinkles with hundreds of tiny white lights. It is very relaxed and informal. If you want a taste of a "real" Mississippi experience, this is the place to go. The Lighthouse Restaurant is located at 2142 Water St. It is open only during the boating season. Call (563) 264-8682 for hours.

One of my favorite parks is located near Muscatine: **Wildcat Den State Park,** a beautiful area with winding trails and some lovely river views. Here you will also find the **Pine Creek Grist Mill.** The mill, originally built in 1848 at a cost of $10,000, was bought by the state of Iowa in 1927 for $87.50 after

# The Pearl of the Mississippi

Muscatine's nickname, the Pearl of the Mississippi, recalls its former status as the world's center for pearl-button production. Though the first major industry in Muscatine was lumber, by the late 1890s button making had become the city's main source of revenue.

John Boepple is credited with launching the industry. Not satisfied with the quality of buttons he could make out of animal horns in his native Germany, Boepple experimented with freshwater clams he had obtained from the Illinois River. He was pleased to find that their iridescent interior produced a sturdier and more attractive button. Eventually he immigrated to Muscatine, where, he had heard, there was a rich supply of clams that collected naturally along the Mississippi River.

Boepple opened Muscatine's first pearl-button factory in 1897, and by 1905 the area was producing nearly 40 percent of the world's annual production of buttons. Button making was a labor-intensive operation requiring a great deal of handwork. More than forty factories employed 3,500 people—more than 50 percent of the local work force—and Muscatine became known as the Pearl Button Capital of the World.

The invention of the zipper and the development of plastic buttons, alas, stifled this thriving industry. Today only three button-making companies remain in Muscatine.

it had gone out of business. It is open May through Oct (call for hours). For more information call (563) 263-4337.

If it's late in the city and you're looking for a place to stay, chug on up IA 22 to **Montpelier,** home of **Varners' Caboose,** a genuine Rock Island Lines caboose, which now sees service as a unique bed-and-breakfast. It has a self-contained bath and shower, a complete kitchen, and can accommodate up to four people. If you rent by the day, a fully prepared breakfast is left waiting for you in the kitchen. For stays of more than five days, the caboose may be rented as a "housekeeping" cabin. Varners' Caboose is open May through Nov at 3911 IA 22. For reservations call (563) 381-3652.

IA 22 will lead you to the largest metropolitan area in Iowa, the Quad Cities. The name is misleading, for there are five cities that come together here on the Mississippi: **Davenport** and **Bettendorf** line the Iowa side, while Rock Island, Moline, and East Moline hug the Illinois bank.

The first thing to realize is that these are river towns, each with a rich history that stretches back some 200 years. The area was a trading center for the American Fur Company and a battleground during the War of 1812. Davenport was the first city in Iowa to have railroad service, and it was here that the first train crossed the Mississippi in 1856. (The railroad bridge was later the cause of a historic lawsuit between the river trade and the railroad. Successfully defending the railroad interests was a young Illinois lawyer who would later make quite a name for himself—Abraham Lincoln.) During the Civil War, a prison camp for Confederate soldiers was located in the area, and nearly 2,000 Southern soldiers, far from their homes, are buried here. In the years following the war, the area became a major port for river travel between New Orleans and St. Paul.

*Arsenal Island,* the largest island in the upper Mississippi, is an excellent place to learn more about the history and military importance of the Quad Cities. The arsenal was established by the U.S. Army in 1862 and continues to manufacture weapons parts and military equipment. With 7,000 civilian and military workers, the Rock Island Arsenal is one of the area's largest employers. Because of increased security measures, you may be asked to provide a photo ID card.

There are a number of attractions here worth a visit. The ***Rock Island Arsenal Museum*** is the second-oldest U.S. Army museum after West Point and contains one of the largest military arms collections in the nation. The building is open daily except for Mon, and admission is free (309-782-5021). Also of historical interest on the island are the National Cemetery, the Confederate Cemetery, and the Colonel Davenport House. The house, which was built in 1834, is open May through mid-Oct, Thurs through Sun from noon to 4 p.m.

The ***Mississippi River Visitors Center*** is located at the west end of the island at Lock and Dam No. 15 and offers a bird's-eye view of the workings of the dam, plus interpretive displays on river navigation and the work of the U.S. Army Corps of Engineers. The Channel Project was developed in the 1930s to maintain at least a 9-foot depth in the Mississippi River channel. The result is an "aquatic staircase" created by twenty-six locks and dams on the river. The visitor center is open daily. Call (309) 794-5338 for more information.

Arsenal Island lies in the Mississippi River channel between Davenport and Rock Island and can be reached through two entrances, one on the Illinois side in Moline and one via the Rock Island Bridge.

Downtown Davenport is enjoying a renaissance thanks to a multifaceted redevelopment project along its riverfront. The ***Figge Art Museum*** houses the former Davenport Museum of Art, which was founded in 1925 as the first regional art museum in Iowa. The $47 million structure more than triples the size of the former facility and is the first civic project in the United States designed by the British architect David Chipperfield. The architect's work can be seen in many significant buildings across Europe and Asia, including the Neues Museum in Berlin and the River and Rowing Museum in London.

Rising dramatically from the riverbank, the Figge is a work of art in itself, a simple block form enveloped by glass surfaces that reflect the movements of sun and clouds. Its interior includes exhibit and educational spaces, a library and resource center, lecture hall, and a two-story Winter Garden that offers spectacular views of the Mississippi.

The Figge is particularly known for its Regionalist collection, an art movement that, beginning in the 1930s, explored the landscape and themes of small town and rural America. The museum also boasts one of the most significant collections of Haitian art in the world. Its Mexican Colonial collection, which is one of the largest outside of Mexico, is also highly regarded. Other prominent works include pieces by artists Salvador Dalí, Andy Warhol, and Winslow Homer, as well as landscapes from the nineteenth-century Hudson River School and European works presenting every major artistic period from the Renaissance to Fauvism.

The Figge Art Museum is at 225 W. Second St. and is open Tues through Sun. For more information call (563) 326-7804 or see www.figgeartmuseum.org.

The **Putnam Museum** is another major attraction in the Quad Cities. The museum's $5 million expansion has greatly increased its space. Inside you'll find exhibits on the region's heritage and the wildlife of the Mississippi River valley, as well as Asian and Egyptian galleries and a hands-on science lab. The Putnam also boasts an IMAX 3-D Theater. The Putnam Museum (563-324-1933; www.putnam.org ) is open daily. It is located at 1717 W. Twelfth St. in Davenport.

The **Family Museum** in Bettendorf is a fun stop whether or not you have young children in tow. I recommend borrowing a child for the day if you don't have one of your own; watching kids explore the exhibits within is as much fun as looking at them yourself. The museum features exhibits designed with curious young children in mind. While most museums say, "Don't Touch," this one says, "Please Do!" During your visit you can go down a rabbit hole, visit an old-fashioned farm kitchen from 1940, and turn into a bird in the Kinder Garten. The Family Museum is open daily. It is located at 2900 Learning Campus Dr. For more information call (563) 344-4106 or see www.familymuseum.org.

**Vander Veer Botanical Park** (214 W. Central Park Ave., Davenport) is a peaceful place to recover from all your sightseeing. The Rose Garden is considered one of the finest in the Midwest, with 1,800 roses representing nearly 145 varieties. The peak blooming period normally begins in early June and continues through the summer. The conservatory presents five special floral displays throughout the year, and at any time it's a lush and quiet place to wander through and enjoy.

One stop you shouldn't miss during your visit here is the **Machine Shed**, one of the state's best restaurants. The walls are filled with old farm implements and antiques (including a large collection of seed corn hats), and the food is home-style midwestern cooking at its best: dinners of crispy fried chicken, thick pork chops, and tasty stuffed pork loin; savory soups; and mouthwatering desserts, all served family style with big bowls of vegetables and freshly baked bread.

The Machine Shed is open for breakfast (don't miss their huge cinnamon rolls), lunch, and dinner and is located off I-80 at exit 292, at 7250 Northwest Blvd. in Davenport. Prices are moderate; call (563) 391-2427 for information or see www.machineshed.com.

Another attraction in the Quad Cities is the *Village of East Davenport,* an area of historic shops and homes that date back to 1851. Here you'll find nearly forty unique shops and boutiques.

You can experience the power and mystique of the Mississippi River by stepping on board the **Celebration Belle** (see page 4), which offers a variety of cruises, including lunch and dinner, sightseeing, and specialty cruises. Call (800) 297-0034 or log onto www.celebrationbelle.com for more information.

Another way to see the river is on board the Quad Cities' **Channel Cat Water Taxi** ride. This wonderful transport functions as a "water bus," departing from and returning to five landings at various spots along the river. Each landing is visited approximately every half hour. It serves as a watery link between Quad Cities' bicycle trails (each taxi has space for seven bicycles), but non-bikers are welcomed as well. Tickets are for all-day unlimited use. The Channel Cats run from Memorial Day to Labor Day. Call (309) 788-3360 for schedule information and ticket prices.

*Walnut Grove Pioneer Village,* located 9 miles north of the Quad Cities near the town of *Long Grove* on US 61, is a pleasant place to unwind after visiting the Quad Cities. Walnut Grove was a crossroads settlement in the pioneer days of Scott County in the 1860s. Today, the three-acre site contains eighteen historic buildings, including a blacksmith shop, a schoolhouse, a church, and pioneer family homes. The surrounding *Scott County Park* offers nature trails, camping facilities, playground equipment, and a nature center.

Walnut Grove Pioneer Village is open daily from 9 a.m. to sundown from Apr through Oct. Admission is free.

While you're in the Quad City area, plan a stay at the *Beiderbecke Inn,* 532 W. Seventh St. in Davenport. This magnificent Victorian "painted lady" was built by local legend Bix Beiderbecke's grandparents. As every visitor to this area knows or will soon find out, Bix was a world-famous jazz cornetist, pianist, and composer. (Davenport hosts the Bix Beiderbecke Festival the third week in July.) In this grandly spacious bed-and-breakfast, you can truly sample the life of the well-to-do of yesteryear. Not only that, it is close to the river and even has a tower room! Rates are moderate. Call (866) 300-8858 for more information or to make reservations.

A few miles north of the Quad Cities lies the charming river town of *Le Claire.* Founded in 1833, Le Claire was once a boatbuilding center and home to many steamboat captains who used to hire on with riverboats traveling past the treacherous rapids near the Quad Cities. Today it's a pleasant town of 3,000 people who take great pride in Le Claire's history and historic homes and buildings.

The town's most famous son is "Buffalo Bill" Cody, who was born on a farm near Le Claire in 1846. Cody became a Pony Express rider at the age of fourteen and later gained fame as a buffalo hunter who supplied meat for the workers building the railroad lines. In 1872 he began his long career as a showman, taking his Wild West Show to all parts of the United States and Europe.

There are several sites to visit in the Le Claire area if you're interested in the life of this colorful man. The *Buffalo Bill Cody Homestead* (28050 230th Ave., Princeton; 563-225-2981) is located about 10 miles northwest of Le Claire near the town of *McCausland.* Buffalo, burros, and longhorn cattle graze the land around the homestead, and the house is furnished with nineteenth-century items. The site is open from 9 a.m. to 5 p.m. daily from Apr 1 to Oct 31.

In Le Claire visit the *Buffalo Bill Cody Museum* (200 N. River Dr.; 563-289-5580) on the bank of the river next to the dry-docked stern-wheeler *Lone*

## The Tug!

The states of Iowa and Illinois have been fighting it out each August since 1987 in a rip-roaring tug-of-war contest. What line defines the loser? Why, the mighty Mississippi, of course! That's right—contestants from Le Claire, on the Iowa side, and from Port Byron, on the Illinois side, pit their strength against one another with ropes stretched across the width of the river. These will have to be the longest ropes you've ever seen, for the river is a half mile across at this point. I am informed that there used to be weight restrictions for the participants, but in the fierce heat of rivalry, these restrictions have collapsed. I am also informed (by an Illinois resident) that Illinois holds the edge in these competitions and that the traveling trophy currently resides in Illinois. It's time to step up to the plate and cheer on the Iowa team. There are fun things to do in both communities before and after the tug—boat flotillas, craft exhibits, and food vendors abound—and the evening explodes in fireworks when the two sides join together to host a gigantic fireworks display from barges moored in the middle of the river. This is competition and cooperation at its finest—come and join the fun!

*Star.* Along with memorabilia relating to Cody's life, the museum also has exhibits on Native Americans, early pioneers, and the history of Le Claire. The museum is open daily from May 15 to Oct 15 and on weekends during the rest of the year.

For a brochure highlighting these and other local sites relating to Cody's early life, as well as a wide variety of other tourism material, visit the ***Mississippi Valley Welcome Center*** at 900 Eagle Ridge Rd. Located high on a bluff overlooking the Mississippi, the center also features educational displays, a gift shop, and a multimedia slide presentation.

Le Claire is also home to the **Twilight,** a paddle-wheel riverboat that offers a two-day cruise along one of the prettiest sections of the entire Mississippi.

I've taken a number of cruises on the Mississippi, and I consider the trips offered by the *Twilight* to be among the very best. The food is delicious, the scenery magnificent, the live entertainment enjoyable, and the boat itself lovely. River cruises on the *Twilight* depart from Le Claire in the morning, travel upriver all day, and dock at Dubuque, where guests spend the night. The next day you can tour Dubuque and then board the boat again for a leisurely trip back to Le Claire. Cruises run mid-May through mid-Oct, and reservations are required. Tickets are $329 (double occupancy) and include all meals, entertainment, and lodging. For more information call (800) 331-1467 or log onto www.riverboattwilight.com.

An excellent restaurant in Le Claire is the ***Faithful Pilot*** (563-289-4156), overlooking the river at 117 N. Cody Rd. Here you'll find a changing and creative menu, along with homemade breads and desserts. Prices are moderate to expensive.

And then go get lost! Visit the ***Amazing Haunted Maize Maze*** at Carter Farms in Princeton, just north of Le Claire on US 67. Open during Oct (naturally!), this is a labyrinth carved from growing corn—four acres, to be exact, with a 2-mile network of paths. Don't worry; there are clues to lead you around, as well as a lookout bridge and other navigational aids. This is truly an Iowa experience—don't miss it! The maze is open on weekends and some weekdays. Call (563) 289-9999 for hours and more information.

From Princeton head north to the river port of ***Clinton.*** Like the Quad Cities, Clinton is a town dominated by the Mississippi River. During the late nineteenth century, Clinton became an important transportation and lumbering center. Today it continues to be an active industrial area.

Clinton takes great pride in its history as a river town, and you can enjoy an echo of that past at the ***Clinton Area Showboat Theatre.*** This is a theater group that performs each summer aboard the *City of Clinton* showboat—an authentic paddle wheeler permanently dry-docked on the riverbank in

# Amaizing Mazes

As a full moon rises over a cornfield in central Iowa, a rustling noise can be heard amid the stalks. Something big is racing through the plants, a creature whose pounding feet make a rhythmic sound as it runs at full speed. Its gasping breath grows louder as it nears the edge of the field, until suddenly it bursts into a clearing.

"I won!" shouts the young man in triumph as a group of his friends emerge from the corn a few seconds later, their laughter filling the evening air.

Similar scenes are repeated across Iowa each fall, as a growing number of farmers are finding a new use for corn, that most quintessential of Iowa crops.

The first corn maze in Iowa opened in the late 1990s, and today there are more than twenty scattered around the state. Farmers install the mazes to bring in some extra income, but also to introduce the public to farm life.

Humans have long loved mazes (the most famous of ancient times was built in the Minoan palace on the island of Crete some 4,000 years ago). In Europe, mazes were often created on the grounds of wealthy estates using boxwood shrubbery or yew trees. The American maze craze, which took root in the early 1990s, uses more temporary building materials, most often stalks of corn. Because the plant grows to a height of 12 feet, the intricate, looping paths of a maze create a genuine challenge, especially because of the many dead ends that are incorporated into most designs. Once the growing season is over, the corn that forms the maze is simply harvested along with other crops.

Some farmers create their own design, and others rely on companies that specialize in maze designs. The pattern is cut with a garden tractor into a cornfield when the plants are about 6 inches high. Most mazes are between four and twenty acres. Visitors are provided with maps that help them navigate the paths, and often clues and puzzles are given within the maze itself. A modest admission fee is charged, typically ranging from $4 to $8.

Most corn mazes are open only in the fall, with October being the busiest month. Many farmers combine them with additional attractions like pumpkin patches, hayrides, and petting zoos. For many visitors, corn mazes have become a fall tradition as beloved as trick-or-treating.

Major mazes in Iowa include:

- **Bloomsbury Farm,** near Cedar Rapids, (319) 446-7667, www.bloomsburyfarm.com.

- **Dan-D Farms Corn Mazes,** near Knoxville and Ames, (641) 891-8166, www.dandfarms.com.

- **Geisler Farms,** near Des Moines, (515) 964-2640, www.growingfamilyfun.com.

- **Pumpkinland,** near Orange City, (712) 737-8364, www.pumpkinlandiowa.com.

- **Korn Krazy Maze,** near Council Bluffs, (712) 366-1982.

Clinton's Riverview Park. Recalling the days when lavish showboats plied their way up and down the river, the theater is the perfect place to complete a day's touring along the Mississippi.

These aren't amateur productions, either. Each spring the theater recruits nationally to produce its June-through-August summer stock season. Performances are given in a 225-seat air-conditioned theater and include contemporary works as well as old standards. Musicals, comedies, and dramas are offered each season.

The *City of Clinton* showboat is docked along the Mississippi at 311 Riverview Dr. Call (563) 242-6760 for more information.

Travel to the north end of Clinton, and you'll find **Eagle Point Park,** a recreation area perched high on a bluff overlooking the river. The park itself contains 200 acres with numerous hiking trails and picnic areas. Be sure to see the 35-foot observation tower built of locally quarried stone that stands on a promontory above the river.

Another lovely nature area is the **Bickelhaupt Arboretum** at 340 S. Fourteenth St., Clinton. This fourteen-acre horticultural showplace features more than 2,000 plants and 600 trees and shrubs. It is open from sunrise until sunset, year-round, and no admission is charged.

From Clinton travel north on US 67 and US 52 to **Bellevue,** one of the Mississippi River's most charming towns. Begin your tour at Lock and Dam No. 12 in the middle of town, and then wander through Bellevue's shopping district, an area lined with century-old stone and brick buildings. Many now house stores selling antiques, collectibles, and arts and crafts.

For a treat of a different sort, visit the **Garden Sanctuary for Butterflies** at **Bellevue State Park.** And just what is a butterfly garden, you ask? From a butterfly's point of view, it's heaven. This one-acre garden is carefully planned to provide for the care and feeding of nature's most beautiful and delicate creatures. In it is a mixture of plants that range from radishes and carrots to milkweeds and stinging nettles—plants that play host to some sixty species of butterflies that hover here each spring, summer, and fall. Interspersed among the plants are large rocks that make ideal basking spots for butterflies, plus a small pond where they can get water. The Butterfly Garden is located in Bellevue State Park, ½ mile south of town off US 52.

One of Bellevue's magnificent old mansions is **Mont Rest,** a bed-and-breakfast inn built in 1893. Nestled into a wooded hillside overlooking the town and river, Mont Rest is owned by Christine Zraick, who has restored the house to its original elegance. A dozen bedrooms are open to guests, each beautifully decorated and furnished with antiques. On Christmas Eve in 1996, Mont Rest was almost totally destroyed by a tremendous fire. Firefighters from five fire stations battled the blaze all night, dumping more than 200,000 gallons of water on the structure. Christine was not sure whether Mont Rest could be rebuilt, but due to an overwhelming response from the people of Bellevue and her own feelings of stewardship toward the property, in the spring of 1997 she decided to rebuild. Today Mont Rest has been reborn in all its Victorian splendor.

Everything that the fire destroyed has been replaced with vintage woodwork, chandeliers, and furniture that Christine searched the world to find.

Mont Rest is located at 300 Spring St.; (877) 872-4220. Rates are in the expensive category. The inn's Web site is www.montrest.com.

Before you leave Bellevue, pay a visit to ***Potter's Mill,*** a restaurant and bed-and-breakfast located in a six-story former mill built in 1843. During the

# Iowa's Island City

The mighty Mississippi rolls past hundreds of towns and cities on its long journey from northern Minnesota to the sea, but none is as intimately tied to the river as the small town of **Sabula.** Located on a narrow island reached only by bridge, causeway, or boat, the town of 700 residents is a haven for people who have Mississippi River water flowing in their veins.

Sabula's many links to the surrounding river are visible throughout the town. Many of the modest houses that line its quiet streets have a fishing boat or a speedboat parked on their lawns, and on warm summer days the town empties as nearly everyone heads for the water.

Thanks to Sabula's location, they don't have to travel far. The town, which is just 4 blocks wide and 9 blocks long, covers the entire island. To the east lies the main channel of the Mississippi, its powerful current carrying massive barges loaded with grain bound for New Orleans, Jet Skiers out for an afternoon spin, and fishing boats trolling at a leisurely pace. The rest of the island is surrounded by a maze of backwaters, perfect habitat for the hundreds of great blue herons and other birds that nest in the area. A portion of these backwaters just north of town forms the 3,500-acre **Green Island State Wildlife Refuge,** home to recently reintroduced trumpeter swans.

Native Americans were the first inhabitants on the island, which wasn't discovered by white settlers until 1835. In 1864 the town was incorporated, its name taken from the Latin word *sabulum,* meaning "sandy soil." Its location made it a desirable steamboat landing, and the little settlement later grew into a major meat-packing center. Another early industry was the making of buttons, combs, and jewelry fashioned from mussel shells harvested from the river bottom.

Today the town's small business district includes several taverns and restaurants, as well as Ackerman's Grocery Store, the place where locals gather to share news and swap stories.

nineteenth century the mill sold its flour to wholesalers as far away as New York and Boston. Over the years it had fallen into nearly total disrepair but it was refurbished in the 1980s and is now listed on the National Register of Historic Places. Potter's Mill Restaurant serves a menu of moderately priced Midwestern favorites and is open daily from Apr through Oct, with reduced hours in the winter. Overnight guests stay in four rooms (rates are in the moderate category). You'll find the mill at 300 Potter's Dr. Call (563) 872-3838 or see www.pottersmill.net for information.

Travel north on US 52 for 10 miles and you'll reach *St. Donatus,* a small village known for its old-world architecture and traditions. Its settlers were immigrants from Luxembourg who tried to duplicate the architecture, dress, and customs of their native land in their new home.

One of the village's main attractions is the *Outdoor Way of the Cross,* the first of its kind in America. Built in 1861, it consists of fourteen brick alcoves scattered along a winding path behind the St. Donatus Catholic Church. Each alcove contains an original lithograph depicting Christ's journey on Good Friday. At the top of the hill is the Pieta Chapel, a replica of a church in Luxembourg.

# Grant Wood Country

Iowa's most famous native artist, Grant Wood, drew rich inspiration from this part of eastern Iowa, depicting its rolling countryside in many of his paintings. You'll find this region easy to explore on the *Grant Wood Scenic Byway,* a series of county roads and highways that takes you past many attractions relating both to Wood's life and to Iowa history. The byway stretches between Bellevue and Anamosa and is marked by special signs. For a brochure describing the route, call the Iowa Tourism Office at (888) 472-6035.

On your tour of this part of the state, follow the winding roads of the byway to *Maquoketa.* North of town on US 61 is *Banowetz Antiques* (563-652-2359), one of the Midwest's largest antiques shops, with more than two acres of merchandise. And for an introduction to the history of the area, tour the Jackson County Historical Museum on the Jackson County Fairgrounds.

A nice place to stay in Maquoketa is the *Squiers Manor Bed and Breakfast,* located at 418 W. Pleasant St. This lovely, Queen Anne–style mansion was built in 1882. Guests enjoy desserts by candlelight each evening and a full gourmet breakfast every morning. Rates range from moderate to expensive. For more information call (563) 652-6961 or log onto www.squiersmanor.com.

Two miles north of Maquoketa on US 61 are the *Hurstville Lime Kilns,* once the site of the old company town of Hurstville. Built in the 1870s, these formerly active kilns crushed the limestone quarried nearby and heated it with wood fires to produce a lime resin. Preceding the development of concrete, this was one of Iowa's most important early industries. Thanks to a large community volunteer effort, these kilns and an interpretive center (563-652-3873) are open to visitors year-round.

Nearby you'll find **Maquoketa Caves State Park,** one of Iowa's most unusual geologic formations. This 272-acre state park contains a labyrinth of underground caverns and woodland trails. You can reach the thirteen caves scattered throughout the park by well-marked and sometimes rugged trails. Although two of the main caves are lighted, flashlights are needed in the others.

Indian pottery, arrowheads, spears, and other artifacts found in the caves provide proof that they were used by native tribes for hundreds of years. When the caves were first discovered before the Civil War, lovely stalactites and stalagmites were found, but unfortunately, souvenir hunters have robbed the caves of most of these. Two monuments that remain are a balanced rock and a natural bridge.

Camping and picnic sites are available in the park. Call (563) 652-5833 for more information.

For some local color and hearty food, visit **Bluff Lake Catfish Farm,** at 9343 Ninety-fifth Ave. It is 1 mile from Maquoketa Caves at the end of a long and winding gravel road (follow the signs once you leave the park). This bustling establishment specializes in all-you-can-eat dinners. On weekends hundreds of people flock here for the fish fries; on other nights, barbecued ribs, chicken, and shrimp are served. Its owner is the friendly Linda Wells, whose father built the restaurant in 1971.

Bluff Lake Catfish Farm is open Thurs through Sun for dinner, and prices are moderate. Call (563) 652-3272 for more information.

Ten miles west of Maquoketa on IA 64 lies the town of **Baldwin.** From Baldwin, follow the signs 1 mile north and 1 mile west to the **Tabor Home Vineyards and Winery.** Its owner, Paul Tabor, caught the winemaking bug early. Growing up on a farm that has been in his family for more than a century, he enjoyed winemaking as a hobby. Later Tabor earned a doctorate in microbiology and worked as a professor at Indiana State University, but his interest in winemaking continued. He enjoyed experimenting with different varieties of vines on the home farm and eventually hatched the idea of establishing a commercial winery there. In 1996, Tabor Home Vineyards and Winery became the first Iowa winery with its own vineyard to be established since Prohibition. It is a family operation that includes Paul Tabor, his wife, children, mother, and brother.

From the beginning, the family's goal has been to grow the very best varieties of winemaking grapes for this area, and then to make the very best wines from them. "We want to create truly distinctive Iowa wines, not wines made from grapes grown somewhere else in the country," says Tabor.

The Tabor family grows six acres of grapes on their property and also buys grapes from about forty eastern Iowa farmers, a number that continues to grow as people realize that grape growing can be a good supplemental source of farm income.

There are approximately twenty varieties of grapes that are well-adapted to the Iowa climate, says Tabor, including native varieties like Catawba as well as hybrids developed in the wine-growing regions of France and Eastern

## Iowa Wine Country

Thanks to a creative and hardworking group of vintners and farmers, the Iowa wine industry is blossoming. And as wineries prosper, Midwestern travelers are discovering the sensual pleasures of wine country: the chance to sample diverse vintages, chat with vintners about their complex art, observe the steps that go into the harvesting of grapes and bottling of wine, and enjoy the inviting ambience of a well-tended vineyard.

The growth of Iowa wineries is actually a rebirth, for during the early years of the twentieth century Iowa was the sixth-largest grape producer in the nation. The industry declined as a result of Prohibition, the growing market for corn and soybeans, and damage to grape vines caused by the drift of corn herbicides. For decades the industry was kept alive mainly in the small wineries of the Amana Colonies, establishments that buy most of their juice from outside the state to create primarily sweet dessert wines.

The past decade, however, has seen a remarkable renaissance in the Iowa wine industry. Today there are more than sixty wineries and nearly 400 commercial vineyards scattered across Iowa, numbers that are growing each year.

One of the best ways to sample Iowa vintages is to follow the *Iowa Wine Trail,* a consortium of eight wineries in eastern Iowa. The trail extends from West Branch near Iowa City north to Decorah, a route that winds through a pastoral landscape of tidy farms and rounded hills immortalized in the paintings of Grant Wood.

The Wine Trail sponsors two annual events. The November Wine and Foods Weekend is held on the first weekend in November. Travelers will find a selection of wines paired with a variety of holiday foods at each winery. On the last weekend in April, the establishments hold an April Wine Trail Event, when guests are invited to sample gourmet cheeses that are matched with compatible wines and can also enjoy the emerging spring on vineyard tours.

For more information see www.iowawinetrail.com.

Europe. Today the Tabor winery produces fifteen varieties of wine, of which about 75 percent are reds and 25 percent whites. Wines from the Tabor Home Winery have won more than 200 national and international awards.

Visitors to the winery can sample these award-winning vintages in a light-filled tasting room. The shop overlooks the winery's indoor production facilities and also includes a touch-screen kiosk with information about grape and wine production in Iowa. Outside there are large grape arbors for picnicking and two interpretive vineyards: one features varieties popular in Iowa in the early 1900s and another has varieties that are used in Iowa winemaking today. Guests are welcome to pluck grapes off the vine and compare the flavors. The winery also sponsors a variety of special events. In the summer, free live entertainment is offered on many Sunday afternoons on the veranda of a century-old barn that overlooks the vineyard.

For more information on the Tabor Winery, call (877) 673-3131 or see www.taborhomewinery.com.

From the Tabor Winery travel west on IA 64 to the town of **Anamosa,** site of the **Grant Wood Art Gallery.** At the center you can see Grant Wood prints and murals and view videos about Wood's life and art, as well as a large display of *American Gothic* caricatures. The center also stocks tourism information and sells a large selection of Grant Wood prints, books, note cards, T-shirts, and other memorabilia. The gallery (319-462-4267) is at 124 E. Main St. It is open daily from 1 to 4 p.m.

Before leaving Anamosa take note of the impressive architecture of the **Iowa State Men's Reformatory** located at the west end of the downtown. Beginning in 1873 prisoners labored to construct the prison using stone quarried from the nearby Stone City area. Upon its completion, Iowans dubbed it the White Palace of the West, a tribute to its imposing architecture, beautiful stone walls, and immaculate landscaping. The prison today looks much the same as it did a hundred years ago, down to the regal stone lions guarding its entrance. During the summer months a formal garden in front of the prison is filled with blooming flowers. For more information about this striking landmark, visit the **Anamosa Penitentiary Museum** on North High Street, a stone building on the prison grounds that displays artifacts and historical information. The museum (319-462-2386) is open Memorial Day weekend through Labor Day, from noon to 4 p.m. Fri through Sun.

West of Anamosa lies lovely **Stone City,** once a thriving quarry area and later the site of several summer art colonies run by Grant Wood during the early 1930s. The best time to visit the village is on the second Sunday in June, when Stone City hosts the **Grant Wood Art Festival.** Area artists come to demonstrate and sell their work, tours of the town's historic ruins are offered, and strolling entertainers perform throughout the village. For more information call (319) 462-4879.

Next head south to the major city in this part of the state, **Cedar Rapids.** The city made international headlines in June of 2008 when it suffered a devastating flood. More than 10 square miles (about 14 percent of the city) was inundated when the Cedar River overflowed its banks. Since then the people of Cedar Rapids, aided by volunteers from around the nation, have worked valiantly to rebuild and improve the city. While some tourist landmarks have been affected, many more have reopened or were fortunate enough to have escaped the flood waters in the first place.

**Czech Village** was one of the hardest hit areas, but rebuilding is happening fast. This three-block area of Czech shops and restaurants on Sixteenth Avenue Southwest serves as the heart of historic Cedar Rapids. One-third of the population in Cedar Rapids is of Czech origin, making it the dominant ethnic group in the city. The village area is a center for preserving that heritage and is the site of several ethnic businesses as well as the **National Czech and Slovak Museum.** The museum was flooded in 2008 but will be relocated to a nearby site.

Thankfully, many other city treasures were unaffected by the flood, including the **Cedar Rapids Museum of Art,** a $10-million structure that houses an outstanding regional collection, including the nation's largest collection of works by Grant Wood and Marvin Cone. The museum also operates the **Grant Wood Studio** at 5 Turner Alley, where the famous artist lived and worked from 1924–35 (*American Gothic* was painted here in 1930). The museum (319-366-7503) is at 410 Third Ave. Southeast. It is open Tues through Sun, and the Grant Wood Studio is open on weekends from Apr through Dec See www.crma.org for more information.

## thecherrysisters

The famous Cherry Sisters spent most of their lives in Cedar Rapids. The name doesn't sound familiar? The Cherry Sisters (Effie, Addie, and Jessie) were stage performers at the turn of the twentieth century whose act was so bad that it sometimes had to be "presented behind nets to protect the sisters from vegetables, fruit, and other missiles hurled at them," according to one Iowa history book. Nevertheless, their performances were so popular that they enabled the Oscar Hammerstein Theatre in New York to pay off its mortgage in one season. The Cherry Sisters then returned to Cedar Rapids, where they spent the rest of their lives—safe, one hopes, from flying vegetables.

Travelers with a love for the past should hop on board the time machine leading to **Ushers Ferry Historic Village,** located on the northeast side of Cedar Rapids. The site interprets life in á small Iowa town during the years from 1890 to 1910 and is named after Dyer Usher, who operated a ferry on the Cedar River near here in the 1840s. While the site was damaged in the 2008 flood, it is being restored. It features more than thirty historic structures, including a one-room schoolhouse, saloon, blacksmith shop, general store, livery stable, and train depot. On a self-guided tour visitors can try their hand at activities like scrubbing clothes on a washboard, feeding chickens, or sewing a quilt.

A variety of special events highlight the calendar at Ushers Ferry, including a Civil War Reenactment in Sept, CelticFest in Oct, Thanksgiving Candlelight Tour, and Parlour Theater Series, which re-creates entertainments enjoyed by nineteenth-century audiences.

Ushers Ferry is open from May through Oct, and a small admission is charged. You'll find the site at 5925 Seminole Valley Trail Northeast. Call (319) 286-5763 or see www.cedar-rapids .org/ushers for more information.

## newdealmurals

During the Depression, the Works Progress Adminstration commissioned artists to paint murals across the state. You can see these WPA murals in towns that include:

**Cedar Rapids:** Harrison School

**Monticello:** Post Office

**Marion:** Post Office

**Tipton:** Post Office

**DeWitt:** Post Office

A Cedar Rapids landmark is *The Vernon Inn,* located at 2663 Mount Vernon Rd. Southeast. It offers an outstanding Greek menu, as well as eclectic American food. The Vernon Inn (319-366-7817) is open for lunch and dinner, and the prices are moderate.

Other sites of interest in Cedar Rapids include the restored Brucemore Mansion, Indian Creek Nature Center, and Duffy's Collectible Cars, a car dealership with dozens of restored automobiles dating from the 1940s to the 1960s. For more visitor information on Cedar Rapids, call (800) 735-5557, or visit the Cedar Rapids Visitors Bureau Web site at www.cedar-rapids.com.

Before you leave the Cedar Rapids area, check out the *Cedar Valley Nature Trail,* a 52-mile route that follows a former railroad line between Cedar Rapids and Waterloo. Opened officially in 1984, the trail is the longest one of its kind in Iowa.

One advantage of the trail is that its grade is never more than 3 percent, making it an easy place to hike, bike, or cross-country ski. The path winds through grasslands, woods, wetlands, and farms, with abundant wildlife along the way, from wild turkeys to white-tailed deer. It also passes through the towns of Gilbertville, La Portè City, Brandon, Urbana, Lafayette, and Center Point. Water and restrooms are available at various locations along the trail.

# The Days of Corn and (Sunburned) Noses

Imagine this: the beautiful cloudless days of an Iowa July, a good hot sun, plenty of fresh country air, plenty of friends, gallons and gallons of lemonade, the song of meadowlarks and red-winged blackbirds, the low whir of cicadas, the distant lowing of grazing cows, the smell of green things growing. Perfect working conditions, right? The ideal job, right? Wrong. At least, that is, if you're corn de-tasseling.

I am lucky to have the hardest job I hope I will ever have behind me. From the time I was twelve until I was fifteen (at the age of sixteen I became eligible, under then current Iowa law, to get a "real job"), I spent ten to fourteen of these beautiful cloudless July days out in the country, with plenty of fresh air, plenty of friends, gallons and gallons of lemonade, etc., pulling tassels out of field corn. Those of us foolhardy enough or greedy enough (why, you could make at least a hundred dollars for only ten days' work!) climbed on board a school bus at our local high school at six or seven in the morning and bounced out to a farmer's field where the corn awaited us. One person to a row, we marched (or strolled or crawled, whimpering) pulling tassels out of (I think) the "female" rows. This had something to do with pollination or fertilization or something. (I'm afraid I wasn't that interested in biology in those days. At least not that kind of biology.)

There were days the temperature reached a hundred degrees or more, days it poured rain and we slogged through mud up to our ankles, days we had aphid-infested corn and had to pull tassels out of their black jelly, gagging. We got blistered, sunburned, and stung. We worried about our "farmers' tans." We got to know one another, our weaknesses and strengths, well. We had tassel fights—which were forbidden—mud fights, and water fights. We sang songs, some of them not very nice. We ate lunches our moms packed that never tasted better and drank barely cool lemonade that also never tasted better. I will admit there were probably days we could have smelled better. At night, a bed had never felt better. All in all, I suppose it could have been a lot worse . . . but not much.

—T. S.

To enter the trail from Cedar Rapids, drive north on I-380, take exit 25, and follow the signs to the trailhead. See www.cedarvalleytrail.com for more information.

No visit to this part of Iowa is complete without a visit to **Mount Vernon,** the home of **Cornell College.** Cornell boasts the fact that it is the only college in the nation whose entire campus is on the National Register of Historic Places. A very pleasant afternoon may be spent wandering through this lovely old hilltop campus and the adjacent downtown area, where there are several antiques shops and places to eat. In the winter make sure you bring your sled along because when there's snow, Third Avenue North's "Pres Hill" is blocked off and left unplowed for some winter fun.

Mount Vernon is also home to one of Iowa's finest restaurants, *The Lincoln Café*. The downtown establishment is owned by Matt Steigerwald, a chef who came to Mount Vernon when his partner was hired by Cornell College. Formerly a chef at the famed Magnolia Grill in Durham, North Carolina, Steigerwald has built a devoted following in eastern Iowa. The luncheon menu features an attractive array of inexpensive sandwiches and salads, but the cafe's gourmet dinners attract the most attention. The menu changes frequently, but past favorites include such entrees as roasted duck with mushroom arancini and scallops with lobster hash, lemon oil, and lettuce cream. "I'm here eighty hours a week," says Steigerwald, "but I love it." So do eastern Iowa diners!

The Lincoln Café is at 117 First St. West. Call (319) 895-4041 or see www .foodisimportant.com for information. It is open for lunch and dinner from Tues through Sat and for brunch on Sun.

Next door, the *Silver Spider* (319-895-9977) stocks an eclectic range of collectibles, jewelry, and items ranging from quirky to bizarre. You'll find it at 117½ First St. West.

For more information about Mount Vernon and its environs, call (319) 210-9935.

Take US 30 West out of Mount Vernon to end your trip to this region with a visit to the *Palisades-Kepler State Park,* located 10 miles east of Cedar Rapids. During the autumn months especially, this beautiful park skirting the banks of the Cedar River makes an ideal picnicking spot and a wonderful place to while away a Sunday afternoon. For more information call (319) 895-6039.

## Places to Stay in Cultural Crossroads

**AMANA**

**Annie's Garden Guest House**
716 Forty-sixth Ave.
(319) 622-6854
www.timeandtides.com
moderate

**CEDAR RAPIDS**

**Belmont Hill Victorian Bed & Breakfast**
1525 Cherokee Dr.
Northwest
(319) 366-1343
www.belmonthill.com
moderate to expensive

**DAVENPORT**

**Renwick Mansion**
901 Tremont Ave.
(563) 324-9678
moderate to expensive

**IOWA CITY**

**hotelVetro**
201 S. Linn St.
(800) 592-0355
www.hotelvetro.com
expensive

**Smith's B&B**
314 Brown St.
(319) 338-1316
http://smithsbandb.home
.mchsi.com
inexpensive to moderate

**MAQUOKETA**

**Decker Hotel & Restaurant**
128 N. Main St.
(563) 652-6654
www.deckerhotel.us
moderate

## Places to Eat in Cultural Crossroads

**AMANA**

**Ox Yoke Inn**
4420 220th Trail
(800) 233-3441
www.oxyokeinn.com
moderate

**Ronneburg Restaurant**
4408 220th Trail
(888) 348-4686
www.ronneburgrestaurant
.com
moderate

**CEDAR RAPIDS**

**Irish Democrat Pub & Grille**
3207 First Ave. Southeast
(319) 364-9896
www.irishdemocrat.net
inexpensive

**Zinn's**
227 Second Ave.
Southeast
(319) 363-9467
www.zinsrestaurant.com
moderate

**CLINTON**

**Rastrelli's Restaurant**
238 Main Ave.
(563) 242-7441
www.rastrellis.com
moderate

**CORALVILLE**

**Wig & Pen Pizza Pub**
1220 US 6 West
(319) 354-2767
www.wigandpeneast.com
moderate

**DAVENPORT**

**Front Street Brewery**
208 E. River Dr.
(563) 322-1569
moderate

**IOWA CITY**

**Atlas World Grill**
127 Iowa Ave.
(319) 341-7700
www.atlasworldgrill.com
moderate

**Linn Street Café**
121 N. Linn St.
(319) 337-7370
www.linnstreetcafe.com
expensive

**SOLON**

**Redhead**
240 E. Main St.
(319) 624-5230
www.myspace.com/
redheadrestaurant
moderate

# RURAL CHARMS

Southeast Iowa is rich in rural pleasures. In the Kalona area you'll find the largest **Amish-Mennonite Community** settlement west of the Mississippi, while a few miles south lies Mount Pleasant, home of the Midwest Old Threshers Reunion that celebrates the state's agricultural heritage. The southern part of this region has been shaped in countless ways by two great rivers: the mighty Mississippi and the scenic Des Moines. In this part of southern Iowa, you'll find that many legacies from the nineteenth century still remain in the villages of Van Buren County and in the Mississippi River ports of Fort Madison and Keokuk.

## Amish Country

Begin your tour of Amish country in **Kalona,** a place where buggies travel the highways next to cars, Amish farmers work the land with horse-drawn equipment, and on the downtown sidewalks women in black dresses and bonnets mingle with those in blue jeans and T-shirts. About 1,200 Amish people live in the area, as well as many Mennonites.

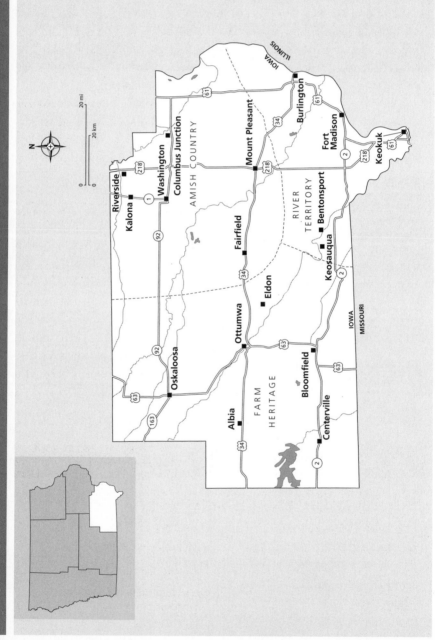

Although the Amish live in the countryside and limit their contact with the outside world, Kalona itself welcomes visitors to its tidy and prosperous downtown. Here you'll find a wide selection of antiques, bakery goods, and locally made gifts and craft items, including the hand-stitched quilts for which the area is famous. In late April the town hosts the *Kalona Quilt Show and Sale,* which is one of the Midwest's largest quilt shows. Each year several thousand people attend this nationally advertised event featuring hundreds of new and antique quilts made by the local Amish and Mennonite women. The show is held at the Kalona Community Center located at 307 Sixth St. A small admission fee is charged. Call (319) 656-2240 for information.

At any time of year, you can tour the *Kalona Quilt and Textile Museum.* Each year the museum presents three or four shows that showcase the creativity of generations of women. Past exhibits have included "feed-sack quilts" made during the Depression and crazy quilts made of tiny scraps of material. The museum (319-656-3232) is located in Kalona Historical Village at 715 D Ave. (see page 68) and is open Mon through Sat.

Don't miss a stop at the *Kalona Cheese House* at 2206 540th St. Southwest. While you are here you can watch cheese being made and pay a visit to the tasting room (there are plenty of samples) and gift shop. Whatever you do, make sure you buy a bag of their cheese curds. They may look funny and they may "squeak" when you bite into them, but they are absolutely delicious. If you continue east on 540th Street from the cheese house, you will find the *Stringtown Grocery* (2266 540th St. Southwest), a fascinating Mennonite-run store featuring a huge variety of products sold in bulk. Don't leave here without getting some of their raspberry chocolate chips—they make incredible cookies.

Another charming place to visit is *Sisters Garden,* about 2½ miles north of the Cheese House at 4895 IA 1, Kalona. An old farmhouse has been

## AUTHORS' FAVORITES

| | |
|---|---|
| Lacey-Keosauqua State Park | Mars Hill |
| Old Fort Madison | Snake Alley |
| Ghost Hunting at the Mason House Inn | Stringtown Grocery |
| American Gothic House | Columbus Junction Swinging Bridge |
| Cafe Dodici | Toolesboro Indian Mounds |

converted into a shop that sells both the delightfully old and the delightfully new. During the spring and summer months, you can also buy potted herbs, annuals, and perennials. Among the things you can find here are handcrafted willow furniture pieces and many unique items with a garden theme. There are also a few picnic tables scattered about the yard so you can relax and enjoy yourself in this rural setting. Call (319) 683-2046 for their schedule.

For further insight into the history and culture of the area, visit the **Kalona Historical Village** at 715 D Ave. The village contains seven restored nineteenth-century buildings that include a one-room schoolhouse, a general store, a log house, a buggy shop, and an old railroad depot. Also on the grounds is the Iowa Mennonite Museum and Archives, a repository for the documents and history of the Mennonite community in the area.

## Art for the Ages

*Max-Cast* is Iowa's only art foundry not connected with an educational institution and a fascinating place to see the complex process of metal casting.

While the foundry casts objects ranging in size from just a few inches across to dozens of feet tall, the most challenging are the larger pieces. The process begins with the creation of small models that allow the artist to determine the correct pose and proportions of the finished piece. An intermediate model is often constructed as well, including a finer level of detail. The artist then constructs a full-scale model of wood, cardboard, plastic foam, or paper, carefully determining the dimensions of the armature that will be needed to support the completed metal piece.

Using this final model, a mold is created. Next comes the most dangerous and dramatic part of the process, the heating and pouring of the metal. As the furnace roars, the metal inside the crucible becomes hotter and hotter. When it reaches a temperature of about 2,000 degrees, workers carefully maneuver a crane into position, lift the crucible from the furnace, guide it to the mold, and pour the metal into the receptacle.

Once the metal has hardened, the molds are removed and the piece is ready for the finishing process. Imperfections and the lines where two pieces are bonded together are ground off, and the surface is smoothed and polished. The polishing process makes the foundry reverberate with the sounds of grinding and drilling, making it sound like some mad dentist's office.

In the final step, a patina is applied to the surface of the piece. Chemical patinas react with the surface metal to create various types of colors and finishes, or the artist can use heat to create other effects.

The finished product has a durability unmatched by any medium. "We like to say that we give a 5,000-year guarantee on our work," says Doris Park. "There are statues from the Bronze Age that have been recovered from under the sea and they're still beautiful."

Another fascinating introduction to the area can be had on a **Kalona Byways Tour.** Sponsored by the Kalona Historical Society, the narrated tour winds through back roads and includes stops at local stores. The cost is $12 for adults, $6 for children. Call (319) 656-2660 for information.

The best time to visit the village is during its annual **Fall Festival,** a down-home celebration with plenty of delicious food, homemade crafts, and demonstrations of old-time skills like spinning, weaving, cornmeal grinding, and wood sawing. For me the smells alone are worth the trip: Big pots of bubbling apple butter send a heavenly aroma through the crisp air, a smell rivaled only by that of bread baking in the village's outdoor oven.

The Kalona Fall Festival is held the last Fri and Sat in Sept, and the Historical Village is open Mon through Sat from 9:30 a.m. to 4 p.m. Apr 1 to Oct 31. The rest of the year, hours are 11 a.m. to 3 p.m. Mon through Sat. Admission is $7; $2.50 for children ages seven to twelve; call (319) 656-3232 for more information.

Downtown Kalona is also home to the **Max-Cast Foundry,** where Stephen Maxon and Doris Park have been creating metal works of art since 1988. Inside the industrial-looking building is a warren of rooms overflowing with metal scraps, tools, molds, half-finished projects, and vats of peculiar smelling chemicals, a laboratory where humble materials are transformed into objects of beauty.

Visitors can shop in a gallery located at the front of the foundry. If Maxon and Park have time, you can also take a guided tour of the operation. The two work primarily with cast iron, aluminum, and bronze. Park draws much of her inspiration from the natural world, creating sculptures of unusual or underappreciated animals like snapping turtles and toads. Maxon has a more eclectic style, often creating fantastical creations that blend diverse elements. Many pieces display a sly sense of humor—including toes that look like they're peeking out of the ground and bookends sculpted in the shape of brains— while others take ordinary objects like scissors and a well-polished apple as inspiration for works of art. You can also see the couple's work in downtown Iowa City at the corner of Iowa Avenue and Linn Street, where their statue of local historian Irving Weber waves jauntily at passersby.

Max-Cast Foundry is at 611 B Ave. It's typically open Mon through Fri, but it's best to call ahead before visiting its gallery. For more information call (800) 728-9339 or see www.max-cast.com.

East of Kalona in the small town of **Riverside** lies an Iowa landmark of interest to all *Star Trek* fans: the **Future Birthplace of Captain James T. Kirk.** In 1985 the Riverside City Council voted unanimously to declare a spot behind what used to be the town's barbershop as the place where Captain Kirk of *Star Trek* fame would one day be born.

## TOP ANNUAL EVENTS

**JANUARY**

**Bald Eagle Appreciation Days**
Keokuk, third weekend in Jan
(800) 383-1219

**APRIL**

**Civil War Reenactment/Battle of Pea Ridge**
Keokuk, last weekend in Apr
(800) 383-1219

**Kalona Quilt Show and Sale**
Kalona, last weekend in Apr
(319) 656-2660

**JUNE**

**Burlington Steamboat Days**
Burlington, mid-June
(800) 827-4837
www.steamboatdays.com

**Trek Fest**
Riverside, last weekend in June
(319) 930-8735
www.trekfest.com

**SEPTEMBER**

**Albia Restoration Days**
Albia, weekend before Labor Day
(641) 932-5108

**Midwest Old Threshers Reunion**
Mount Pleasant, Labor Day weekend
(319) 385-8937

**Centerville Pancake Day**
Centerville, last Sat in Sept
(800) 611-3800

**OCTOBER**

**Oktoberfest**
Ottumwa, first weekend in Oct
(800) 479-0828
(641) 682-3465

**DECEMBER**

**Parade of Lights**
Fort Madison, Fri after Thanksgiving
(800) 210-8687

Riverside has some official proof to back up its claim. Gene Roddenberry's book, *The Making of Star Trek,* says that Kirk "was born in a small town in the State of Iowa." The town contacted Roddenberry and received a certificate confirming its birthplace status, and thus was born one of Iowa's most famous future historical sites.

On the last weekend in June, Riverside celebrates Kirk's future birth date in the year 2228 by holding its *Trek Fest.* This gathering includes a talent show, carnival rides, and costume contest, plus sports events, a beer garden, and a parade on Main Street. Captain Kirk will undoubtedly be proud (once he's born). For more information about Trek Fest, call (319) 930-8735 or see www.trekfest.com.

South of Riverside in the town of Washington, you'll find one of Iowa's destination restaurants: *Cafe Dodici.* Located on the town's central square at 122 S. Iowa Ave., the restaurant has the ambience of an art gallery, with chandeliers handmade in Florence and artwork from around the world. Its menu includes many Italian pasta dishes, from tortellini bianco to shrimp asiago, as well as entrees such as pistachio-encrusted lamb and raspberry salmon. The restaurant uses locally grown produce and meats as much as possible, varying dishes with the seasons.

The cafe's European style reflects the backgrounds of its owners. Lorraine Williams grew up in Washington but later spent twenty-five years living in Italy, where she married her husband, Alessandro Scipioni. On a typical evening, Cafe Dodici hums with conversation and laughter, a welcoming atmosphere set by its extroverted owners. "A restaurant is about much more than just food," says Williams. "It's a place where you should be greeted like an old friend."

Entrees are moderate to expensive. For reservations or more information, call (319) 653-4012 or see www.cafedodici.com.

From Washington, head east to **Columbus Junction,** where you'll find the **Columbus Junction Swinging Bridge.** A 262-foot suspension bridge made of steel cable and wooden boards, it stretches across a deep, wooded ravine and provides a suitably scary feeling as you stand in its center and sway back and forth.

The bridge's nickname is the Lover's Leap Bridge, a reference to a local legend that says that an Indian maiden jumped to her death in the ravine after hearing that her warrior sweetheart had been killed in battle. The bridge itself was first erected in 1896 so that citizens could travel between Third and Fourth Streets in Columbus Junction without making a detour around the ravine. Since then, the bridge has been replaced several times, most recently in 1921 when a professor of engineering at Iowa State University designed a new bridge for the town. To reach the bridge, follow the signs on IA 92 on the west end of Columbus Junction.

From Columbus Junction head east to the **Port Louisa National Wildlife Refuge.** Located adjacent to the Mississippi River, its 8,375 acres include pristine wetlands, grasslands, and bottomland forests. During the spring and fall migration season, more than 60,000 waterfowl can be found here, including mallards, pintails, canvasback, Canada geese, and snow geese. At any time of year, the refuge provides a haven for hundreds of fish, reptile, and amphibian species, as well as deer, muskrat, river otters, bobcats, mink, coyotes, and beaver.

While wildlife refuges can be found throughout the length of the Mississippi River, the Port Louisa Refuge has unique topographical characteristics. More than most refuges along the Mississippi, it's able to closely mimic the ebb and flow of water that existed here for millennia before the lock and dam system was installed. That means that its diverse habitats are regularly replenished by the waters of the river. The health of the refuge also benefits the surrounding area, helping to make Louisa County one of the premier

## Water Wilderness

Exploring the mazelike backwaters of the Mississippi can be intimidating to anyone unfamiliar with the area, but thanks to the *Odessa Water Trail,* paddlers can enjoy easy access to this water wilderness. The marked trail winds through 6,400 acres of marshes, ponds, lakes, and timbered chutes, an area that is home to thousands of waterfowl, shorebirds, and other animals, from playful river otters to basking turtles. The route is the third water trail in Iowa, and it's the only one that takes paddlers through a variety of water habitats rather than just on a river or stream.

The Odessa Trail is an interconnected set of routes that wind through both the Port Louisa National Wildlife Refuge and the adjoining Odessa Management Area. In all, the various segments of the trail include almost 70 miles of marked routes.

Parts of the trail are closed during the winter months, and changing water levels can affect paddling conditions. For more information call (319) 523-8381 or see www .naturallylouisacounty.com.

waterfowl hunting and bird-watching areas in the state. The refuge is home to a number of rare and endangered species, including piping plovers, least terns, and peregrine falcons. For information call (319) 523-6982 or see www .fws.gov/midwest/portlouisa.

Next head west to the small community of **Swedesburg,** home of the **Swedish American Museum.** Located in northern Henry County, Swedish settlers began draining the marshy soil for farmland beginning around 1860. The museum tells their story and is the location of several Swedish festivals throughout the year, including Lucia Day and Midsomer. Admission to the museum is free, tours are provided, and Swedish meals are served for travel groups. Make sure you see the Huckster wagon, from which merchants sold their wares to outlying farms, as well as the wicker "cooling basket" used by the undertaker to keep the deceased body in while the casket was being built. The museum is located at 107 James Ave., Swedesburg. For more information call (319) 254-2317. Their hours are 9 a.m. to 4 p.m., closed Wed and Sun.

South of Swedesburg lies the aptly named town of **Mount Pleasant.** A prosperous community of 8,500, Mount Pleasant is an Iowa success story with a thriving economy and friendly small-town atmosphere.

But what makes this town well known throughout the state belongs as much to the past as it does to the present: the **Midwest Old Threshers Reunion,** a celebration of old-time agriculture that draws more than 100,000 visitors each Labor Day weekend. The event began in 1950, when a small group of enthu-siasts got together at the Henry County Fairgrounds to exhibit steam-powered equipment. (Before the development of the gas-engine tractor in the 1920s, smoke-belching steam engines provided the power that ran America's farms.)

Today the reunion has grown into a five-day event that draws visitors from throughout the country. Many are drawn by the wonderful old behemoth machines on display here: antique tractors and trucks, electric trolleys, steam trains, and all kinds of engines. Other attractions include live entertainment by nationally known performers, a log village, craft demonstrations, and food tents staffed by local church and civic groups that serve platefuls of ham, fried chicken, mashed potatoes, and various fixings. Take a ride on a trolley, attend classes in a one-room school, learn how to make soap, and watch a horse-pull competition—activities all meant to recall a largely vanished way of life.

If you can't make it to the reunion, the Old Threshers 160-acre site is still worth a visit. The permanent ***Heritage Museums*** (405 E. Threshers Rd. in Mount Pleasant) house scores of steam engines, antique tractors, agricultural equipment, and tools. There are also a farmhouse, barn, and exhibits on farm women and the use of water and electricity.

The Midwest Old Threshers Reunion is held each year during the five days ending on Labor Day. Camping and motel accommodations are available. Admission is $20 for a five-day pass and $12 for a one-day pass. The Heritage Museums are open daily Memorial Day through Labor Day from 8 a.m. to 4:30 p.m. (weekdays only in spring and fall). Admission is $5 for adults; children under fourteen are admitted free. Call (319) 385-8937 for more information on the reunion or museums or visit www.oldthreshers.org.

## All Aboard!

The ***Midwest Central Railroad*** proves the old adage that the only difference between men and boys is the size of their toys (though that's not quite accurate, because women are involved with the railroad, too). These toys are indeed big. The volunteer-run railroad's two vintage, steam-powered trains make the ground shake as they rumble by, with great clouds of steam filling the air.

This narrow-gauge railroad preserves a slice of train history on the grounds of the Midwest Old Threshers. The trains operate during the reunion in September and also for special occasions, such as the Fourth of July.

My favorite time to step on board the train is before Halloween, when the ***Ghost Train*** pulls into town. Each year during October weekends, the railroad offers delightfully spooky rides through a haunted landscape of ghosts, ghouls, open coffins, and headless horsemen. The high and lonesome sound of a train whistle in the night adds the perfect atmospheric touch to the scene. For more information call (319) 385-2912 or log onto www.mcrr.org.

Also on the Old Thresher grounds is the **Theatre Museum of Repertoire Americana** (405 E. Threshers Rd.), one of my favorite museums in the state. The facility houses the country's largest collection of tent, folk, and repertory theater memorabilia—show business that's in the rural, rather than Hollywood, style. Before the days of radio, movies, and television, hundreds of traveling theater companies crisscrossed the nation, bringing live entertainment to even the smallest of towns. This museum provides a colorful introduction to that forgotten past.

The museum owes its existence to Neil and Caroline Schaffner, former owners of the Schaffner Players. The two are best known for their stage characters of Toby and Susie, the wise country bumpkin and his sharp-tongued girlfriend. For nearly forty years their company performed throughout the Midwest, and after they retired they dreamed of establishing a museum to save the memories of early popular theater.

Mount Pleasant and the Midwest Old Threshers Association came to their rescue, and in 1973 the new museum opened its doors. Inside is a fascinating collection of costumes, advertising sheets, scrapbooks, scenery, pictures, and newspapers relating not only to the Schaffners' careers, but to all forms of early American theater. (Don't miss the beautiful hand-painted opera house curtains that were used as scenery for plays.)

The Theatre Museum of Repertoire Americana is open Memorial Day through Labor Day, Tues through Sun. Call (319) 385-9432 or visit www.the theatremuseum.com for information.

While visiting Mount Pleasant, include in your plans a lunch or dinner at the **Little Mexico Restaurant.** Hostess and owner Ana Pang has created a bright and festive environment in which to enjoy great Mexican food. The walls are just the color of the mango margaritas and are enlivened by murals in the Mexican folk tradition. Her shredded beef tacos have received several awards. Located at 107 S. Jefferson St., Mount Pleasant; call for more information at (319) 385-8424. Prices are inexpensive to moderate.

Just south of Mount Pleasant lies the small community of **Salem,** home of the **Lewelling Quaker Museum,** 401 S. Main St. Built in the 1840s, this stone house served as a stop on the Underground Railroad; two of the hiding places can still be viewed. In 1847 a band of mounted men from Missouri, seeking revenge against Salem's Quaker community for helping Ruel Dagg's slaves to escape, positioned a cannon in front of the house (a replica of this cannon now rests on the grounds). They threatened to fire upon the house but word was dispatched to the Henry County sheriff, who managed to disperse the men without violence. The museum is open on Sun from 1 to 4 p.m. May through Sept, or by appointment. Call (319) 385-2460 for more information.

From Salem drive west on US 34 to the town of *Fairfield,* home to the state's most unusual institution of higher learning, *Maharishi University of Management (MUM).* Much of the university looks like any tranquil mid-western college campus—until you drive past its two huge, golden domes rising out of the Iowa prairie. The contrast symbolizes the interesting mixture at MUM, which combines traditional academic disciplines with the practice of transcendental meditation. Twice each day, students and faculty gather in the domes to practice a meditation technique that they say reduces stress and increases their creativity and productivity.

When representatives of the Maharishi Mahesh Yogi bought the campus of bankrupt Parsons College in Fairfield in 1973, many locals worried that their peaceful community would become a haven for leather-fringed hippies. Instead, MUM has helped stimulate an economic boom in Fairfield that has made it one of the most dynamic small towns in the state. Many new busi-nesses have been started by people associated with MUM, from health-food stores and restaurants to financial consulting firms and art galleries.

One of Fairfield's favorite gathering places is *Revelations* at 112 N. Main St., just off the town square. The multiple rooms of this combination book-store/coffeehouse/cafe are filled with used and new books and comfortable chairs, perfect for browsing the volumes you've pulled from the shelves (don't miss the section on "Afterlife, Tarot, Channeling, and Prophecy"!). The cafe has a wood-fired pizza oven and also serves tasty homemade desserts. Call (641) 472-6733 for information.

For dinner, try Vivo's at 607 W. Broadway. This moderately priced, casu-ally elegant restaurant serves an array of international entrees, from Tuscan

## Ayurvedic Luxury

One of Fairfield's most successful enterprises is *The Raj,* a luxury hotel and health center that offers the indulgent delights of a full-spa experience. Housed in a French country-style manor house, The Raj is set on one hundred acres of rolling meadows and woods. Its treatments are based on *ayurveda,* an ancient system of preventive health care originally reserved for the royal families of India. It emphasizes prevention as the key to health and explores the relationship between mind and body through diet, exercise, meditation, relaxation, and purification procedures. Western-trained physicians working in conjunction with Indian doctors (called *vaidyas*) devise individualized treatment rou-tines for guests looking to lose weight, reduce stress, and improve their health.

If you don't want to sample the spa, you can still visit *The Raj Restaurant,* which is open for lunch Sunday through Thursday. The vegetarian buffet is moderately priced. The Raj is located at 1734 Jasmine Ave. Call (800) 864-8714 or see www.theraj.com.

artichoke chicken to coconut curry–crusted tofu. For information call (641) 472-2766 or see www.vivofairfield.com.

Before leaving the area, take a short drive north of town to **Maharishi Vedic City,** which in 2001 became Iowa's newest city. You'll quickly see that this isn't your typical Iowa small town, for all the homes in this community are built according to the principles of Vedic architecture. All face east and have a central open space as well as a golden roof ornament. The town also includes the Maharishi Vedic Observatory, a one-and-a-half-acre, open-air site with sundial-like instruments said to illustrate the inner structure of the universe. This is also the first (and I would guess the last) town in Iowa where the street signs are in Sanskrit.

## Farm Heritage

Begin your tour of this predominantly rural part of southeast Iowa with a visit to the small town of **Eldon.** There you'll find the **American Gothic House** (300 American Gothic St.), a home whose image is one of the most reprinted in the country, thanks to Grant Wood's having used it as a backdrop for his painting *American Gothic.* The picture of the grim, pitchfork-bearing farmer and his equally sour wife is one of the most familiar (and parodied) images in American art, and it has brought fame to the modest house that inspired it.

The home's brush with fame was entirely coincidental. While on a motor trip through southeastern Iowa in 1930, Wood saw the house and made a rough sketch on the back of an envelope of its Gothic-arched window and two long-faced people in front. Later he looked around his home of Cedar Rapids for a farmer who would fit his ideal, but none was quite right. Finally he persuaded his sister, Nan, and his dentist, Dr. B. H. McBeeby, to be his models. Nan must have had a sense of humor, however, because she collected parodies of this painting during her lifetime and donated them to the Davenport Museum of Art.

After many years as a private residence, the home is now owned by the State Historical Society of Iowa and has been restored to its 1930s appearance. Follow the signs through town to find it, and don't forget to pack your camera. (It helps if you have a friend along who can take your picture in front of it, and you might bring a lemon along so you can achieve the proper facial expression.) Call (641) 652-3352 for more information.

From Eldon travel north on IA 16 for 6 miles and then west on US 34 for 10 miles to **Ottumwa.** Whereas Riverside is the future birthplace of Captain James T. Kirk, Ottumwa can claim a famous citizen of its own: Radar O'Reilly of *M*A*S*H* fame.

Ottumwa is home to an attraction certain to delight children: **The Beach Ottumwa.** Why go to Florida when you can enjoy southeast Iowa's own beach, without all those pesky alligators? This indoor/outdoor facility has a wave pool, thrilling waterslides, kayaks and paddleboats, sand volleyball, and millions of gallons of water. The surf's always up at The Beach Ottumwa, 101 Church St. Call (641) 682-SURF for information.

The **Pioneer Ridge Nature Area and Nature Center,** located 6 miles south of Ottumwa on US 63, offers fun of a drier sort. The site includes a two-story nature center, three stocked ponds for public fishing, and 10 miles of hiking trails. The center is open from 8 a.m. to 4:30 p.m., Mon through Fri. Call (641) 682-3091 for more information.

Another attraction in the area is the **Air Power Museum,** at 22001 Bluegrass Rd. The museum is home to nearly fifty old-fashioned aircraft and is the site of an annual reunion of antique-airplane enthusiasts each Labor Day weekend. The museum is a labor of love for its founder and president, Bob Taylor, an aviation buff who soloed just before Pearl Harbor, served in World War II and Korea as a crew chief, and then returned to his hometown of Ottumwa to open a flying service in 1953. That same year he founded the Antique Airplane Association, an organization that claims members from throughout the United States and twenty-two foreign countries.

At the museum you can see airplanes from the 1920s through the 1940s, plus various flight memorabilia. Most of the planes are civilian craft, with a few homebuilt ones on display as well. There's also a library for people doing research and renovation of antique aircraft.

The Air Power Museum is located west of Ottumwa, 3½ miles northeast of **Blakesburg.** It is open from 9 a.m. to 5 p.m. on weekdays, from 10 a.m. to 5 p.m. on Sat, and from 1 to 5 p.m. on Sun. Call (641) 938-2773 or see www .antiqueairfield.com for more information. Admission is by donation.

Southeast of Ottumwa and north of Floris (off CR J15) and located on the Wapello-Davis county line is **Mars Hill,** the oldest log church in the United States still in use, as well as the state's largest remaining log structure. Built in 1857, it was one of Iowa's earliest religious buildings. It is constructed of hewn oak and walnut logs, some of them as large as 16 feet high and 8 inches thick, while others are as long as 28 feet. Services are held once each year on the third Sunday in June. Mars Hill was also a stop on the Underground Railroad. The adjoining cemetery has many old tombstones, the oldest dated 1846. This building is really amazing;

## amishcountry

Davis County is home to more than 600 Amish. Here, as elsewhere, please do not take pictures of these fine, hardworking people.

go out of your way to pay it a visit (but be careful, for the site is said to be haunted!).

Travel US 63 south to the town of **Bloomfield,** home of the **Davis County Historical Museum** on Franklin Street, which is open from 1 to 4 p.m. on Sat during the summer. The museum complex contains a hand-hewn log cabin built by Mormons traveling west in 1848, a one-room schoolhouse, and a livery barn built in 1920. Inside the barn is a great mural painted by a local high school art teacher, which depicts the Civil War Guerrilla Raid of 1864, during which twelve raiders marched across Davis County, stealing horses and guns and killing three men in the process. In addition, there is a unique feed-sack display. Call (641) 664-1512 for more information or to schedule a tour.

Nearby (about 13 miles northwest of Bloomfield off IA 273) is pretty **Lake Wapello State Park.** It has fourteen family cabins with bathroom and cooking facilities, which may be rented by making reservations with the park ranger. Call (641) 722-3950 for more information.

From Lake Wapello State Park, travel north to **Oskaloosa,** one of the prettiest-named towns in Iowa. It's named after the wife of Chief Osceola of the Seminole tribe, and its meaning is as lovely as it sounds: "Last of the Beautiful." Legend has it that Oskaloosa's husband believed that her beauty could never be surpassed.

In Oskaloosa's downtown, stop by **Smokey Row Coffee** on the town square. The old-fashioned soda fountain, coffee shop, and cafe occupies a vintage building with high ceilings, scuffed wooden floors, and cozy booths. On open-mic nights, musicians perform underneath an old theater marquee installed on one wall. Call (641) 676-1600 for more information.

Adjoining Smokey Row is **The Book Vault,** a well-stocked, independent bookstore housed in a former bank. The old security vaults are now lined with best sellers, and in the back you'll find cooking and baking items. Ask the helpful clerks for a book recommendation—they're very friendly. For more information call (641) 676-1777 or see www.bookvault.org.

A major attraction 2 miles off US 63 north of Oskaloosa is the **Nelson Pioneer Farm and Museum** (2294 Oxford Ave.; 641-672-2989), a complex of restored buildings developed around the original pioneer homestead of Daniel Nelson, who acquired the land from the U.S. government in 1844. The land was farmed by the Nelson family until 1958, when it was given to the Mahaska County Historical Society. The Nelson home and barn are both designated as National Historic Sites, and there are also a number of other buildings open for tours, including a log cabin, summer kitchen, meat house, post office, a voting house, school, and a Friends meetinghouse. Guided tours are available. Their Web site is www.nelsonpioneer.org.

A good time to visit the Nelson museum is during its annual Pioneer Festival held on the third Sat in Sept. More than thirty pioneer skills are demonstrated each year, along with special exhibits and musical entertainment. The farm is open May to Oct, Tues through Sun. Admission is $7 for adults and $2 for children.

From Oskaloosa head south on IA 137 to *Albia,* which at one time had the dubious distinction of being known as the ugliest town in Iowa. What once had been the center of a prosperous coal-mining region had gradually slipped into decay and neglect, and years of grime and coal dust coated the downtown's once-elegant Victorian buildings.

Then came Operation Facelift in the early 1970s, when the community banded together to save its historic buildings using funds that came almost entirely from local sources. Visit Albia today and you'll see a town square far different from the shabby district of years past. Brightly painted, refurbished storefronts, tree-lined sidewalks, and a general air of prosperity announce that Albia is a town that intends to survive and grow. In 1985 the town received a sweet reward for all its restoration efforts when the entire ninety-two-building business district was named to the National Register of Historic Places—the largest such district in the state.

One of the most impressive historic buildings is *First Iowa State Bank,* located on the north side of the town square. This is a working bank but also a place to *ooh* and *aah* over gorgeous antiques, all donated by Robert T. Bates, the town benefactor who spearheaded the decades-long restoration efforts. The bank includes five interconnected buildings, each filled with Victorian-era furnishings and artwork. The staff is happy to give tours to visitors. There's no other bank like this in Iowa—and perhaps not in the entire country!

## didyouknow?

The Nelson Pioneer Farm and Museum is the site of the only mule cemetery in Iowa, the final resting place of Becky and Jennie, two white mules owned by Daniel Nelson that served in the U.S. Artillery during the Civil War. They lived out the rest of their days on the farm and now have a special plot near the museum.

A couple of doors down from the bank is the *Skean Block Restaurant,* also housed in a historic building on the town square. Moderately priced steaks, sandwiches, pasta dishes, and pizzas are served in a casually elegant atmosphere. For information call (641) 932-3141 or see www.attheblock.com.

Just around the corner at 11 N. Main St., pull up a chair at *Main Street Cafe.* Only four tables and a counter fill the tiny space, which has been a restaurant since the 1940s. Owner Frances Manley is famous for her pies,

## An Unusual Friendship

Near the town of **Agency,** you'll see a sign for **Chief Wapello Memorial Park,** a little rest area that marks an important spot in Iowa's history. The park was once the site of an Indian agency (hence the town's name) where the 1842 Sac and Fox treaty was signed to complete the Indian cession of Iowa lands to the U.S. government. This set the stage for the homesteading of Iowa in 1843.

The site is also a reminder of the unique friendship that sprang up between Chief Wapello, a principal leader of the Sac and Fox Nation, and General Joseph Street, director of the Indian agency. After being forced from his home along the Mississippi by the government, Wapello led his people to settle near the Indian agency, due to his friendship with Street. The general died in 1840, and before Wapello died two years later, he asked to be buried beside him. Their graves rest undisturbed in the park to this day.

particularly the caramel apple and blue goose (a combination of blueberry and gooseberry, served only in season). "And if someone brings in a recipe, I'm happy to try it," says Frances. You can also order burgers and sandwiches, but a piece of pie really is essential here. Call (641) 932-5911 for information.

Each year on the weekend before Labor Day, the town celebrates its rebirth during **Albia Restoration Days.** A parade, talent shows, antiques auction, art show, and ethnic food booths are all part of the festivities, along with guided tours of many of the restored buildings. For more information about Albia or Restoration Days, contact its chamber of commerce at (641) 932-5108 or www.albiachamber.org.

In the rolling, wooded countryside south of Albia, you'll find one of Iowa's premiere new attractions: **Honey Creek Resort State Park,** which is located on **Rathbun Lake,** one of the state's largest bodies of water. The idea for a resort park was hatched nearly forty years ago, but it took until 2009 for it to become a reality. The 850-acre site includes a beautifully designed lodge and twenty-eight elegant cottages overlooking an 11,000-acre lake. The 105-room lodge—which is decorated in Arts and Crafts style and includes a massive stone fireplace in its main lobby—features an indoor water park, fine-dining restaurant, outdoor patio, and meeting facilities. Outside lie multipurpose trails, scenic overlooks, picnic areas, a sand beach, boat slips, an RV campground, and an eighteen-hole golf course. The property is owned by the Iowa Department of

## furryfriends beware

Albia is home to Kness Manufacturing, maker of what many consider to be the world's best mousetrap (that adjective is bestowed by humans, not mice).

Natural Resources and offers interpretive programs such as hiking, fishing, biking, stargazing, outdoor cooking, geocaching, and bird-watching.

Honey Creek is one of the finest resort parks in the country and represents a decades-long investment of time and money by the state of Iowa and private citizens. If you like your nature served with a little bit of luxury, this is the place for you. For more information about Honey Creek Resort, call (877) 677-3344 or see www.honeycreekresort.com.

Near the resort you'll find **Rathbun State Fish Hatchery,** Iowa's largest warm-water fish hatchery. Catfish, walleye, saugeye, and largemouth bass by the millions are raised here each year before being released into Iowa streams, ponds, rivers and lakes.

You can view the facility's operations on an elevated walkway. The hatchery is on CR J5T; call (641) 647-2406 for information. It is open Mon through Fri.

South of Honey Creek Resort lies **Centerville,** the county seat of Appanoose County. For many years the area was the site of a thriving coal-mining industry. Commercial mining began in 1863 and peaked in 1917, when 400 mines were operating in the area. Old-timers here can still tell stories of leaving school after eighth grade and joining their fathers in the mines.

Though the last coal mine closed in 1971, you can learn more about the industry's history at the **Appanoose County Historical and Coal Mining Museum** in Centerville. Located at 100 W. Maple St., the museum (641-856-8040) is located in the town's former post office, built in 1903. It houses a coalmine replica on its lower level, with mining tools and equipment that show the difficult working conditions endured by the early miners. The museum also includes information on the Mormon exodus that passed through here in 1846, as well as other aspects of southern Iowa history. The museum is open Memorial Day through Sept, Tues through Sat, and on weekdays only in Apr, Oct, and Nov. A small admission fee is charged. For information call (641) 856-8040.

After touring the museum, stop by **The Shoppes at Bradley Hall** (519 Drake Ave.). This mansion, built in 1909, includes four floors of specialty shops, from jewelry and art galleries to baby items and Christmas decorations The thirty-two-room Bradley home was once the social center of Centerville, and a creative renovation of the building has made it once again a bustling hive of activity. For information call (641) 856-5345.

Another historic home has found new life as a shopping mecca called **The Columns.** The white-columned mansion was built in 1895 and once served as a dormitory for college football players before finding new life as a gift galleria. Its many rooms are filled with antiques, crafts, artwork, and decorative items. You'll find The Columns at 107 E. Washington St. For information call (641) 437-1178 or see their Web site at www.thecolumns.info.

Fans of old-time music will enjoy the ***Rathbun Country Music Theater,*** located 1¼ miles north of the Rathbun Dam on CR J5T. For more than thirty years the theater has been presenting live music each Saturday night from Apr through Oct. Call (660) 344-2310 or see www.countrymusictheater.com for information.

There may be no such thing as a free lunch, but if you go to Centerville on the last Saturday in September, you'll sure get your fill of free pancakes! Why? Because it's ***Pancake Day!*** This wonderful festival, still entirely free of charge, began in 1949 when local merchants got together to say "thanks" to their customers. It started small, but now twenty-six griddles cook up more than 80,000 pancakes. If pancakes aren't enough for you, there is also a parade with floats and bands, ongoing entertainment, and the crowning of the Pancake Day Queen. For more information call (800) 611-3800.

A few miles south of Centerville lies the village of Exline, home to the ***Exline Old Country Store.*** Inside you'll find antiques, a cafe, and a soda fountain, plus T-shirts emblazoned with I Love My Ex! (not sure they sell very many of those). By the potbellied stove you'll find an area marked as the "Sit

## The Wonders of Buxton

In the first two decades of the twentieth century, a unique community lived and prospered in northern Monroe County north of Centerville. At a time when coal was king in southern Iowa—Iowa ranked fifteenth in coal production at that time in the United States—the Consolidation Coal Company established the coal camp of **Buxton.** In this planned community, each house sat on a quarter acre of land, with ample room for gardens and porches. The site of the town was chosen with care, and considerations for drainage, hygiene, and comfort were made priorities. The year was 1900. By 1905 African Americans made up 55 percent of Buxton's labor force.

In an era that witnessed the increasing oppression of blacks in the American South and their segregation in northern ghettos, Buxton was, according to former black residents, "the black man's utopia in Iowa." Because of the town's size (around 5,000 residents), Buxton afforded opportunities for professional occupations and leadership roles for the African-American population in medicine, law, education, and business. The community was integrated—schools, stores, churches, and community centers accommodated both blacks and whites. Black residents and white residents (mostly of Swedish, Slavic, and Italian descent) worked side by side for equal pay, equal housing, and equal opportunities, with very little racial tension. And the name of the community's baseball team? The Buxton Wonders, of course! By 1925, however, with the demand for coal decreasing, Buxton was abandoned, and its inhabitants dispersed to find jobs and homes elsewhere. Though some wonders may cease, they should never be forgotten.

& Spit Corner," though inexplicably, no spitting is allowed. In the summer, you can relax in one of the rocking chairs on the front porch. The store is at 102 W. Main St. and is open daily. Call (641) 658-2399 or see www.exlinecountrystore .com for more information.

# River Territory

Next travel to scenic Van Buren County. **Keosauqua,** its county seat, has a grand total of 1,066 people (when everyone is home), and the pace in the county's other towns is just as slow. Visitors agree that the quiet is part of the area's allure—that and an old-fashioned atmosphere that's authentic, not manufactured.

Back in the mid-nineteenth century, however, life was more hectic in **Van Buren County.** The meandering Des Moines River that flows through the center of the county was a busy passageway for steamboats, and the villages on its banks were bustling ports. Mills, stores, and hotels filled the towns, and an active social life kept both locals and visitors entertained. Unfortunately, the years of prosperity ended abruptly when the U.S. Congress decided that the locks and dams along the river would no longer be maintained, thus making the river un-navigable by the larger boats. Soon the towns settled into faded obscurity, as all but a few residents packed up their bags and moved away.

Within the past twenty years, the area has experienced a renaissance that has preserved its historical character and charm while still making it a favorite destination for growing numbers of visitors. Keosauqua is a good place to begin your tour. The name comes from an Indian word meaning "great bend," a reference to the loop the Des Moines River takes around the town. Keosauqua was once a stop on the Underground Railroad and was also a fording spot for the Mormons on their westward trek in the late 1840s.

Today the best-known landmark in Keosauqua is the **Hotel Manning,** a two-story brick structure with wide verandas for watching the Des Moines River flow by. The hotel was built in 1899 and through the ensuing years has withstood no fewer than four floods. I enjoy staying at the Hotel Manning

## distinguished hotelguest

The great poet T. S. Eliot was one of the Hotel Manning's famous guests. He signed the hotel register on September 13, 1919.

because it's like slipping into an old, comfortable shoe. The floors creak, the doors don't always match, and there's a delightful air of faded gentility about the place that makes it easy to imagine how it must have been when river travelers stayed here a hundred years ago. The hotel's nineteen rooms are furnished with antique furniture and brightly patterned quilts, braided rugs line the floor, and steam radiators keep the building toasty warm in winter. The Hotel Manning is located at 100 Van Buren St. Rates range from inexpensive to moderate; call (800) 728-2718 for reservations.

Also in the area is *Lacey-Keosauqua State Park,* one of the state's largest parks, with more than 1,600 acres. The great horseshoe bend the river makes here offers beautiful vistas for hikers and campers.

Next travel east to *Bentonsport,* a tiny village with a number of restored buildings and stores on its main street, which has been designated a National

## Passion and Precision in the World of Tony Sanders

It is not uncommon to find both passion and precision in the work of a skilled craftsperson. Less common is to find the same passion and precision applied to two apparently unrelated crafts. Rarer still is to find these two crafts wedded together in a work of consummate artistry. But such is the world and work of Tony Sanders.

Since he was seven or eight years old, Sanders found himself drawn to river and creek beds, looking for arrowheads and spear-points to collect. Working for most of his adult life on a dairy farm near Fort Madison, Sanders kept on looking and collecting when spare time and weather conditions allowed. Sanders learned more with every find, until finally he was able to retire and pour his passion into a long-sought dream: establishing a museum for his extensive collection. A small building in Bentonsport became available for himself and his more than four thousand artifacts and animal horns. Here he was also able to pursue woodworking. Sanders designed and inlaid the interior of his one-room museum with the wood of naturally felled trees of all varieties. The work is intricate and various, paying homage to the designs and motifs of the Native Americans who long ago crafted the artifacts that he has spent a lifetime finding, collecting, and respecting. He designed and built the display cases in which the artifacts are housed; the inlaid walls of the cases complement the ancient designs found within. The oldest artifact is 12,000 years old, but this is young in comparison to the piece of petrified palm wood that Sanders found that dates to the time when Iowa was in the tropics. One of the artifacts in which he takes the most pride is an effigy of a snake, not more than 3 inches long, which he first mistook for the gnarled root of a tree. But he soon discovered he had found something unique. Sanders's accumulated knowledge about such artifacts is profound.

The *Bentonsport Museum of Indian Artifacts and Horns* is located on Des Moines Street, next to the Graf General store. It is open daily, and Sanders will be happy to take you on a tour and explain his work. But don't expect to find him if it's raining or immediately following a big rain. He will be out doing what he loves so passionately—scouring the creek and river beds for arrowheads, spear-points, and horns.

Historic District. Take special note of the Greef General Store, a structure built in the Federal style in 1853 that now serves as a showcase for local antiques and crafts. The town also is home to a growing community of artists, including potter Betty Printy. She has established a regional reputation with her distinctive Queen Anne's lace pottery. Using hand-dug local clay, Printy molds the pottery and then presses the wildflower Queen Anne's lace into the clay while it's still wet. The result is a beautiful tracery of lines and flowers. You can find her work at Iron and Lace. For information call (319) 592-3222 or see www.ironandlace.com.

Down the river from Bentonsport is the village of *Bonaparte,* also the site of historic preservation efforts. In 1989 its downtown area was named a National Historic Riverfront District, a tribute to the hard work of the village's citizens. Stop by the *Aunty Green Museum,* which was once a hotel and now houses historical displays and a library. It is located at 602 Second St.

The best-known restoration in Bonaparte is *Bonaparte's Retreat* at 813 Front St. It is a fine restaurant housed in a nineteenth-century gristmill. Owned by Ben and Rose Hendricks, the restaurant is known for both the quality of its food and its decor, and a pleasing mixture of steamboat and gristmill relics. The restaurant's menu includes steak, pork, and seafood.

Bonaparte's Retreat is open Mon through Sat for lunch and dinner, and on Sun for lunch. Call (319) 592-3339 or see www.bonaparteretreat.com. Prices are moderate to expensive.

For more information about other attractions in the area, call the Villages of Van Buren at (800) 868-7822 or see www.villagesofvanburen.com.

West of Bonaparte on IA 2 lies the small village of *Cantril.* There you'll find *Dutchman's Store* (319-397-2322), a bulk grocery, dry-goods, and fabric store operated by a local Mennonite family. The old-fashioned establishment is open Mon through Sat.

The *Wickfield Sales Pavilion* lies 2½ miles north of Cantril on Old Highway 2. Built in 1918, the distinctive, round, brick structure was used as a site for hog auctions staged by Wickfield Farms, once the largest breeders of purebred Hampshire hogs in the world. The Van Buren County Historic Preservation Commission is restoring the site, which is opened on select weekends. For information on special events and tours, call (319) 796-2253.

From Van Buren County travel to *Keokuk,* a city that lies at the southeastern tip of the state. Keokuk was once known as the Gate City because of its position at the foot of the Des Moines rapids on the Mississippi. In the early days of settlement, steamboats were unable to go beyond this point, and all passengers had to disembark here, either to continue their journey on land or board another boat upriver. The city played an important role in the Civil

# Ghost Hunting 101

Iowa's most famous haunted house sits on the banks of the Des Moines River in the small village of Bentonsport. The *Mason House Inn* is said to be haunted by no fewer than twenty spirits, including a ghostly cat. After initially wanting to keep its spectral inhabitants secret, owners Joy and Chuck Hanson now welcome publicity about the inn's haunted reputation. In 2006 the Mason House was featured on a *Today Show* segment on America's most haunted houses.

When the Hansons purchased the Federal-style brick structure in 2001, they were told by the previous owner that the inn had a ghost. "That didn't bother us, but we soon began to suspect there was more than one spirit because there was so much strange activity in the house," says Joy. "Doors locked themselves, we'd hear our names being called when no one was there, and alarm clocks kept going off when we hadn't set them. Also, guests would often come to breakfast with stories of odd things happening at night, like door handles jiggling and tapping on the walls."

Today the Inn offers several ghost-hunting courses throughout the year. A typical class includes a primer in investigation techniques, an overview of the house's history, and a description of the spirits who have previously made appearances. In the evening, class members go from room to room seeking to make contact with the ghosts.

Why do so many spirits congregate at the Mason House? The Hansons speculate that part of the reason is that the house has been a gathering place for the local community since it was built in 1846, and that many happy times happened within its walls. They also believe that the spirits watch over the house and that they enjoy the parade of people who come to stay in it. Guests who are leery of supernatural encounters can stay in the nonhistorical part of the inn, which isn't believed to be haunted.

"We have great respect for the spirits who live here, and I think they like that," says Chuck. "We know that they're the longtime residents here, and we're just temporary."

The Mason House Inn is at 21982 Hawk Dr. For more information call (800) 592-3133 or see www.masonhouseinn.com.

War, when seven hospitals were established here to care for the wounded transported up the Mississippi from southern battlefields.

The *Keokuk National Cemetery* was one of the first national cemeteries designated by the U.S. Congress and is the resting place for both Union and Confederate soldiers. It was also the first national cemetery west of the Mississippi and is the only one in Iowa. It's located at 1701 J St. and is open from dawn to dusk daily.

The city's most famous citizen was Mark Twain, who worked here as a young man in the printing shop of his brother, Orion Clemens. Most of the type for the city's first directory was set by Twain, who listed himself in its pages as an "antiquarian." When asked the reason for this, he replied that he always thought that every town should have at least one antiquarian, and since none had appeared for the post, he decided to volunteer.

The **George M. Verity _Riverboat Museum_** will take you back to those days when Keokuk was a busy river port. Built in 1927, the _Verity_ was the first of four steamboats built to revive river transportation on the Mississippi. In 1960 it was retired and given to the city of Keokuk for use as a river museum. Today it contains many old-time photographs of riverboats and the river era, as well as other artifacts and historical items.

The _Verity_ is berthed in Victory Park at the foot of Main Street on the Mississippi River. It is open daily from 9 a.m. to 5 p.m., Memorial Day through Labor Day, and a small admission is charged. Call (800) 383-1219 or see www .geomverity.org for information.

More history comes to life during the **_Battle of Pea Ridge Civil War Reenactment,_** which includes mock battles, a military ball, period music and dancing, and a ladies' tea and fashion show. The event is held each year on the last weekend in April in Rand Park, and most events are free. Call (800) 383-1219 for more information.

While you're in Keokuk, take a walk. **_On the Avenue_** is a self-guided walking tour that takes in thirty beautiful old houses built at the end of the nineteenth and the beginning of the twentieth centuries. The houses are all located on Orleans and Grand Avenues along the river and were built for the elite of this once-booming town. Don't miss 925 Grand Ave. (No. 21 on the tour). This house was built in 1880 by Howard Hughes Sr., father of the famous junior and the inventor of the oil well drill. Hughes built the house for his

## newdealmurals

During the Depression, the Works Progress Adminstration commissioned artists to paint murals across the state. You can see these WPA murals in towns that include:

**Columbus Junction:** Post Office

**Mount Pleasant:** Post Office

**Sigourney:** Post Office

**Bloomfield:** Post Office

mother, and constructed it entirely without closets because she was panicked by the fear that they were breeding grounds for disease. The tour ends at the lovely Rand Park. To get a wonderfully detailed map and brochure of this informative tour, contact the Keokuk Area Convention and Tourism Bureau at (800) 383-1219 or (319) 524-5599.

Also of interest in Keokuk are the Miller House Museum (once home to U.S. Supreme Court justice Samuel Miller) and the Keokuk Power Plant/U.S.

## City of Christmas

The North Pole isn't the only place where elves work year-round to prepare for the holidays. In Keokuk, Santa's helpers come in the form of volunteers who stage the *City of Christmas,* a spectacular light extravaganza featuring more than one hundred handcrafted displays in the town's Rand Park.

Begun in 1989 with just a few displays, Keokuk's City of Christmas has grown to become a beloved holiday tradition. Financed by donations and run by volunteers, the event is truly a celebration of holiday—and hometown—spirit.

The people who *ooh* and *aah* from inside the 12,000 vehicles that pass through the park each year may not realize the large amount of work that makes the City of Christmas possible. Most of the displays are constructed in the basement of Keokuk's senior center, with a half-dozen volunteers working steadily throughout the year. Several new designs are added each Christmas, and existing ones are improved.

While many of the designs feature familiar holiday themes, a growing number reflect the town's unique identity. One of the newest displays, for example, features a hand reaching down toward six lighted globes. The design pays tribute to three Keokuk children who were killed in a house fire in 1999 and to the three firefighters who died trying to save them.

Lock and Dam No. 19. When the power plant was completed in 1913, it was the largest electric generating plant in the world. Later a 1,200-foot lock, the largest on the Upper Mississippi, was constructed to accommodate modern river traffic.

Thanks to the lock and dam, Keokuk is one of the most important winter feeding areas for the American bald eagle. As the birds' primary feeding spots in Canada and Alaska begin to freeze, they fly south to find food. As many as 1,400 bald eagles winter along the Mississippi between Minneapolis and St. Louis. Keokuk enjoys one of the highest populations because the lock and dam keep the water from freezing, thus enabling the birds to hunt for fish.

Eagles can be seen in the area from October to early April, but the best time for viewing them is from mid-December to mid-February. Early morning is the ideal time, when they can be seen soaring and diving for fish. During **Bald Eagle Appreciation Days** each January, the Keokuk Area Convention and Tourism Bureau sponsors shuttle-bus service to and from observation areas, as well as seminars, lectures, exhibits, Native American activities, and films on the magnificent birds. It also puts out a brochure listing prime viewing areas; call (800) 383-1219. If you do go eagle viewing on your own, bring a pair of binoculars and stay either in or next to your car. It's important that resting eagles not be disturbed; when they fly off, they burn up energy badly needed during the cold weather.

Overnight visitors to Keokuk should make reservations at the ***Grand Anne Bed and Breakfast,*** which overlooks the Mississippi at 816 Grand Ave. The twenty-two–room showplace was built in 1897 and offers four guest rooms furnished with period antiques. Freshly baked desserts and beverages are served at bedtime, and a full breakfast is served each morning. Rates are expensive; call (800) 524-6310 for information.

From Keokuk travel north on US 61 to ***Fort Madison,*** a river town first established in 1808 as a government trading post and one of three major forts guarding the Northwest frontier. Rozanna Stark, the first white child to be born in the state, was born here in 1810. In 1813 the fort was attacked by Indians and its settlers were forced to flee, burning the fort as they left so that all that

# The (Not-So-Famous) Honey War

In December of 1839 troops gathered in Farmington, Iowa, and in Waterloo, Missouri, prepared to go to war—against each other. Like a lot of other wars, this one was set off by a seemingly innocuous incident: A Missourian had cut down three bee trees on what was thought to be Iowa land. But honey was very important to the early settlers, and bee trees were valuable.

The problem behind the bee trees was this: Surveys since 1819 had confused the boundary between the two states. Some marked it from the Des Moines River rapids, some from the so-called Des Moines rapids of the Mississippi. At issue was a 2,600-square-acre region, and both states wanted it. A further complication was the fact that the Missouri Compromise of 1820–21 had allowed Missouri into the Union as a slave state while Iowa remained a free state. Of course, there was also the issue of taxation; taxes were as important to the governors of each state as the honey was to the settlers. Iowa settlers had resisted paying taxes to Missouri. Next, Iowa's Van Buren County sheriff arrested Missouri's Clark County sheriff during one of his tax collection rounds. As a result, Missouri's governor called for militia support and Iowa's governor responded by summoning volunteers. Fortunately, war never actually erupted, but the problem was getting stickier and stickier, and things continued to buzz on both sides of the border until the U.S. Supreme Court finally decided the issue in favor of Iowa in 1851.

You can call the Honey War a foreshadowing of the Civil War, you can call it a mere footnote in the history books, you can call it anything you like, but in 1839 it was definitely one honey of a problem. But all's well that ends well, and I have read, though I haven't been able to confirm, that it did end happily for one farmer whose land was in the disputed territory. She is reputed to have said that she was glad her land turned out to be in the state of Iowa after all, because she had heard that the Iowa climate was much better for crops than the climate of Missouri. So there!

—T. S.

remained was a blackened chimney (the chimney is now a monument on Avenue H and US 61).

On the riverfront in Riverview Park, you can tour the rebuilt stockade of **Old Fort Madison,** which vividly evokes the town's origins as a remote frontier outpost. Constructed on the riverfront in 1983 (partly with labor provided by inmates at the Iowa State Penitentiary in Fort Madison), the rough-hewn fort brings to life the often-precarious existence of its original inhabitants. Costumed interpreters describe how the residents coped with frequent Indian raids, diseases such as malaria and typhoid fever, and the constant threat of starvation.

## didyouknow?

The statue in Rand Park honoring Chief Keokuk, the famous leader of the Sac and Fox tribe, was modeled after the style of the Sioux chiefs, some of Keokuk's most hated enemies.

The tyrannical nature of the fort's commander, Horatio Stark, proved to be another hardship (a popular T-shirt in the gift shop bears the slogan, "The floggings will continue until morale improves"). Volunteer interpreter Nick Colbert says "Even by the standards of the day, Stark was considered a harsh disciplinarian of his men."

Special events are held at the Old Fort throughout the year, including period dinners, candlelight tours, and a military history reunion in June. Old Fort Madison (800-210-8687) is open Wed through Sun from 9 a.m. to 5 p.m. from Memorial Day through Aug and on weekends in May and Sept.

After leaving the riverfront area, take a stroll down Fort Madison's adjoining five-block downtown area. Be sure to stop by Faeth's (where five generations of customers have been coming for beer, fishing advice, and billiards games), and Pendemonium, a haven for pen collectors who appreciate the beauty of an elegant writing instrument.

Next pull up a chair at the **Ivy Bake Shoppe & Café** (319-372-9939), a nineteenth-century clothing store at 622 Seventh St. that now houses the town's favorite meeting place. Owners Susan Welch Saunders and Martha Wolf, who started their business in 1992 by selling baked goods out of their homes, have a loyal following of customers devoted to their made-from-scratch treats. Don't miss the warm onion pie, a house specialty, but leave room for dessert such as caramel apple tarts and blackberry scones.

For dinner, head to **Alpha's on the Riverfront** (319-372-3779) at 709 Ave. H. The award-winning restaurant is part of a complex that includes the elegantly restored **Kingsley Inn,** an eighteen-room hotel overlooking the Mississippi (rates are moderate). Call (319) 372-7074 for reservations.

# The Toolesboro Indian Mounds

Seven Indian mounds are situated on a bluff overlooking the Iowa River near its junction with the mighty Mississippi. The largest one measures 100 feet wide and 8 feet high. Two thousand years ago, between 100 B.C. and A.D. 200, Native Americans constructed these mounds as sacred burial sites for the highest-ranking members of their nation, probably the chiefs and priests. The names of the tribes are lost to us, for no written language survives. They—or rather, their system of burial practices—are known to the modern world as the "Hopewell tradition." No village site has ever been found, perhaps because of the shifting course of the Iowa River over the centuries. We only know that these cultures shared a widespread system of belief and worship. They probably lived along river flood plains and buried their dead on the high bluffs as they did here. They had an extensive trade network; artifacts including marine shells, Chesapeake Bay sharks' teeth, Rocky Mountain obsidian, Great Lakes copper, Appalachian mica, and Gulf of Mexico pearls have all been discovered.

After A.D. 500 the mound builders disappeared from the archaeological landscape. Many of these ancient peoples' mounds were damaged or ruined by European-American land clearing, plowing, and clumsy excavation techniques. Fortunately, this has been stopped in the last fifty years or so. Current archaeological exploration prefers nonintrusive studies, using such methods as aerial photography, surface surveys, and a technique known as "remote sensing," which takes pictures that function a lot like X-rays.

Visitors are welcome to the mounds anytime. The admission is free. They are located on IA 99 between Wapello and Oakville. The fine Educational Center is open from 12:30 to 4:30 p.m. daily except for Mon, Memorial Day through Labor Day, and on Sat and Sun, Labor Day through Oct. Call (319) 523-8381 for more information.

Each year on the weekend after Labor Day, Fort Madison hosts the *Tri-State Rodeo.* Since 1947 it has been one of the nation's top professional rodeos, performed in a 10,000-seat outdoor arena. For more information about Fort Madison, contact the Fort Madison Area Convention & Visitors Bureau at (800) 210-8687 or see www.visitfortmadison.com.

From Fort Madison head north on US 61 to the Mississippi River port of *Burlington.* The Indians called the great bluffs bordering the river here *Sho-quoquon,* a name meaning "flint hills." Many tribes gathered flint from area hillsides in the early nineteenth century for use in their weapons and hunting tools. Their days in the area were numbered, however, for in 1805 Zebulon Pike landed in what is now the city of Burlington, and within thirty years the territory was thrown open to white settlers. Burlington was the first capital of the Iowa territory from 1838 to 1840 and an important steamboat, lumber, and railroad center in the nineteenth century.

A good place to begin your tour of the city is the **Port of Burlington Welcome Center** at 400 N. Front St. Located on the bank of the river, the 1928 building once was a coal-loading site for barges. Now it houses an information center with historical displays and a video of local attractions. The center (319-752-8731) is open daily.

Next take a stroll along Burlington's most famous landmark, **Snake Alley.** *Ripley's Believe It or Not* has dubbed Snake Alley the "crookedest street in the world," and each year it continues to draw many visitors. The alley and the Victorian homes that surround it have been named to the National Register of Historic Places. You can approach the top of Snake Alley along North Sixth Street between Washington and Columbia Streets.

Just off Snake Alley is the **Schramm House Bed and Breakfast,** 616 Columbia St. This beautiful old house, built in the 1860s by the founder of Schramm's Department Store, offers four guest rooms. It is conveniently located for sightseeing throughout Burlington. Call (217) 852-3652 for more information.

A Burlington dining landmark is **Big Muddy's.** The 1898 structure was once a railroad freight station and now houses an excellent restaurant (prices are moderate to expensive). You'll find Big Muddy's (319-753-1699) at 710 N. Front St. Drive in or boat in—it makes no difference.

Visit **Mosquito Park,** named for its size, not its bite! You will find this little gem tucked away at Third and Franklin Streets. Set on bluffs just north

## The Crookedest Street in the World

Building a town along the steep hillsides surrounding the Mississippi River required considerable ingenuity. In 1894 Snake Alley was constructed as an experimental street connecting the downtown business district and the neighborhood shopping area on North Sixth Street. This 275-foot-long, zigzagging street rises nearly 60 feet up the bluff and is constructed of tilted bricks designed to allow better footing for horses. The switchback design proved to be less successful than was hoped, however, as drivers often lost control of their horses on its steep curves. Plans to construct more streets on its model were abandoned.

Snake Alley nevertheless proved useful. Horses were "test-driven" up the winding curves at a gallop, and those that reached the top with the least difficulty were deemed fit enough to haul the city fire wagons. When cars were first offered for sale, they had to endure the same test, as auto dealers used Snake Alley to show off the vehicles' power, with prospective buyers clinging in terror to their seats. While Snake Alley is no longer open to cars, it continues to be the town's most distinctive landmark.

of the downtown district, it offers a captivating view of the rolling Mississippi below.

Another jewel is located at St. Mary's Catholic Church in West Burlington at 420 W. Mount Pleasant St. *Our Lady of Grace Grotto,* completed in 1931, was constructed of thousands of imported and native stones and features split-rock sidewalks and crystal-rock walls. Forty different varieties of trees are found in its garden. For more information call (319) 752-4035.

Burlington's newest visitor destination is *Fun City,* a resort complex that includes a wide range of attractions for both adults and children. If you can't find something to do here, you probably lack a pulse. Huck's Harbor Water Park delights younger kids with its lazy river, dump buckets, water cannons, and slides, while teens flock to a game arcade that includes a 3-D roller-coaster ride, laser tag, cosmic bowling, and an indoor go-kart speedway. The complex also includes Catfish Bend Casino and the Catfish Bend Inn and Spa, where you can enjoy massages, facials, and other body-pampering treatments. Four on-site restaurants offer a variety of dining options, while the nearby Spirit Hollow Golf Course is rated as one of the top courses in the state. You'll find the resort complex at 3001 Winegard Dr., at the intersection of US 34 and US 61. For information call (866) 792-9948 or see www.thepzazz.com.

## longgreenlegacy

Pioneering conservationist Aldo Leopold was born in Burlington on January 11, 1887. His book *A Sand County Almanac* continues to inspire people to treasure and protect the natural world.

The biggest annual event in this river city is *Burlington Steamboat Days,* when nationally known rock, country, pop, rhythm and blues, jazz, big band, and oldies groups perform daily on outdoor stages in June. More than 100,000 visitors converge in Burlington for the event, which also includes fireworks, parades, a carnival, sports competitions, the Snake Alley Art Fair, and plenty of good food and drink. See www.steamboatdays.com for more information.

The *Snake Alley Art Fair,* held during Steamboat Days, offers craft demonstrations and sales by more than one hundred artists. On Memorial Day weekend, the *Snake Alley Criterium* draws cyclists from around the nation to race up Burlington's most famous street.

For more information on Burlington, call (800) 827-4837or you can visit www.growburlington.com.

# Places to Stay in Rural Charms

## BONAPARTE
**Kountry Kottage**
31965 235th Rd.
(319) 592-3431
moderate

## BURLINGTON
**Candlelight Manor Bed & Breakfast**
303 S. Sixth St.
(319) 758-0428
www.candlemanor.net
moderate

## CENTERVILLE
**One of a Kind Bed & Breakfast**
314 W. State St.
(641) 437-4540
www.oneofakindbedand
breakfast.com
inexpensive

## FAIRFIELD
**The Main Stay Inn**
300 N. Main St.
(641) 209-3300
www.mainstayfairfield.com
expensive

## FORT MADISON
**Auntie Ann's B&B**
2626 Ave. H
(319) 463-7200
www.auntieannsbandb
.com
inexpensive

## KALONA
**Carriage House Bed and Breakfast**
1140 Larch Ave.
(319) 656-3824
www.carriagehousebb.net
moderate to expensive

## KEOKUK
**The River's Edge Bed & Breakfast Inn**
611 Grand Ave.
(888) 581-3343
www.riversedgeiowa.com
expensive

# Places to Eat in Rural Charms

## ALBIA
**Casa Agave Mexican Restaurant**
24 Washington Ave. East
(641) 932-2997
inexpensive

## BURLINGTON
**The Drake**
106 Washington St.
(319) 754-1036
www.thedrakerestaurant
.com
moderate to expensive

**La Tavola**
316 N. Fourth St.
(319) 768-5600
moderate

## CENTERVILLE
**The Continental**
217 N. Thirteenth St.
(641) 437-1025
www.thecontinental.info
moderate

## FORT MADISON
**The Palms Supper Club**
US 61 West
(319) 372-5833
moderate to expensive

## KEOKUK
**Beef, Bread & Brew**
2601 Main St.
(319) 524-7476
moderate

## MOUNT PLEASANT
**Iris Restaurant**
915 W. Washington St.
(319) 385-2241
inexpensive to moderate

## OTTUMWA
**Canteen Lunch in the Alley**
112 E. Second St.
(641) 682-5320
inexpensive

# BRIDGE COUNTRY

South central Iowa can be thought of as "bridge country" in two different ways. In Madison County you can discover the sites made famous by the popular novel and film *The Bridges of Madison County*. In Des Moines and its neighboring cities—a region sometimes called the "golden circle"—you can explore the metropolitan area that serves as a bridge between Iowa's rural communities and its increasingly urban central core.

South central Iowa is also home to the ethnic enclave of Pella, where Dutch traditions remain strong, as well as other rural treasures along the southern border.

## Golden Circle

Begin your tour in the town of *Grinnell.* J. B. Grinnell, the founder of the town and the nationally acclaimed Grinnell College located here, was the recipient of Horace Greeley's famous dictum: "Go West, young man, and grow up with the country." Josiah Bushnell Grinnell was active in the early educational concerns of Iowa's legislature as well as an ardent abolitionist. He made Grinnell a stop on the Underground Railroad; more than 1,000 freedom-seeking slaves passed through

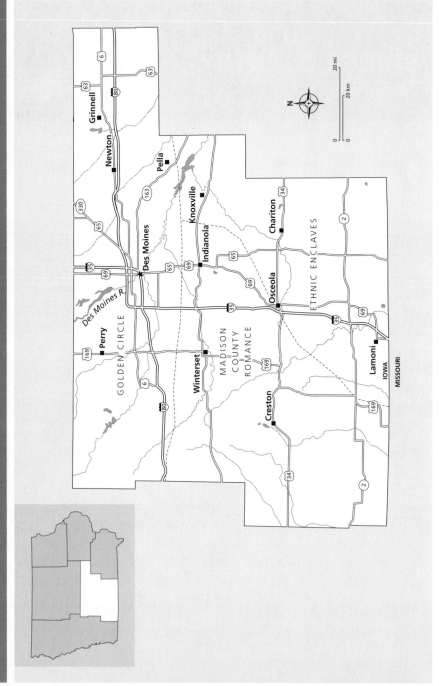

Grinnell in the pre–Civil War years. In 1859 he gave refuge to John Brown following his raids in Kansas and Missouri. Learn more about this influential man and this community when you visit the **Grinnell Historical Museum,** which is housed in a ten-room late-Victorian residence at 1125 Broad St. Besides the furniture and artifacts of an earlier era, there is a barbed-wire collection and several carriages (including a surrey with fringe on top) made by the old Spaulding Carriage and Automotive Works of Grinnell. Call (641) 236-7827 or see www.grinnellmuseum.org for more information.

For a real treat (and maybe even a few tricks) visit **Carroll's Pumpkin Farm** during October. There's so much to do here, it's hard to go wrong. You can pick a pumpkin, get lost in a corn maze, climb into a tree house, burst with laughter as you slide into bales of straw, and see an honest-to-goodness pumpkin tree. If you have children along, you may want to devote an entire afternoon to Carroll's. There's a small concession stand that serves seasonal treats like caramel apples, popcorn, and cider, and you're welcome to bring in a picnic lunch. With advance notice, a bonfire can be built so you can roast your hot dogs and marshmallows. On

## didyouknow?

The first intercollegiate football game played west of the Mississippi took place in 1889 when the University of Iowa and Grinnell College teams met on the gridiron.

weekends there are shows in the barn loft and unlimited hayrides, and if you were lucky enough to be born in October, you will be specially honored. Carroll's Pumpkin Farm is located at 244 400th Ave. in Grinnell. It is open Mon through Sat from 10 a.m. to 7 p.m. and on Sun from 1 to 7 p.m. during Oct. The farm also has a nice gift shop. A small admission is charged. Take IA 146 south of Grinnell to 400th Avenue and turn right. For more information call (641) 236-7043 or see www.carrollspumpkinfarm.com.

## AUTHORS' FAVORITES

| | |
|---|---|
| Neal Smith National Wildlife Refuge | Carnegie Library Museum |
| Iowa State Fair | Cutler-Donahoe Covered Bridge |
| Iowa State Capitol | Des Moines Metro Opera |
| Living History Farms | Mount Pisgah |
| Kin Folks Eatin' Place | Iowa Hall of Pride |

## Twister Alert!

On June 17, 1882, the state of Iowa almost lost the town of *Grinnell.* Storms had been raging across the state all day and were to meet with a furious uproar in Grinnell. Ten miles away in Kellogg, two black clouds united and formed a tornado that swept northeast to Grinnell. In the west, in Carroll County, another tornado was moving swiftly to the southeast.

As if by appointment, the two twisters met in the very center of the town of Grinnell. It was a clash of titanic proportions that sent at least six smaller tornadoes spiraling downward. Thirty-nine people were killed and the college was in ruins. The only property salvaged was the college bell.

Seven years later in 1889, the downtown district was again almost destroyed by a devastating fire. We are lucky to have this town still on the map. J. B. Grinnell, the founder, was instrumental in rebuilding the town twice. Earlier he had given lots to the college, stating that they would have to be given back to him or his estate if liquor was ever sold on them. Could it be that the tornadoes knew more about what was going on than he did?

Continue west to *Newton.* At the *Jasper County Historical Museum* (1700 S. Fifteenth Ave. West) you can view displays on local history. The museum's largest exhibit tells the story of the Maytag Company, which began manufacturing washers here in 1907. The company dominated the local economy until recently, when operations were moved to other parts of the nation. The museum (641-792-9118) is at exit 164 off I-80 and is open daily from 1 to 4:30 p.m. from May 1 to Oct 1.

E. H. Maytag, son of the founder of the Maytag Company, established another of Newton's well-known industries, the *Maytag Dairy Farms.* Maytag Blue Cheese is acclaimed by connoisseurs as one of the country's finest gourmet cheeses. Stop by the cheese shop to sample some; then view a ten minute video and tour the packaging area. The Maytag Dairy Farms (800-247-2458) are located north of Newton;. The farms are open Mon through Fri from 8 a.m. to 5 p.m. and on Sat from 9 a.m. to 1 p.m. Take exit 164 off I-80, and then go 3 miles north on IA 14 and follow signs to the farms.

## clothesline capitalofiowa

Newton was once the home of nine washing-machine companies and was called "the Washing Machine Capital of the World."

A culinary treat in Newton can be found at *La Corsette Maison Inn,* a gourmet restaurant and country inn housed in an opulent Spanish mission–style mansion built in 1909. Owner and chef John Gerken uses locally raised ingredients whenever possible to create prix fixe meals with either four or six courses. Reservations are required. The inn also offers five guest rooms for overnight visitors. La Corsette is located at 629 First Ave. East. Prices are in the expensive category, but well worth it. Call (641) 792-6833 or see www.lacorsette.com for more information.

From Newton travel west to *Trainland U.S.A.* (3135 IA 117 North in Colfax), a must-see for anyone who loves model railroading. Located a few miles north of the town of *Colfax,* Trainland is the fulfillment of a dream for its owner, Leland "Red" Atwood. After many years of collecting Lionel trains, Atwood tore down his family home in 1976 and replaced it with a building designed to house both a museum and living quarters. Friends and neighbors devoted hundreds of hours of labor to help him turn the building's ground floor into a huge display depicting the development of railroads in the United States.

The exhibit represents three eras of railroading: frontier, steam, and diesel. All the scenery is hand-painted and includes details such as a miniature Mount Rushmore, White House, Statue of Liberty, and Kentucky coal mine, plus a drive-in movie with animated cartoons projected on a tiny screen. More than twenty electric trains operate simultaneously over nearly a mile

## Prairie Wonders

When pioneers first saw the endless grasslands that covered much of the heartland of the United States, they reasoned that the soil must be poor because there weren't many trees here. Some even called it a desert. Only later was it discovered that the prairie plants had in fact created the richest soil on earth, rich loam that extended to a depth of 4 feet in places.

Within a few short decades settlers had plowed the prairie and sowed the land with crops like corn and wheat. Prairie plants remained only in a few scattered remnants. In Iowa alone the loss was catastrophic: When pioneers first came to the state, tallgrass prairie covered 85 percent of Iowa's 36 million acres. Today, less than 1 percent of that prairie remains.

A mature tallgrass prairie provides an abundance of life: hundreds of plant, insect, and bird species, plus scores of mammals, amphibians, reptiles, and even fish species. Each is precisely adapted to the extremes of temperature and precipitation found in the Midwest, from blazing summer heat and frigid winters to great floods and lingering droughts. Some prairie plants exhibit amazing ingenuity. Needlegrass, for example, has a seed with a sharp point and a tail that changes with the weather. When it's dry, it twists; when it's wet, it untwists. Thus the changing weather creates a seed that literally screws itself into the ground.

of track, with the sound of steam locomotive whistles and diesel air horns playing in the background. It's all a monument to Atwood's lifelong passion, a love that began at the age of five when he received his first model train as a Christmas gift.

Trainland U.S.A. is located on IA 117, 2½ miles north of the Colfax exit on I-80. It is open daily from 10 a.m. to 6 p.m., Memorial Day through Labor Day. A small admission is charged. Call (515) 674-3813 for more information or visit www.trainlandusa.com.

From Colfax drive 7 miles to Prairie City, home to the *Neal Smith National Wildlife Refuge.* This is one of the few places in the nation where you can close your eyes and listen to an ancient sound: the restless, melodic swish of prairie grasses swaying in the wind. Founded in 1990, the 5,200-acre site is the largest reconstruction of a tallgrass prairie ecosystem in the nation. It is named after Neal Smith, a former congressman from Iowa with a long-standing interest in environmental preservation.

"We're about ten years into a thousand-year project," says Pauline Drobney, research biologist at the refuge. "It took a long time for these landscapes

## TOP ANNUAL EVENTS

**FEBRUARY**

**BRR (Bike Ride to Rippey)**
Perry, first weekend in Feb
(515) 465-4601

**APRIL**

**Red Bud Festival**
Chariton, mid-Apr
(641) 774-4059

**MAY**

**Tulip Time Festival**
Pella, first weekend in May
(641) 628-4311
www.pellatuliptime.com

**AUGUST**

**National Balloon Classic**
Indianola, early Aug
(515) 961-8415
www.nationalballoonclassic.com

**Corydon Old Settler Celebration**
Corydon, second weekend in Aug
(641) 872-1536

**Sweet Corn Festival**
Adel, second weekend in Aug
(515) 993-5472

**Iowa State Fair**
Des Moines, third week in Aug
(800) 545-FAIR
www.iowastatefair.org

**OCTOBER**

**Madison County Covered Bridge Festival**
Winterset, second weekend in Oct
(515) 462-1185

to evolve, and bringing them back is also a long-term effort. This is the first time prairie restoration has been tried on this large a scale, and there's a lot that we have to learn as we go along."

In the middle of the refuge sits the ***Prairie Learning Center,*** an airy, light-filled building that shows why this landscape is worth saving and how it is being restored. In the Fire Theater visitors can learn more about the engine of destruction and rebirth that makes prairies possible. Fire is essential because it clears away old thatch, releasing seeds and allowing new growth to flourish. It also keeps the prairie free of trees. Before the arrival of the pioneers, some fires were set by lightning, but the native peoples of the region also periodically burned the prairie, knowing that it kept the land attractive to grazing animals like buffalo and elk.

After touring the center, experience the prairie firsthand by either car or foot. An auto tour route and several hiking trails wind through the refuge, each providing lovely views of a rolling landscape of swaying grasses, blooming flowers, and expansive sky. You can also view the refuge's herds of buffalo and elk. Animals like these play a role in the ecosystem of the prairie, for their grazing, trampling, and manure stimulate plant growth. Visitors may also see another prized species at the refuge: regal fritillary butterflies, an endangered species that has been reintroduced in the past two years. Other rare and endangered animal species here include the Indiana bat, Henslow's sparrow, northern harrier hawk, short-eared owl, and upland sandpiper.

The Prairie Learning Center is at 9981 Pacific St., Prairie City. The entrance is at the southwest corner of Prairie City, at the IA 163–Prairie City interchange. The center is open Mon through Sat, 9 a.m. to 4 p.m., and on Sun from noon to 5 p.m. The refuge trails and auto tour route are open daily from sunrise to sunset. Admission is free. For more information call (515) 994-3400 or see www.tallgrass.org.

From the wildlife refuge head west to ***Des Moines,*** Iowa's capital city. If you think the phrase "hip Des Moines" sounds as strange as "jumbo shrimp" or "working vacation," you're way overdue for a visit to the capital city of Iowa.

Consider the fact that in the city's lively East Village neighborhood, you can have a passionate conversation about the virtues of Huo Shan Yellow versus Wuyi Shan Ti Kwan in the elegant, minimalist atmosphere of Gong Fu Tea. After enjoying a steaming cup of tea, you can cross the street to browse through the upscale specialty stores in the neighborhood, including Sticks, a gallery that's been lauded on national television for its trendsetting style. Come evening, head across the Des Moines River to dance to the pulsing beat of a rock concert in the city's new, 17,000-seat arena, or sip chardonnay at an event sponsored by the Des Moines Art Center Downtown.

Frankly, this isn't your grandmother's Des Moines (unless, of course, you have an exceedingly cool grandmother).

The city's ongoing transformation is due in large part to a $2.85 billion infusion of private and public development money. During the past fifteen years a host of new attractions have kept construction crews busy, including a new Iowa Events Center with multiple venues for concerts, athletic events, and conventions; the dazzling new Science Center of Iowa; a revitalized East Village neighborhood; and a continuing reclamation of the riverfront with pedestrian paths and parks.

The new developments—in combination with established city landmarks such as Living History Farms, the Des Moines Art Center, and Blank Park Zoo—are luring increasing numbers of visitors to a city whose staid image is getting an extreme makeover.

Of all the new attractions, the **Wells Fargo Arena** is the most visible: a gleaming, glass-sided structure that dominates the Des Moines riverfront just north of the downtown. The space plays host to some of the nation's hottest touring acts. The arena is connected to the city's enclosed 4-mile skywalk system, so that no matter what the weather is like outside, you can easily walk to all the attractions in the downtown. You can find the arena at 730 Third St. Call (515) 564-8300 or see www.iowaeventscenter.com for a listing of upcoming events.

Adjacent to the arena is another new attraction, the **Iowa Hall of Pride.** The site celebrates the best of the state in twenty-six interactive, multimedia stations. Included are displays on famous Iowans ranging from plant researcher Norman Borlaug to artist Grant Wood, as well as exhibits that celebrate the excellence of the state's high school system, which is ranked as one of the best in the nation.

Throughout the hall, visitors are put in the center of the action. In the Spirit of Competition Theater, for example, a 180-degree, panoramic screen surrounds visitors with the sights and sounds of a variety of intense sporting events. Other displays allow people to call the balls and strikes in a three-dimensional baseball game, sing along with the Iowa All-State Choir, and take part in an Iowa girls basketball game via virtual reality.

The Iowa Hall of Pride is open daily except for Mon and is located at 330 Park St. Admission is $5 for adults and $4 for students (Iowa kids get in free). For more information call (515) 280-8969 or see www.iowahallofpride.com.

More technological wizardry is on display at the **Science Center of Iowa,** a gleaming, $62 million facility near the Des Moines riverfront on the south end of the downtown. Instead of exhibits, the center has six "experience platforms" that bring the wonders of science to vivid life, as well an IMAX Dome Theater and a state-of-the-art "Cosmic Jukebox" that allows visitors to customize their own star shows. Throughout the facility, the focus is on self-guided exploration and the ties between science and our everyday lives.

Because science changes so rapidly, the center is not a static place. Its calendar includes more than sixty live programs ranging from Kitchen Chemistry to Fire and Ice, an exploration of thermodynamics. In addition, its experience platforms will be changed on a rotating basis in the coming years, with the result that there will always be something new at the Science Center.

The Science Center of Iowa is open daily and is located at 401 W. Martin Luther King Jr. Parkway. Admission is $10 for adults, $7 for children. For more information call (515) 274-6868 or see www.sciowa.org.

Des Moines is also drawing renewed energy from the revitalization of existing neighborhoods. A prime example is the *East Village,* a six-block area that sits below the gold-domed Iowa Capitol, the center for state government. For decades the area had been in decline, until a flood of new investment flowed into the district to restore old buildings, build loft-style apartments, and install new street lighting.

Visitors to the East Village should begin with tours of its two best-known landmarks: the granite-and-glass *State Historical Museum,* a treasure trove of exhibits that tell the story of the state, and the *Iowa State Capitol,* a

## A Bell of Friendship

On the grounds of the Iowa State Capitol, you can see a bell house and large bronze bell that are a gift to Iowa from the people of Yamanashi, Japan. The landmark is a testimony to the generosity of Iowans and to the remarkable friendship that has blossomed between the two lands.

The friendship between Yamanashi and Iowa began in 1959 when Yamanashi suffered two devastating typhoons. Richard Thomas, an Iowan who had served in the U.S. military in Japan after World War II, helped organize an Iowa Hog Lift that sent thirty-five pigs and 1,500 tons of corn to Yamanashi to help rebuild its shattered agricultural industry. That act of generosity laid the foundation for America's first sister-state relationship with Japan, a bond that continues to this day with frequent visits and exchanges.

The bell and bell house were sent to Iowa in 1962. The bell house was built in Japan and shipped to Iowa in boxes for assembly here. The bell, which weighs 2,000 pounds, is similar to those found in temples in Japan.

The story of the Iowa Hog Lift is told in the children's book *Sweet Corn and Sushi: The Story of Iowa and Yamanashi* by Lori Erickson.

showcase for nineteenth-century craftsmanship that is considered one of the nation's most beautiful capitol buildings. Completed in 1886, the building has a twenty-three-carat golden dome and is filled with ornate mosaics, intricate wood carvings, and hand-painted murals. Admission is free to both attractions.

East Village is home to an inviting array of stores, galleries, and restaurants. Don't miss the Sticks Gallery, Kitchen Collage, Accenti, and (for a tasty, inexpensive lunch) *Noodle Zoo* at 601 E. Locust S.

Just across the Des Moines River lies another revitalized area, the *Court District.* Each Saturday during the growing season, the neighborhood hosts the city's large farmers' market, but at any time of year visitors enjoy its eclectic array of restaurants, clubs, and stores. Popular spots include Court *Avenue Restaurant and Brewing Company,* a microbrewery and eatery at 309 Court Ave., and *Spaghetti Works,* a casual dining spot at 310 Court Ave. known for its Italian specialties. Both offer moderately priced meals.

The neighborhood also provides easy access to another major city project, the *Principal Riverwalk.* Upon its completion in 2011, the route will connect the east and west sides of Des Moines with a series of walking paths and bridges. It will also serve as a hub for the many bike trails that fan out through the city.

The new attractions join an impressive roster of existing Des Moines landmarks, including *Terrace Hill,* the official residence of the Iowa governor and one of the finest examples of Second Empire–style architecture in the country. The home was constructed at a cost of $250,000 in the 1860s and was home to a couple of the city's most prominent citizens for many years. It was built for the state's first millionaire, B. F. Allen, who sold it to the F. M. Hubbell family, who donated it to the state in 1971. Since then more than $3 million has been spent on its renovation. Much of the effort has gone into refurbishing the home's main-floor rooms to their original Victorian splendor. The lower two floors are included in the tour open to the public, with the exception of one room on the second floor used as quarters for visiting families and dignitaries. The third floor houses the offices and family quarters of the governor. Terrace Hill is located at 2300 Grand Ave. It is open Tues through Sat, except during Jan and Feb. Call (515) 281-3604 or see www.terracehill.org for tour times.

*Salisbury House* is another Des Moines mansion that will bring you back in time—to Tudor England, not nineteenth-century Iowa. The home is at 4025 Tonawanda Dr. It is modeled after a centuries-old Tudor dwelling in Salisbury, England, complete with a great hall with beamed and raftered ceiling, rich tapestries, Oriental rugs, stained-glass windows, and ornate wall paneling. It was built by a wealthy cosmetics manufacturer, Carl Weeks, who purchased many of the home's furnishings in England and who also collected art objects as well as a 3,500-volume library that includes such treasures as a page from the Gutenberg Bible and a copy of the Kelmscot Chaucer produced by William Morris. Call (515) 274-1777 for a tour schedule.

For a quiet treat on a frosty winter day, stop by the **Des Moines Botanical and Environmental Center** (909 Robert D. Ray Dr.), an 80-foot geodesic dome, 150 feet in circumference, filled with lush tropical and semitropical plants as well as a variety of major floral shows. Don't miss the bonsai collection, rated one of the ten best in the United States. Some of the plants have been in training for more than a hundred years! On pleasant days you can spend an enjoyable time wandering through the outdoor gardens. Call (515) 323-6290 for information.

The **Blank Park Zoo** (7401 S.W. Ninth St.) displays more than 800 animals from five continents in exhibits that simulate the animals' natural habitats.

## Presidential Politics

If you're a political junkie, you already are well familiar with the *Iowa caucuses.* Every four years the national spotlight focuses on these January political meetings, the first significant test of the presidential candidates' appeal to voters.

The word *caucus* comes from a North American Indian word meaning "a gathering of tribal chiefs." Even before Iowa became a state, caucuses—rather than the more-common primaries—were used to nominate candidates here. The belief was that caucuses encouraged grassroots democracy and participation. Though caucuses are held in Iowa every two years, the ones held during presidential-election years are better attended and receive far more media attention. During caucus season, Iowans get the rare opportunity to meet and question candidates in a way nearly unheard of in an age dominated by sound bites and paid commercials.

The caucuses aren't the state's only connection to presidential politics, however. Several presidents have ties to Iowa:

**Herbert Hoover,** the only Iowan to become president, was born in West Branch. The town is the site of his presidential library and museum.

**Mamie Doud Eisenhower,** the wife of President Dwight Eisenhower, was born in Boone. Her birthplace has been restored and is open to visitors.

**Abraham Lincoln and his son Tad** are depicted in a statue on the grounds of the Iowa State Capitol. The monument was dedicated in 1961 on the one-hundredth anniversary of the Gettysburg Address. Tad died at the age of fourteen, and the statue is a rare image of Lincoln as a family man.

Trees at the Living Heritage Tree Museum in Storm Lake have connections to Abraham Lincoln, George Washington, Ulysses S. Grant, and John F. Kennedy.

The zoo's new Discovery Center features indoor habitats for bats, butterflies, snakes, and fish. The **Des Moines Art Center** (4700 Grand Ave.) is nationally recognized both for its art collection and for its futuristic architecture created by the internationally known architects Eliel Saarinen, I. M. Pei, and Richard Meier. Downtown, visit the new **Pappajohn Sculpture Park,** which includes twenty-four works in Western Gateway Park. Included are works by Willem de Kooning, Louise Bourgeois, and Martin Puryear.

Located in Union Park on the Des Moines River, the **Heritage Carousel** features thirty animals and two chariots that are accessible to wheelchairs. Note the handsome hand-painted local scenes as you ride. The fine wooden carousel runs on a variable schedule; call (515) 323-8200 for more information.

For an afternoon of browsing, shopping, and munching, check out **Historic Valley Junction** in **West Des Moines.** The area was settled by coal miners and was once a bustling railroad center with a wild reputation, but as the importance of the railroad faded, so did the town's spirit. Then in the late 1960s, the area began to come to life again, as small-business owners (many of them antiques dealers) opened their doors in the area's historic old storefronts. Today Valley Junction has become a popular shopping district filled with more than a hundred businesses, which include upscale restaurants, fancy boutiques, antiques stores brimming with mismatched treasures, and specialty stores selling everything from lace to jewelry to kitchen tools. On Thursday evening mid-May through Sept, Valley Junction is also the site of a farmers' market. Call the Valley Junction Foundation at (515) 222-3642 for more information.

The Valley Junction district is located on Fifth Street and the surrounding area in downtown West Des Moines. Take I-235 to the Sixty-third Street exit, and then go south and follow the Valley Junction signs.

One other stop, just west of Des Moines, is definitely worth a visit before you leave Polk County: **Living History Farms,** 2600 Northwest 111th St. in Urbandale. This is a 500-acre agricultural museum that tells the story of farming in the Midwest, from a 1700 Ioway Indian village to displays on twentieth-century farming. In between, several eras are highlighted, including an 1850 pioneer farm, an 1875 town, and a 1900 farm. The artifacts come to life through the efforts of interpreters dressed in historical clothing who re-create the daily routine of early Iowans. On each farm the buildings, planting methods, and livestock are authentic to the time periods represented, and visitors are invited to try their hand at old-time skills like wool carding and apple-butter making. Tractor-drawn carts transport visitors between the five period sites on a regular schedule, and walking trails through native woodlands are also open between the sites.

## Come to the Fair

As the inspiration for a novel (Iowan Phil Stong's *State Fair*), three motion pictures, and a Rodgers and Hammerstein's Broadway musical, the **Iowa State Fair** is undoubtedly the nation's most celebrated fair. It is also the single largest event in the state, attracting nearly one million people to Des Moines each August.

The eleven-day fair showcases midwestern life at its most wholesome. Here you can see hundreds of buffed and groomed animals raised by 4-H kids, marvel at behemoth farm equipment, devour turkey legs big enough to feed a family of four, scream on a neck-snapping roller coaster, take in a superstar stage show, and try the latest gadgets hawked by fast-talking barkers.

The fair's most celebrated attraction is its butter cow created by sculptor-in-residence Sarah Pratt. Pratt uses about 550 pounds of butter to craft the animal, which is exhibited in a forty-degree cooler in the Agriculture Building. Each year she also creates an additional sculpture, which has ranged from Garth Brooks and Elvis to Grant Wood's *American Gothic* couple. Now that's fat put to a good use!

For more information on the annual extravaganza, call (800) 545-FAIR or visit www.iowastatefair.com.

Throughout the year special events and festivals are held at Living History Farms, from bobsled parties and hayrides to pioneer craft shows and early twentieth-century plowing exhibitions. On July 4 there's an old-fashioned Independence Day celebration, and during the fall there are several events centered on the harvest. Another popular attraction at Living History Farms is the 1900-farm-supper program. November through April interpreters prepare and serve authentic meals based on early twentieth-century recipes. Reservations are required (and the suppers are often booked well in advance).

To reach Living History Farms, take exit 125 (Hickman Road, US 6) off the combined I-35 and I-80. The farms are open daily May through the third Sun in Oct from 9 a.m. to 5 p.m. Admission is $11.50 for adults, and $7 for children. Call (515) 278-5286 for more information or visit www.lhf.org.

Every April, Des Moines hosts the **_Drake Relays,_** bringing together track competitors of all skill levels, from high school to professional, to compete with their peers. On a lighter note, Drake College, whose mascot happens to be a bulldog, hosts the **_Bulldog Beauty Contest_** in which fifty bulldogs compete for the title. But don't get your hopes up—it does not include a swimsuit competition. The contest serves as a kickoff to the relays and is held the third week in Apr; call (515) 243-6625 for more information or an entry blank.

Finally, one more exciting Des Moines–based event needs to be mentioned: *RAGBRAI* **(Register's *Annual Great Bicycle Ride Across Iowa*).** The seven-day bike ride is sponsored by the Des Moines *Register* newspaper and draws thousands of participants who toil up and down Iowa's hills at the end of each July. The event began in 1973 and was the first statewide bicycle ride in the country. A mixture of endurance test, parade, and party, RAGBRAI has become an Iowa tradition that's well loved both by its participants and by the small towns that feed and shelter the riders as they pass through. For information visit www.ragbrai.org.

For more information about attractions in the Des Moines area, call the Greater Des Moines Convention and Visitors Bureau at (800) 451-2625 or visit www.desmoinesia.com.

Northwest of Des Moines lies the small town of *Perry.* In its downtown, visit the *Carnegie Library Museum,* which serves as a hymn of praise to that most glorious of American institutions, the public library system. Located in the town's original Carnegie Library, a graceful stone building built in the Beaux Arts style in 1904, the museum celebrates libraries and their most important American patron, Andrew Carnegie. Beginning in 1896, Carnegie (a Scottish immigrant who became the wealthiest industrialist in America) built nearly 1,700 libraries across the United States, so that even the poorest citizens could be introduced to the world's literary riches.

Filled with light from large windows, the library museum is a cozy and inviting place, furnished as it was in its early years with a fireplace, oak desks, Windsor chairs, wooden book stacks, and cast-iron radiators. Its shelves include books and displays that tell the story of the important role libraries have played in the nation's history. Browsers can learn more about topics that include midwestern authors, bestsellers of the early nineteenth century,

## Inside Pitch

Where will you find the *Bob Feller Museum* you've been looking for? Well, in *Van Meter,* of course. You won't need directions because you can't miss the mural of Rapid Robert painted on the side of the museum devoted to this famous Hall of Fame pitcher for the Cleveland Indians. Dominated by Bob's smiling face, this mural depicts him in various stages of his pitch. Inside you'll be able to catch a glimpse of his old uniforms, special awards, and rare photos. Van Meter is deservedly proud of its native son. To get there take exit 113 off I-80 and proceed to 310 Mill St. The exhibit is open Mon through Sat from 10 a.m. to 5 p.m. and on Sun from noon to 4 p.m. Adult admission is $5; $3 for seniors and children. Call (515) 996-2806 or see www.bobfellermuseum.org for more details.

banned books, and the importance of libraries to immigrants. The displays show that throughout their history, public libraries have been both lending institutions and also places that nurture community spirit, gathering spots where farm wives visited with town women, young men and women courted, and the issues of the day were debated.

You'll find the library museum at 1123 Willis Ave. It's open Thurs, Fri, and Sat, and admission is free. For more information call (515) 465-2481.

Just outside the library museum's doors lies the **Hotel Pattee,** a jewel-like property luxuriously restored to its original Arts and Crafts style. The AAA Four Diamond Award property, which first opened in 1913, was completely restored in 1997.

Each of the hotel's forty guest rooms is meant to celebrate a different aspect of Iowa and the Midwest. Some are named after personages important to the town and state, while others, like the Dutch and Mexican rooms, pay tribute to Iowa's immigrant heritage. The hotel features more than 130 pieces of original art, most by midwestern artists. Its award-winning restaurant, **David's Milwaukee Diner,** features decor that re-creates a luxury train-dining experience from years past.

The Hotel Pattee is at 1112 Willis Ave. Rates are moderate to expensive. Call (888) 424-4268 or see www.hotelpattee.com for more information.

Perry visitors can relax in **Soumas Court,** an outdoor gathering place next to the Hotel Pattee. The shaded enclave is named after former mayor George Soumas, a son of Greek immigrants and World War II hero. A bronze statue of the well-loved town character sits at one of the tables, holding court over a coffee cup as he often did in life. The court is also the site of the "Wall of Witnesses," a tribute to Perry citizens such as Flora Bailey, the town's first librarian, and jazz musician Roy "Snake" Whyte.

Just a few blocks away lies another Perry landmark: the **Perry Tea Room and Calico Shops.** Visitors can browse through its eleven interconnected rooms filled with gifts, decorative items, and clothing, and then enjoy a meal in the tearoom decorated in lavish Victorian style.

The Perry Tea Room (515-465-2631) is located at the corner of First and Otley Streets. Entree prices are moderate. For more information see www.perry tearoom.com.

## Madison County Romance

Author Robert James Waller's decision to set his first novel in **Madison County,** Iowa, has sparked a remarkable series of events that have helped revitalize this primarily rural region. First the book landed a seemingly permanent spot on the national best-seller lists, then Hollywood decided to turn the love story into a movie, and then, before the town quite knew what was happening, Clint Eastwood and Meryl Streep were exchanging passionate kisses on Roseman Bridge. Since then, **Winterset** has become a mecca for fans who travel from around the country and the world to see the sites immortalized in the book and movie. This formerly sleepy town may never be the same, but few in Winterset are complaining.

The covered bridges of Madison County were a tourism attraction long before the book was written (though hardly on the scale they are now). Nineteen bridges were built in Madison County between 1855 and 1885, and they were covered to help preserve their large flooring timbers, which were more expensive to replace than the lumber used to cover the bridge sides and roof. Most were named after the resident who lived closest. Six of these covered bridges remain today, all of which are listed on the National Register of Historic Places. For many years the bridges have been the focus of the **Madison County Covered Bridge Festival,** held each year on the second full weekend in October, when bus tours to all the bridges are offered and the town square comes alive with food and craft booths, a car show, a parade, and other entertainment.

A visit to Winterset is enjoyable at any time of year, however—especially if you happen to be enamored of the story of Francesca and her photographer friend. Begin your tour with a visit to the **Madison County Welcome Center** (800-298-6119), which is located on the town square at 73 Jefferson St. There you can pick up brochures on the area's attractions as well as a map that lists the locations of all the bridges in the surrounding countryside.

A few doors down from the welcome center is an establishment that played a role in the movie: The **Northside Cafe** was the setting for a scene in which Robert Kincaid learns more about the town and its attitudes. The cafe has been a Winterset institution since 1876 and has become a popular spot for *Bridges* fans (who are quick to caress the fourth seat from the door, the one that was used by Clint). The food is hearty and inexpensive, and the waitresses can tell you stories about the filming. The Northside Cafe (515-462-1523) is at 61 Jefferson St.

## didyouknow?

During the past decade Madison County has become a favorite spot for weddings in Iowa. Hundreds of couples have tied the knot on one of the county's many picturesque bridges.

Another hallowed spot for fans is the **Roseman Bridge,** where Francesca left a note inviting Robert to dinner. The bridge is located about 10 miles southwest of Winterset and spans a picturesque bend in the Middle River. In the woods near the bridge is a gift shop that sells *Bridges* memorabilia. Another lovely spot is the **Cedar Bridge,** which is located a few miles northwest of Winterset and is surrounded by a park with picnic tables. In the novel, Cedar Bridge is where Francesca goes to observe Robert taking photographs.

A good place for a picnic is the **Cutler-Donahoe Covered Bridge** located in the Winterset City Park. This little park is perfectly charming and is also the site of Clark's Tower, a three-story limestone structure that serves as a pioneer memorial and offers outstanding views of the surrounding countryside.

Winterset has other attractions in addition to sites relating to the book and movie. Before Robert James Waller ever came to town, the **John Wayne Birthplace** put the town on the map. The famous actor was born here in a modest frame house on May 26, 1907. Back then he was called Marion Robert Morrison, son of a pharmacist who worked in a local drugstore. The Morrison family lived in the home until Marion (or John or the Duke) was three, when they moved to nearby Earlham in northern Madison County.

## theroseman bridgeghost

In 1892 an outlaw escaped from jail, and a posse had him cornered on Roseman Bridge. They broke into two groups and came at him from both sides, only to watch him rise up through the roof and disappear. He was never seen again, but to this day some folks say you can hear his footsteps and laughter on the bridge.

Restoration of the tiny four-room house began in 1981, funded by the local community and by the actor's fans and family, who have donated many items to the site. Since then it has been visited by thousands of people, including Wayne's wife, six of his seven children, and former president Ronald Reagan. Two of the rooms are furnished as they might have been in 1907, and the other two contain a collection of John Wayne memorabilia (including the eye patch he wore in *True Grit*).

The John Wayne Birthplace is located at 216 S. Second St. It is open daily from 10 a.m. to 4:30 p.m. A small admission is charged. Call (515) 462-1044 or see www.johnwaynebirthplace.org for more information.

At the Madison County Historical Complex, you can learn more about the local history of the area. This impressive eighteen-acre historical site contains a museum, an 1856 restored mansion, a log schoolhouse, a post office, a general store, an 1870 train depot, a blacksmith shop, a stone barn, and what is probably the only outhouse in the state of Iowa to be listed on the National Register of Historic Places (made of stone, the privy was at one time wallpapered and heated for the comfort of its users). Also on the property is the Zion Federated

## For the Love of Quilts

Colorful, intricately stitched quilts are an Iowa tradition, and thanks to Marianne Fons and Liz Porter of Winterset, a new generation of Americans is learning this pioneer art.

Marianne and Liz met in 1976 when they took a local quilting class together. Eventually they became teachers themselves, collaborating on designs and techniques and stimulating new ideas in each other. Thirty years later their partnership has grown into what you might call a quilting empire in Winterset.

Since 1995 Marianne and Liz have taught quilting on public television, most recently as hosts of the nationally broadcast show *Fons & Porter's Love of Quilting.* They are also editors of a quilting magazine of the same name and have written more than a dozen books. Their best-selling *Quilter's Complete Guide* has been hailed as the most comprehensive quilter's reference book ever written. These two Winterset entrepreneurs have found a profitable niche through a unique blend of friendship and devotion to a time-honored craft.

You can shop for quilting designs, fabrics, and notions at the women's retail store, **Fons & Porter Quilt Supply,** at 54 Court Ave. The store is open from 10 a.m. to 5 p.m., Tues through Sat. Call (888) 985-1020 for more information. You can also shop on their Web site at www.fonsandporter.com.

Church, an 1881 structure that was moved to the complex in 1988 through the support of local residents.

In the complex's museum you can view exhibits on local history, including vintage clothing, quilts, farm equipment, and Indian artifacts. In the basement is another treasure, a huge collection of fossils and minerals that the Smithsonian Institution offered to buy before it was donated to the museum.

The **Madison County Historical Complex** is located at 815 S. Second Ave. It is open May through Oct. Its hours are Mon through Sat from 11 a.m. to 4 p.m. and Sun from 1 to 5 p.m. Call (515) 462-2134 for more information.

Don't overlook the **Winterset Art Center,** the circa-1854 brick house located at 224 S. John Wayne Dr. It once served as a stop on the Underground Railroad, and features a display dedicated to George Washington Carver, renowned scientist and educator. He is also honored in a memorial park next to the fire station. This is the site of the old hotel where he once worked. The art center offers classes and displays the work of local artists. Its hours vary; call (515) 210-3286 for more information.

From Winterset travel east on IA 92 to **Indianola,** home of Simpson College and the site each summer of the **National Balloon Classic.** The event is one of the most visually spectacular festivals you are likely to find any place in the country. Each August some one hundred pilots are invited to bring their magnificent balloons to Indianola and compete for cash and prizes. Throughout the festival the skies of Indianola are filled with brilliant-colored balloons, attracting thousands of visitors who crane their necks for hours on end to view the serene craft. Balloon flights are scheduled morning and evening (weather permitting), and during the day special demonstrations and competitions are held. After dark there's a Nite-Glo Extravaganza, when the bursts of flames that power the balloons light up the colored fabrics above them, creating vivid patterns against the night sky.

Other events at the festival include balloon rides, musical performances, fireworks, wine festival, parade, and children's activities. The Indianola Arts and Crafts Festival is held on the first weekend during the festival.

A few tips for balloon spectators: Wear comfortable shoes and bring a lawn chair or blanket to sit on. And you'll be sorry if you don't bring your camera along—the sight of the balloons rising above the area's lush rolling hills is unforgettable.

The National Balloon Classic is held in early August. You can purchase tickets for either a single day or the entire event. Visitors should be aware that weather conditions must be right before the balloons can fly. You may want to call ahead before you leave for the event. Call (515) 961-8415 or see www .nationalballoonclassic.com for more information.

## Bundle Up

When Winterset residents were trying to come up with a name for their community, they originally tried to decide between Summerset and Sommerset. Because it was a particularly cold day, someone suggested that the name Winterset would be more appropriate, and so it was called.

This bit of information triggered a memory I have of a visit to a former Iowan who owned a small motel in West Yellowstone. Looking around the lobby, I was mesmerized by the seemingly hundreds of photographs of family and guests frolicking in the towering drifts of snow of Montana and Wyoming.

In most cases these drifts topped 10 or even 20 feet, and I felt like I was looking at pictures of the North Pole. "Why?" I asked him. "Why did you ever move out here?" Without hesitating for an instant, he replied, "Easy. To get away from the cold. There's no colder state in the nation than Iowa." I don't know if this is true or not, but there are sure times when it feels like it is. All I can tell you is that if you're visiting our state in January, you'll have something to brag about when you get home.

—T. S.

If you can't make it to Indianola for the balloon classic, you can still visit its *National Balloon Museum.* The architecture of the structure is a reason to visit in itself. The motif suggests two inverted balloons, which are approached through entrance arches that accentuate the feeling of entering a balloon. The exterior is trimmed with blue and yellow ceramic tiles that recall the color, serenity, and gracefulness of balloons.

Inside you'll be able to view exhibits that chronicle more than 200 years of ballooning history. On display are balloon envelopes, inflators, gondolas, and other equipment used in both hot-air ballooning and gas ballooning. Other items include memorabilia associated with scientific, competitive, and record-setting flights, including trophies, photos, and an extensive pin collection. The gift shop is fun to browse through as well, with its displays of posters, calendars, mobiles, and mementos relating to ballooning.

The National Balloon Museum is located on US 65/69 on the north side of town at 1601 N. Jefferson Way. It is open daily except during the month of January. A small admission is charged. Call (515) 961-3714 for more information or see www.nationalballoonmuseum.com.

Balloons aren't the only reason to travel to Indianola during the summer. Another attraction is the *Des Moines Metro Opera,* one of the top twenty summer opera companies in the world. Each season the Metro Opera presents three grand operas at the Blank Performing Arts Center on the Simpson College campus in Indianola. The singers are drawn from the ranks of the country's top young performers and present both classic and contemporary operas. Since its founding in 1973, the Metro Opera has attracted national and international attention for the quality of its performances. Iowans are fortunate to have such a premier cultural resource in their midst.

The Des Moines Metro Opera presents three operas in repertory during June and July. Single or season tickets are available, as well as weekend packages that include your tickets, comfortable lodging, and elegant dining. For more information call (515) 961-6221 or check its Web site at www.des moinesmetroopera.org.

Iowa's growing wine industry is on display at the *Summerset Winery,* also in Indianola. Owner Ron Mark discovered a love for winemaking while growing up on a farm near Rising Sun, Iowa. As a young adult, four years in Italy deepened his interest in the process. Though Mark later pursued a career as an electronics technician, his dream of becoming a vintner didn't fade. In 1989 he and his family moved to a hilltop near Indianola and Mark began planting grape vines. In 1997 the Marks opened their winery.

Today the Summerset Winery grows more than twelve acres of grapes. Additional grapes are purchased from more than a dozen other Iowa vineyards.

Its winery building includes wine processing equipment, an underground wine cellar, a tasting room, and two large rooms for meetings and banquets. About 150,000 bottles of wine in more than a dozen varieties are produced each year at Summerset. Free musical performances are offered on Sunday throughout the year.

For more information call (515) 961-3545 or see www.summersetwine.com.

# Ethnic Enclaves

Begin your tour of this region of Iowa with a visit to **Pella,** a pristine small town that looks as if it could be the set for a Walt Disney movie. The name *Pella* means "city of refuge," for it was here that a small band of Hollanders came in 1847 to found a new city based on freedom. Today that Dutch heritage is visible throughout Pella, especially in the downtown, with its European-style architecture, a large windmill in the city square, lovely flower beds, and the Klokkenspel, a musical clock with figures that perform five times daily. The gift shops around the square stock imported Dutch treasures, and at Jaarsma's and Vander Ploeg Bakeries, you can buy ethnic specialties that include the ever-popular Dutch letters—puff pastry baked in the shape of an S with an almond-paste filling.

The newest addition to Pella is **Molengracht Plaza,** located in the downtown area a half block southeast of the city square at Main and Liberty Streets. The word *molengracht* means "mill canal" in Dutch, and the area re-creates the canals that are found throughout Holland. The canal appears to emerge from under the street, and then winds through the length of Molengracht Plaza. Shops, restaurants, and a hotel (all with exteriors that resemble eighteenth-century Dutch storefronts) line the Molengracht's bricked pedestrian walkways, making this a lovely place to stroll.

The best time to sample Pella's Dutch heritage is during its annual **Tulip Time** festival held on the first weekend in May. Each spring the town comes to life with hundreds of thousands of tulips, and local residents dress in colorful ethnic costumes as they host thousands of visitors from across the state. Highlights of the festival include folk dancing and crafts, parades, ethnic foods, and the crowning of the Tulip Queen. Another good time to visit is during the Christmas season, when *Sinterklaas* comes to help the town celebrate the season with traditions stretching back a hundred years.

The **Pella Historical Village** (507 Franklin St.) will give you the chance to learn more about the history that has shaped this town. It contains twenty-one buildings, some more than a century old, and an authentic grain-grinding windmill. Here you can see items that the early settlers brought from Holland, an outstanding collection of delft pottery, folk costumes, Dutch dolls, Hinde-loopen folk art painting, and a miniature Dutch village. The buildings include a log cabin, blacksmith shop, gristmill, potter shop, store, and church, as well as the boyhood home of gunslinger Wyatt Earp. Another historic site in town is the Scholte House on the north side of the town square, former home of Dominie H. P. Scholte, the leader of the group of immigrants who founded Pella.

## didyouknow?

Wyatt Earp, the famous gun-slinging western marshal, grew up as an ordinary Pella boy. He and his family came to the town in 1850 when Earp was two years old. At the age of fifteen, he ran away to join the army—and was promptly sent back home to Pella by his father, an army officer.

The newest addition to the historical village is a full-size, functioning 1850 Dutch grain windmill. The mill has been laboriously reconstructed in Pella and houses a welcome and interpretive center where visitors can ride an elevator up four stories to the windmill's outdoor stage.

The Pella Historical Village is located 1 block east of the town square. It is open Mon through Sat, Mar through Dec. Admission is $8 for adults and $2 for children. Call (641) 628-2409 for more information or visit www.pellatuliptime.com.

Southwest of Pella lies the town of **Knoxville,** which calls itself the Sprint Car Racing Capital of the World. Drivers have been racing at Knoxville for nearly a century on a dirt track that is rated as one of the fastest in the nation.

In honor of its racing status, Knoxville has built the **National Sprint Car Hall of Fame and Museum** at the Marion County Fairgrounds off IA 14 at 1 Sprint Capital Place. The facility includes tributes to famous drivers, restored sprint cars, a gift shop, and booths for race viewing. The museum (641-842-6176) is open daily, and admission is $4 for adults and $3 for students. Visit their Web site at www.sprintcarhof.com.

Somehow sprint-car racing and barbecue seem to go together, so once you leave Knoxville head to **Kin Folks Eatin' Place** (1731 High St.; 641-943-2362), which is located in the tiny town of **Attica,** 9 miles south of Knoxville on IA 5. This down-home restaurant offers some of the best barbecue in the state, including succulent ribs, beef brisket, ham, chicken, and turkey. For dessert try the homemade blackberry or peach cobbler with hand-cranked ice cream. Kin Folks Eatin' Place is open for lunch and dinner daily. Prices are inexpensive to moderate.

Southwest of Attica at the junction of US 34 and US 65 lies the town of **Lucas,** home to the **John L. Lewis Mining and Labor Museum.** The

## The Magic Is in the Dirt

The secret to Knoxville's status as sprint-car heaven lies in the sticky, tacky clay that lines its raceway. Cars get great traction on it, which makes for faster and more exciting races.

Racing has been part of Knoxville life since the early twentieth century, but it wasn't until 1954 that the sport began to take off. In that year the Marion County Fair board began holding weekly races and hired Marion Robertson to promote them.

Within a few years sprint-car racing dominated the Knoxville scene. The lightweight, open-wheeled vehicles have a single seat directly behind the engine. In 1958 large "wings" began to be added to the tops of cars, an innovation that forces air pressure downward, creating better traction and improving safety if the car rolls.

As their name implies, sprint cars are designed for short bursts of speed. At just 1,200 pounds and packing more than 700 horsepower, the cars have one of the highest power-to-weight ratios of any motor sport. Each race is between twenty and thirty laps and is as short as seven minutes.

Knoxville vibrates with racing action for approximately thirty-five nights from mid-April to mid-September, with 5,000 spectators filling the stands each evening. While many are from the surrounding area, drivers and spectators also flock to Knoxville from around the nation and the world, particularly during the Knoxville Nationals held in early August.

museum pays tribute to one of the most famous union leaders in America. Lewis was born in Lucas in 1880 and worked in the local coal mines before eventually becoming president of the United Mine Workers for forty years. The museum houses exhibits about his life, mining, and labor history.

The Lewis Museum (641-766-6831) is located 2 blocks north of US 34 at 102 Division St. It is open Mon through Sat 9 a.m. to 3 p.m., mid-Apr through mid-Oct. A small admission is charged.

Just south of Lucas lies the major portion of the *Stephens State Forest,* one of the largest tracts of forest land in the state. The forest provides visitors with miles of trails that wind through deeply wooded country, as well as four stocked ponds and numerous campgrounds, three of which are set aside for equestrians.

Two other local park areas deserve mentioning. One is the *Pin Oak Marsh* (located on IA 14 south of Chariton), a 160-acre wetland where nature lovers can spot a variety of wildlife, like muskrat, mink, river otter, beaver, songbirds, shorebirds, and—during spring and fall migrations—ducks and geese. Bring your binoculars! Another favorite is the *Red Haw State Park,* known for its abundance of redbud trees. Visit this park the last Saturday

## warning: buggycrossing

Lucas County is the home of a growing Amish community. Watch for horse-drawn vehicles!

in April for the Redbud Festival and Redbud Walk for inspiring beauty. This 420-acre park is located just 1 mile east of Chariton.

A visit to the town of **Chariton** is definitely in order while you're visiting this area. Take the time to observe the clock in the clock tower of the **Lucas County Court House** (916 Braden Ave.), a lovely sandstone-faced Romanesque-style building. It was purchased—the clock, that is—at the 1893 Chicago World's Fair. When the people of Lucas County go out to shop for souvenirs, they mean business! The sidewalk surrounding the courthouse reinforces the time theme. In other words, look down as well as up if you want to know the time of day.

While you're on the town square, be sure to pay a visit to **Piper's Candy.** Piper's has been a landmark in Chariton since 1903. For many years it operated

## Mount Pisgah

Oddly enough, I visited the **Mount Pisgah Mormon National Monument** in February at the same time of the year, apparently, as Mormon leader Parley Pratt led his followers here in the middle of the nineteenth century. Although the ground was thawing, it was a deeply chilling day, and I must have felt as miserable as they did. And like them, I turned again and looked out over the valleys and saw what a beautiful place this must be at any other time of the year.

The Mormon pioneers settled here, cleared thousands of acres, and dwelled in caves as well as log cabins, hoping for the best. Between 300 and 800 of them died in their struggle for adequate food and shelter. Mount Pisgah lasted as a community, however, for six years, from 1846 to 1852, and served as a stopping point for other Mormons on their westward journey to Utah. At one point they were visited by the Potawatomi chief Pied Riche, whose people had been driven here from Michigan and who felt sympathy for the Mormons because they had also been driven from their homes. He is reported to have said to them, "We must help one another, and the Great Spirit will help us both. Because one suffers and does not deserve it is no reason he shall suffer always. We may live to see it right yet. If we do not, our children will." Let us hope he was right.

Mount Pisgah is quite definitely off the beaten path. From Lorimor, take US 169 south 4 miles, and follow the signs to the monument. Right before you get there, you will think you've accidentally stumbled onto private land and will be tempted to turn around. Don't—you're almost there.

—T. S

as a grocery store, but beginning in 1947 it also began selling handmade candy. Today the store is famous for its fudge, caramels, and toffee, which it ships around the country. Piper's is located at 901 Braden Ave. It is on the northeast corner of the town square. For more information call (800) 479-1343 or see www.piperscandy.com.

Wear off that toffee by taking a hike or a bike ride down the **Cinder Path,** the first Rails-to-Trails location in the state. The grade is even, and the smooth cinder surface makes it easy to enjoy the 14 miles winding from the west edge of Chariton southwest to Humeston.

Your next stop in south central Iowa should be **Lamoni,** site of the **Liberty Hall Historic Center,** an eighteen-room Victorian house that was home to the Joseph Smith III family from 1881 to 1906. Joseph was the oldest son of the founder of the Mormon Church and the first president of the Reorganized Church of Jesus Christ of Latter Day Saints. His father, Joseph Smith Jr., was assassinated in 1844, and in the years that followed, the church divided into two main groups. One group followed Brigham Young to Utah; and the other became known as the Reorganized Church and named Joseph Smith III its leader. In the 1880s Smith and his followers established Lamoni as their headquarters, and Smith's home became the busy center of the new church. Though the church later moved its headquarters to Independence, Missouri, Liberty Hall has been lovingly restored to its original decor and today tells the story of the Smith family and the Reorganized Church. Many of the items inside are the Smiths' original furnishings. Don't miss the fold-down bathtub! Also on the property is a schoolhouse built in 1875, plus a museum shop selling Victorian gifts.

## newdealmurals

During the Depression, the Works Progress Adminstration commissioned artists to paint murals across the state. You can see these WPA murals in towns that include:

**Des Moines:** Callanan Junior High and the Public Library

**Pella:** Post Office

**Knoxville:** Post Office

**Corydon:** Post Office

**Osceola:** Post Office

**Leon:** Post Office

**Mount Ayr:** Post Office

The Liberty Hall Historic Center is located at 1138 W. Main St. Admission is free, and hours are Tues through Sat from 10 a.m. to 4 p.m. and 1:30 to 4 p.m. on Sun. Call (641) 784-6133 for more information.

The last stop to make in this region is **Creston,** west of Afton on US 34. Creston was founded in 1868 as a railroad town and is the county seat of Union County. Don't miss the **C. B. & Q. Railroad Depot** located between

Union and Adams Streets. Inside, you can almost hear old steam engines chugging into town and whistles screeching in the distance. It is open weekdays; call (641) 782-7021 for information.

Equally charming is the **Union County Visitors Center** at 636 New York Ave. Housed in a 1931 Phillips 66 gasoline station, it not only serves as a tourism center but also commemorates Frank Phillips, an erstwhile Creston resident and barber who, with his brother, founded the Phillips Petroleum Corporation in 1917. This is a great place to stop, gather your bearings, and plan your next stops. The visitor center (641) 782-6115 is open 8:30 a.m. to 5 p.m. Mon through Sat, mid-May to mid-Oct.

## Places to Stay in Bridge Country

### ALLERTON

**Inn of the Six-toed Cat**
200 N. Central Ave.
(888) 330-2605
www.6toedcat.com
inexpensive to moderate

### DES MOINES

**Butler House on Grand**
4507 Grand Ave.
(866) 455-4096
www.butlerhouseongrand
.com
expensive

**The Cottage**
1094 Twenty-eighth St.
(515) 277-7559
www.thecottagedsm.com
moderate to expensive

### GRINNELL

**Marsh House Bed & Breakfast**
833 East St.
(641) 236-0132
www.marshhousebandb
.com
moderate

### INDIANOLA

**Garden and Galley Bed and Breakfast**
1321 S. Jefferson Way
(515) 961-7749
www.gardenandgalley.com
moderate to expensive

### PELLA

**Cloverleaf Bed & Breakfast**
314 Washington St.
(641) 628-1496
www.cloverleafbandb.net
moderate

**Royal Amsterdam Hotel**
705 E. First St.
(641) 620-8400
www.royalamsterdam.com
moderate to expensive

### URBANDALE

**Wells Bed & Breakfast**
4724 Seventy-second St.
(515) 251-4724
www.wellsbedandbreakfast
.com
Moderate to expensive

## Places to Eat in Bridge Country

### CLIVE

**Cosi Cucina Italian Grill**
1975 N.W. Eighty-sixth St.
(515) 278-8148
www.cosicucina.biz
moderate

### DES MOINES

**Centro**
1007 Locust St.
(515) 248-1780
www.centrodesmoines
.com
moderate

**Drake Diner**
1111 Twenty-fifth St.
(515) 277-1111
inexpensive

**The Royal Mile**
210 Fourth St.
(515) 280-3771
www.royalmilebar.com
inexpensive

**Splash Seafood Bar & Grill**
303 Locust St.
(515) 244-5686
www.splash-seafood.com
expensive

**GRINNELL**

**Phoenix Cafe**
834 Park Ave.
(641) 236-3657
www.thephoenixcafe.com
moderate

**NEWTON**

**Uncle Nancy's Coffeehouse & Eatery**
114 N. Second Ave. West
(641) 787-9709
www.unclenancyscoffee
.com
inexpensive

**PELLA**

**The Grille on the Green**
2411 Bos Landen
(641) 628-4627
www.boslanden.com/
dining.html
moderate

# FERTILE PLAINS

The rich soil of north central Iowa produces some of the nation's most bountiful harvests, on land that was once tall-grass prairie. In this region you'll find the fascinating railroad history of Boone County, the beauty of Clear Lake, and a host of other treasures that celebrate Iowa's rich past and vibrant present. From the Mesquaki Indian Pow Wow to the Surf Ballroom where the memory of Buddy Holly is celebrated, north central Iowa offers an eclectic range of attractions.

## Diverse Diversions

Begin your tour of this region of Iowa with a visit to the only Native American settlement in the state. The word *settlement* (rather than *reservation*) is important, because the land here was purchased by the Mesquaki, not set aside for them by the federal government. Using money from the sale of furs and ponies, the Mesquaki (also known as the Sac and Fox tribe) first bought eighty acres of land near what is now the town of Tama in 1857. In the following years more land was purchased with tribal funds, and today the Mesquaki own nearly 3,500 acres of timberland and river bottom along the Iowa River in Tama County.

# FERTILE PLAINS

The best time to visit the settlement is during the **Mesquaki Indian Pow Wow,** which is held each year on the second weekend in August. This four-day celebration honors the traditional ways of the Mesquaki people, with various arts, crafts, and exhibits on display, plus old-time foods and authentic costumed dancing. The Pow Wow has its origin in the Green Corn Dance, a religious and social event that was held each year at harvest time. The fresh corn was cooked for feasting, and the bounty of the land was celebrated with dancing, games, and socializing. Around the beginning of the twentieth century, more and more white visitors began attending the ceremonies, and in 1913 the festival gained its official name of the Mesquaki Indian Pow Wow.

The traditions of the Pow Wow remain strong. The center of the festival is dancing, with members from the local tribe (and often guests from other parts of the country) performing dances that have been handed down for generations. The Buffalo Head Dance, for example, honors the magnificent beast that has played a central role in Native American culture and life, and the Swan Dance mimics the beautiful, rhythmical movements of a swan in the water. For the Traditional Women's Dance, the Mesquaki women don elaborately decorated dresses. The Pipe Dance is presented to honor distinguished visitors and warriors, and the Harvest of Bean Dance is performed by young girls and boys to thank the Great Spirit for the abundance of food for the coming winter.

The Mesquaki Indian Pow Wow is held each August at the settlement 3 miles west of the town of **Tama.** For more information call (641) 484-4678 or see www.meskwaki.org.

At any time of the year you can visit the **Mesquaki Bingo and Casino** (1504 305th St.), which operates twenty-four hours daily. You can call (800) 728-4263 for information.

You can learn more about the Mesquaki and the history of the area at the **Tama County Historical Museum,** 200 N. Broadway, **Toledo.** The museum

## AUTHORS' FAVORITES

| | |
|---|---|
| Big Treehouse | Boone & Scenic Valley Railroad |
| Reiman Gardens | Matchstick Marvels |
| Surf Ballroom | Grotto of the Redemption |
| National Hobo Convention | Union Slough National Wildlife Refuge |
| Community Orchard | Mesquaki Indian Pow Wow |

# Traveling the Lincoln Highway

If you are traveling across the state, the route of the first transcontinental highway, the old **Lincoln Highway,** would be a grand route to take. Funded by private industry and wealthy entrepreneurs, the Lincoln Highway spanned the country from Times Square to San Francisco, crossing twelve states and leading right through the heart of Iowa, from Clinton to Council Bluffs. The original idea for this Coast to Coast Rock Highway, as it was originally called, belonged to Carl Fisher, "an enthusiastic motorist," and the founder of the Indianapolis Speedway. Begun in 1913, the route has had many changes through the course of the years but what remains of it now roughly follows US 30. In this section of the state, you can drive from Tama in the east to Ogden in the west. Be on the lookout for old gas stations, cafes, bridges, and buildings. The Lincoln Highway originally passed through forty-nine towns; in forty-four of them, it went right down Main Street. Today you would have to make significant detours to visit all of these towns, but if you've got the time, what an adventure it would be! The Lincoln Highway's Iowa headquarters are located in Ogden. For more information on the Iowa portion of the Lincoln Highway, visit www.lincolnhighway assoc.org/iowa.

is open from 1 to 4:30 p.m. Tues through Sat. The building was built in 1869 and served as the county jail until 1970. Today it houses pioneer tools and utensils, antique toys, musical instruments, furniture, and clothing, plus a display of Mesquaki artifacts. Call (641) 484-6767 for more information.

And while you're in the area, drive to the neighboring town of Tama to see the **Lincoln Highway Bridge** on East Fifth Street near US 30. The bridge was built in 1915 to promote Tama as an oasis along the new transcontinental route of the Lincoln Highway (at that time, most of the highway was dirt). The bridge has a decorative railing that spells LINCOLN HIGHWAY and is listed on the National Register of Historic Places. This is the only remaining Lincoln Highway Bridge. The roadside park next to the bridge makes this a pleasant stop.

Next head west to **Marshalltown,** home to two attractions that will please active travelers. The new **Marshalltown Family Aquatic Center** (641-844-1515) at 212 Washington St. features three waterslides, a lazy river, water basketball, and water toys, making this a perfect place to spend a hot summer day.

The **Grimes Farm** is an unusual combination of nature preserve, working farm, and recreation and educational areas. It's designed to show how agriculture can work in harmony with the various ecosystems that make up the local landscape. The farm, which includes woodlands, prairie, wetlands, and agricultural areas, was purchased in 1964 by Leonard and Mildred Grimes. Over the years they have worked diligently to transform neglected acreage into a productive, profitable, and beautiful farm. The Grimes have significantly reduced soil erosion by planting grasses and using no-till agricultural practices. They have established waterways, constructed terraces, built a farm pond, and planted thousands of trees. They have also donated 160 acres of their land to the Iowa Natural Heritage Foundation, ensuring that future generations will learn about responsible land stewardship.

During your visit to Grimes Farm, you can walk hiking trails and see educational displays in its visitor center. Guided interpretive programs are offered frequently. The conservation center is at 2359 233rd St. It is open Mon through Fri from 8:30 a.m. to 4 p.m., and on Sat from 9 a.m. to noon. For more information call (641) 752-5490 or see www.grimesfarm.com.

No visit to Marshalltown would be complete without a visit to *Lillie Mae Chocolates.* Although their present home at 23 W. Main St. is their third location, Lillie Mae's has been serving up chocolates since 1939. The chocolates were named after the daughter of the original owner, George Demopolus. The current owners, Aimee and Tom Snyder, who bought and expanded the store in 2003, keep her legacy alive by featuring a lily on their boxes of candy. The selection of chocolates is vast—they ship Easter eggs and Valentine's candy all over the country—and the caramels are truly outstanding. The caramels are made the old-fashioned way in a huge copper kettle. They claim that these caramels are so buttery, they won't stick to your teeth. The "tor-tush," Lillie Mae's signature candy, is a different kind of turtle altogether: caramel is poured over walnuts and pecans, then coated with milk chocolate

## TOP ANNUAL EVENTS

**MAY**

**North Iowa Band Festival**
Mason City, Memorial Day weekend
(800) 423-5724
www.nibandfest.com

**JUNE**

**Scandinavian Days**
Story City, early June
(515) 733-4214

**JULY**

**Antique & Classic Boat Show**
Clear Lake, mid-July
(800) 285-5338

**Watermelon Day**
Stanhope, mid-July
(515) 826-3290

**Floyd County Fair**
Charles City, third week in July
(641) 228-1300
www.floydcountyfair.org

**AUGUST**

**Summer Fest**
Hampton, mid-Aug
(641) 456-5668

**Midwest Polka Fest**
Humboldt, late Aug
(515) 332-1481

and dipped in white chocolate. Call (641) 752-6041 or (800) 752-6041 or visit www.lilliemaechocolate.com for more information.

Lick the chocolate off your fingers and head to the **Big Treehouse,** which is guaranteed to captivate anyone who remembers the joy of perching in a tree as a child. Few of us had access to a tree house like this, however; this twelve-level structure has electricity, running water, piped-in music, and a spiral stairway from top to bottom. You'll find the Big Treehouse at 2370 Shady Oaks Rd. Call (641) 752-2946 to schedule an appointment between Memorial Day and Labor Day. A small donation is requested.

Northeast of Marshalltown in the small town of **Gladbrook,** be sure to visit **Matchstick Marvels.** Here you can see how master craftsman Patrick Acton is able to turn ordinary kitchen matchsticks into incredible works of art. *Ripley's Believe It Or Not!* calls Pat Acton "the best matchstick model maker in North America."

Millions of matchsticks and gallons of glue have gone into the creation of the models on display, which include the battleship USS *Iowa,* the space shuttle *Challenger,* and the U.S. Capitol. Don't miss Acton's model of the French cathedral of Chartres, which took two years and 174,000 matchsticks to construct. The model contains 136 hand-carved statues, ornate towers and spires measuring nearly 5 feet tall, and internal lighting.

Originally the collection was a traveling exhibit that appeared at art festivals, woodworking shows, and community festivals. It has now found a home in Gladbrook at 319 Second St. Matchstick Marvels (641-473-2410) daily from Apr through Nov, from 1 to 5 p.m. Admission is $2. See www.matchstick marvels.com for more information.

If you're traveling during the summer months, visit **Rock-n-Row Adventures** in Eldora for a tube float down the scenic Iowa River. Trips last an average of three to four hours and can be a great way to shake off the heat of a hot summer afternoon. The length of the trip varies, depending on the height and swiftness of the river. A shuttle bus drops you off and picks you up. Bring along sunglasses, plenty of sunscreen, and shoes that can't fall off your feet and can get very, very wet. If you're not inclined to the water, there is also a driving range and miniature golf. They are located at 23539 First St. Call (641) 858-5516 for more information o or see www.rock-n-row-adventures.com.

The town of **Eldora** is where part of the 1995 movie *Twister* was filmed. Warner Brothers spent a lot of money and time fixing up a local house and barn only to destroy them again. The house is being fixed up again. See if you can find it.

South of Marshalltown in the small town of **Haverhill,** you'll find the **Edel Blacksmith Shop** (214 First St.; 641-752-6664). The shop was operated by

German immigrant Matthew Edel between 1882 and 1940 and provides a vivid picture of the days before mechanized farming changed agriculture. Here Edel shoed horses, repaired tools and wagons, and manufactured implements like garden hoes and wedge makers. Edel was also an inventor who took out patents on such inventions as a perfection wedge cutter and cattle dehorner. Adjacent to the blacksmith shop is a two-story house constructed in the early 1880s, plus a summer kitchen where food was prepared during the warm months. Like the shop itself, they have been left largely unaltered and help complete the picture of what the life of a skilled craftsman was like some hundred years ago.

The Edel Blacksmith Shop is open daily from noon to 4 p.m. Memorial Day through Labor Day.

Northwest of Haverhill lies the town of **State Center,** which prides itself on being the Rose Capital of Iowa. During the summer the town maintains a lovely rose garden at Third Avenue Southeast and Third Street Southeast, and each year on the third weekend in June, State Center hosts a **Rose Festival.**

After strolling through State Center's rose garden, visit **Watson's Grocery Store Museum,** 106 Main St. This general store looks as if it hasn't changed a bit since 1920. The store was built more than one hundred years ago and was operated as an old-fashioned grocery by Ralph Watson for many years until his death in 1979. At that time his widow locked its doors, and the building remained closed until she died in 1989 and her heirs put the property up for sale. Local townspeople approached the heirs with the idea of turning the store into a museum, but they refused to sell it to them. Instead they scheduled an auction to sell the store and all its contents.

But the people of State Center didn't give up so easily. A fund-raising drive was held, and more than $15,000 in pledges poured in. On the day of the auction, State Center citizens crowded into the little store and emerged successful at the end of the bidding. (When one of the other bidders said that he wanted to use the store as a movie set, the locals told him that they'd let him make his movie, but that they wanted the store.) After the auction came the hard part. Volunteers cleaned, scraped, painted, and refinished the dusty and dirty interior, decorating it with old-time advertising signs and refurbishing it with antique equipment and fixtures.

Watson's Grocery in State Center is open from 1 to 4 p.m. on weekends, Memorial Day through Labor Day (and by appointment). For more information call (641) 483-3002.

Northwest of State Center, near I-35, lies the town of **Story City,** which is home to the only municipally owned carousel in the state. Built in 1913 the **Story City Carousel** first came to the town when its Iowa Falls owner agreed to let Story City use it for its Fourth of July celebrations. In 1938 the town purchased the merry-go-round, which was run each summer until 1979 when it became too dilapidated to use.

Instead of abandoning the carousel, however, the town decided to save it, raising the $140,000 needed to refurbish and repair it. A local antiques store and refinishing business took on the laborious task, and in 1982 the gleaming, revitalized machine was once again offering rides in its new home, a pavilion located in the town's North Park.

The merry-go-round is open daily from Memorial Day through Labor Day and is located in North Park on Broad Street. It is open on weekends only in May and Sept. For more information call (515) 733-4214.

After you ride the carousel, stop by South Park for a pleasant walk across the swinging bridge. The bridge was constructed in the early 1930s under President Franklin Roosevelt's Works Progress Administration (WPA) program, and the park is a delightful place for a picnic lunch.

Also in Story City is the *Factory Stores of America Outlet Center,* where you can find discounts on brand-name merchandised. The mall is located off I-35 at exit 124.

From Story City travel south on US 69 until you reach *Ames,* home to *Iowa State University.* ISU is one of the oldest land-grant institutions in the country and is an international leader in agricultural studies. Some 26,000 students are enrolled here in a wide variety of undergraduate and graduate programs. The campus itself is lovely and full of green areas, with historical markers scattered throughout so that visitors can take their own self-guided tours (ask for a map at the Memorial Union, 2229 Lincoln Way, on the south side of the campus). On your tour, stop by the library to see its large Grant Wood murals, and notice the sculptures by artist Christian Petersen that are located throughout the campus.

A major attraction on the Iowa State campus are the *Reiman Gardens,* 1407 Elwood Dr. The $2 million horticulture display area covers fourteen acres south of Cyclone Stadium on Elwood Drive and includes eleven distinct gardens, including an herb garden, rose garden, wetlands garden, and a campanile garden. The gardens are a beautiful place to stroll, and garden tours are also offered. The newest addition to the Reiman Gardens is the Christina Reiman Butterfly Wing, a beautiful structure that is designed to look like a butterfly in flight. The 2,500-square-foot wing houses a year-round tropical garden filled with exotic and native butterflies from six continents.

The Reiman Gardens and Butterfly Wing are open daily from 9 a.m. to 4:30 p.m. Admission is $7 for adults, $6 for seniors, and $3 for children. For more information on this beautiful site, call (515) 294-2710 or visit www.reiman gardens.iastate.edu.

Two other sites should be part of your ISU tour. The ***Brunnier Gallery and Museum*** in the Scheman Building features a fine collection of decorative arts as well as traveling exhibitions. Also worth a visit is the ***Farm House Museum,*** the oldest building on campus and a fully restored National Historic Landmark that has been furnished to reflect the 1860-1910 period. Located on Knoll Road, the museum is open noon to 4 p.m. Mon through Fri. For more information on Iowa State University and its attractions and events, call (515) 294-4111 or see www.iastate.edu.

Before you leave Ames, take some time to explore the rest of the city. Downtown Ames has a variety of specialty shops, including the Octagon Center for the Arts, a gallery and arts-and-crafts shop with a wide selection of jewelry, pottery, and other works of art. It's located at 427 Douglas Ave. Campustown, an area within walking distance of the university, also has shops and restaurants.

## Farmers' Market Bounty

Each spring, my husband and I have the same argument. As he's calculating how many seeds and sets he can squeeze into our garden plot, I'm urging him to plant more flowers—not because of my reluctance to deal with a bountiful harvest, but because I know that come summer, I'd rather be strolling through our local farmers' market instead of picking our own vegetables.

It's not the work involved, mind you. It's just that we can eat only so many cucumbers, and how can I not buy from the kindly old farmer who always tells me about the latest doings of his grandchildren? And every ripe tomato we grow ourselves is one less I can purchase from the gentle Mennonite family with daughters so shy they never make eye contact. The market, with its overflowing bushels of brilliantly colored apples, peppers, and carrots, its shocks of Indian corn, bouquets of broccoli, gleaming jars of homemade jams, and succulent ears of sweet corn, is a sensory feast that lures me out of the house each Saturday morning from June through October.

A farmers' market is a primer in human relations as well as a place to buy food. Amish women in bonnets sell produce next to Vietnamese immigrants who offer piping-hot egg rolls; overalled farmers in seed-corn caps set up their tables next to long-haired twenty-somethings selling organic garlic; and matronly farm women offer advice on life, in addition to delicious fruit pies.

The rich soil of Iowa nurtures more than a hundred farmers' markets. You'll find major ones in Ames, Cedar Rapids, Des Moines, and Iowa City, but nearly every small town in the state has a farmers' market during the growing season (typically they're held on Saturday mornings, but often at additional times as well). There's no better place to sample the tastes of Iowa.

—L. E.

No visit to Ames would be complete without a stop at **Hickory Park Restaurant.** To find it, follow the crowds: On any given night it seems as though half the city is dining here. That means that you may have to wait a while to be seated, but your patience will be amply rewarded. Hickory Park serves succulent and tender barbecued meats, the kind that fall off the bone with a nudge and melt with a tang in your mouth. Its specialty is huge slabs of pork ribs, but its smoked chicken and beef ribs also have devoted followings. Each dinner comes with your choice of two side orders, which include smoked baked beans, potato, coleslaw, applesauce, and macaroni salad. For dessert try one of Hickory Park's sinfully rich ice-cream treats. Regulars agree that a chocolate mint marvel sundae is the perfect ending to a meal of barbecued ribs.

As you might expect in a college town, the atmosphere here is casual and friendly. Small wooden booths fill the restaurant's interconnected dining rooms, each with a tinplate ceiling and vintage photographs and signs on the walls.

Hickory Park Restaurant is located at 1404 South Duff Ave. It is near the Duff Avenue exit on US 30. Lunches are inexpensive; dinners are inexpensive to moderate. Hickory Park is open daily from 10:30 a.m. to 9 p.m.; Fri and Sat, they are open till 10 p.m. Call (515) 232-8940 or see www.hickoryparkames .com for more information.

For a uniquely Brazilian dining experience, try the **Café Beaudelaire,** 2504 E. Lincoln Way. Close to the campus, this fine cafe specializing in South American-cuisine functions as a restaurant by day and a bar by night. Try to nab a window seat for some great people-watching. Call (515) 292-7429 for more information.

For an overnight stay in Ames, check out the **MonteBello B&B Inn,** 3535 S. 530th Ave. This hacienda-style inn is set on nineteen acres of prairie land, next to MonteBello Lake and overlooking the city of Ames. Designed, built, owned, and operated by Daphne and Jaime Reyes, this place deserves your attention for its unique style and colorful ambience. Decorated with south-of-the-border flavor, the rooms are spacious and light-filled and have king-size beds and private baths. Rates, which fall into the expensive category, include full Mexican breakfasts. For more information or to make reservations, call (515) 296-2181 or visit www.montebellobandinn.com.

## Railroad History

For more than a hundred years, scenic **Boone County** has been the railroad center of Iowa. At one time this was a bustling coal-mining region, with the railroads serving as a lifeline to the rest of the world. That heritage lives on today in the **Boone and Scenic Valley Railroad,** an excursion and dining train based in the town of **Boone** that travels through some of the state's most spectacular scenery. The railroad is operated by the Boone Railroad Historical Society and offers a 14-mile trip through the Des Moines River Valley from Boone to Fraser, passing through densely forested bluffs and valleys.

Rides on the Boone Railroad last about two hours and are offered Memorial Day weekend through the end of October, as well as during December and around Valentine's Day. The train depot is located at 225 Tenth St. (go north on Story Street through the business district to Eleventh Street, west for 5 blocks, south 1 block, and west again for 1½ blocks to parking). Call (800) 626-0319 for schedules and fares or visit www.scenic-valleyrr.com.

A good time to visit Boone is during its annual **Pufferbilly Days.** Held on the first weekend after Labor Day, Pufferbilly Days is a celebration of the town's railroading heritage and a community-wide festival featuring train rides, a parade, antique-car show, live entertainment, a carnival, sports events, an arts festival, and model-train displays. For more information call the Boone Chamber of Commerce at (515) 432-3342.

Another piece of Boone County railroad history is preserved at the Kate **Shelley High Bridge** northwest of Boone and the **Kate Shelley Memorial Park and Railroad Museum** 5 miles southwest of Boone at 1198 232nd St. in Moingona. The two sites are named in honor of a local girl who became a heroine at the tender age of fifteen. In a terrible storm the night of July 6, 1881, Kate crawled across a railroad bridge longer than the length of two football fields to warn an oncoming passenger train of a trestle washout near her home. Two crewmen had already died when a locomotive crashed at the site, and Kate is credited with saving the lives of everyone on the oncoming passenger train. Kate's bravery did not go unrewarded: As word of her adventure spread, the young woman became a national heroine. A Chicago newspaper raised funds to pay off the mortgage on her family home, and a well-known temperance leader of the day arranged to send the girl to college.

In 1901 the North Western Railroad completed the world's longest and highest double-track railroad bridge over the Des Moines River, a marvel of nineteenth-century engineering skill (the bridge is now listed on the National Register of Historic Places). The span was christened the Kate Shelley High Bridge in honor of the local heroine, and in 1903 Kate was named the North Western station agent in Moingona. She held the position until shortly before her death in 1912. Later the Boone County Historical Society bought the depot and opened it as a museum, re-creating a typical passenger station of the late nineteenth century, complete with a period waiting-room bench, a potbellied stove, a ticket window, a telegraph, and a wide variety of railroad memorabilia.

A Rock Island Rocket passenger car parked on the tracks nearby is used as a theater in which a presentation of the Kate Shelley story is given.

The Kate Shelley Museum is open by appointment. The Kate Shelley High Bridge is located 3 miles northwest of Boone. For information on either the museum or the bridge, call (515) 432-1907.

Railroads are not the only attraction in Boone County. The town of Boone is also proud of its status as the birthplace of Mamie Eisenhower, wife of the thirty-fourth president of the United States. You can learn about her life and times at the *Mamie Doud Eisenhower Birthplace,* a modest frame house where she was born in 1896. The home had been privately owned for many years before a town committee was formed in the 1970s to buy and restore it. After five years of work, the birthplace was dedicated in 1980. Though Mamie was originally against the idea of saving the house (out of modesty, it was thought), she later donated a number of items to the site. Today it is one of only a few first ladies' birthplaces that have been preserved.

Though Mamie returned to Boone a number of times as an adult, her stay here as a child was brief. Her father, John Sheldon Doud, came to Boone in the early 1890s and established a meatpacking company with his father. In 1897, one year after Mamie's birth, the family moved to Cedar Rapids and a few years later to Colorado. Mamie met her future husband in 1915 on a vacation in San Antonio, Texas, and began living the traveling life of an Army officer's wife. Later, after eight years in the White House, Ike and Mamie retired to the farm home they had purchased in Gettysburg, Pennsylvania—the first and only home they had ever owned. After Ike's death in 1969, Mamie continued living on the farm until shortly before her death in 1979.

Visit the birthplace today, and you'll gain more insight into the life of the first lady and her husband. The home has been restored to the 1890s period and contains many furnishings that were donated by Mamie's family. The master bedroom has its original furniture, including the bed in which Mamie was born, and there is also a library of Eisenhower-related materials.

The Mamie Doud Eisenhower Birthplace is located at 709 Carroll St. It is open 10 a.m. to 5 p.m., Mon through Sat, June through Oct. A small admission fee is charged. For more information call (515) 432-1907.

For a peaceful place to recover from all your sightseeing, visit the *Iowa Arboretum,* southeast of Boone near the town of *Luther.* The arboretum is an educational facility unlike any other in Iowa. Located on 378 acres in rural Boone County, it contains hundreds of species of trees, shrubs, and flowers in a quiet, scenic setting. Its main goal is to help Iowans appreciate and better understand plant life. Here you can learn which plants are best adapted to the soils and climate of Iowa and how to use these plants properly for landscaping, gardening, conservation, and other purposes. The arboretum also serves as an outdoor laboratory for testing the hardiness and adaptability of newly introduced plants and as a center for the preservation of rare and endangered plant species.

A vital part of the arboretum is its forty-acre Library of Living Plants, where you can view varieties of cultivated trees, shrubs, and flowers. Plants with similar uses are grouped together—small shade trees are located in one area, for example, and trees useful as windbreaks in another. With this arrangement, you can quickly "look up" the best plant for your needs.

The arboretum also contains more than 300 acres of forest, prairie, and meadow, with trails that pass by scenic overlooks, deep ravines, and streams. Labels identify the native trees, shrubs, and wildflowers, and illustrated brochures will help you plan your own self-guided tour. Along the way you're likely to see some of the deer, birds, and wild turkeys that make their home here. Guided tours and educational programs are also offered.

The Iowa Arboretum is open every day of the year from sunrise to sunset. To arrange a guided tour, call (515) 795-3216. The arboretum is located about 30 miles northwest of Des Moines, 2½ miles west of the town of Luther on CR E57. Log onto www.iowaarboretum.com for more information.

West of Boone lies the town of *Jefferson,* where you can pay a visit to the *Mahanay Bell Tower,* a 162-foot structure topped by fourteen cast bells. Take the elevator to the observation platform and you can see a view of seven counties. The tower was built with funds from the estate of William and Dora Mahanay, both residents of Jefferson. William was a sales representative for a surgical-instrument company as well as the owner of a substantial amount of Green County farmland. When he died, he specified that his estate be used for the construction of a tower on the southwest corner of the courthouse square.

The bells on top of the tower were made and installed by a Chicago company. The largest one, middle C, weighs 4,700 pounds and is 5 feet in diameter. The smallest is G, which weighs only 198 pounds. Concerts are played several times each day, as Mr. Mahanay wished.

## didyouknow?

George Gallup, founder of the Gallup Poll, was born and raised in Jefferson, Iowa. Maybe he got his penchant for counting things by counting the walls of his octagon-shaped house, located at 703 South Chestnut St. Whatever you do, don't "gallup" past this one!

The Mahanay Tower is located on the downtown square in Jefferson (it's difficult to miss) and is open to the public from Memorial Day to Labor Day from 11 a.m. to 4 p.m. daily. In May and Sept, it is open on weekends, weather permitting. Admission is $2 for adults, $1 for children. Call (515) 386-2155 for more information.

Jefferson is also home to **Deal's Orchard,** which has been growing tasty apples since 1941. In addition to apples and other fresh produce, the Deal family sells more than 30,000 gallons of fresh cider each year. In mid-October they hold a Fall Festival with horse-drawn hayrides, a corn maze, and live music. Deal's Orchard is at 1102 244th St. Call (515) 386-8279 or see www .dealsorchard.com for more information.

# Frontier Chronicles

Begin your tour of this region of the state in **Fort Dodge.** The city is the county seat of **Webster County**—though if a certain wrestling match in 1856 had turned out differently, Fort Dodge's destiny may have followed another path.

The story begins when John F. Duncombe, described in a newspaper of the day as "an engine in pants," arrived in Fort Dodge in 1855. At that time Fort Dodge was only a tiny settlement in contrast to the nearby thriving town of Homer. Duncombe, however, spearheaded an effort to have Fort Dodge named as the county seat. The citizens of Homer naturally objected, and an election was held to determine which town would get the coveted distinction. When the votes were counted, it was discovered that both sides had stuffed the ballot box—but the citizens of Fort Dodge were more successful in their voting fraud, as their town came out the winner. John D. Maxwell, the leader of the Homer faction, was furious. Then someone made the suggestion that Maxwell and Duncombe settle the issue with a wrestling match. For an hour the two battled it out in Homer's public square in front of a large crowd. Duncombe was declared the winner, and Fort Dodge was named the county seat and as a result became the leading commercial center in the area. Fort Dodge has good reason to be grateful for the athletic prowess of John F. Duncombe.

Fort Dodge's history has many more colorful episodes, and the best place to learn about them is at the city's **Fort Museum.** The site is a re-creation of Fort Williams, a garrison built in 1862 to protect local residents from Indian raids. The fort includes a frontier village with stockade, blockhouse, soldiers' quarters, general store, blacksmith shop, one-room school, log chapel, and drugstore, all with period furnishings. Also on display are exhibits on military and pioneer history.

Various special events are held at the Fort Museum, including **Frontier Days**, which is on the first weekend in June. This citywide celebration of Fort Dodge's past features a parade, Buckskinner's Rendezvous, live entertainment, historic home tours, and much more.

The Fort Museum is located a quarter mile east of the junction of US 169 and US 20. It is open daily from mid-April through mid-Oct. A small

## Fee, Fi, Fo, Fum!

Did you know you were in the land of giants? One of the great American hoaxes had its origin in a great lump of Fort Dodge gypsum. Listening to a sermon in church while visiting in Ackley, George Hull, a native New Yorker, came up with the idea of staging a little resurrection of his own. Somehow he managed to ship a chunk (7,000 pounds' worth!) of Fort Dodge gypsum to Chicago. There, while Hull posed, a sculptor carved the rock into the figure of a 10-foot-tall man. Hull, his cousin, and the sculptor worked with wooden mallets and steel needles to give the giant an ancient and weathered "faux-cade." Then, using a circuitous route, the giant was shipped on to New York and given a midnight burial in a field on the cousin's farm near Cardiff.

About a year later, when some men were digging a well on the farm—surprise!—a huge stone foot appeared, then a leg, then two legs, and soon they had unearthed an amazing stone-like giant! Hull and his cousin didn't let the grass grow under their feet: They put up a fence, erected a tent, charged a ten-cent admission, and went into business. Scientists, scholars, and an Indian medicine man visited the Cardiff giant; theories were advanced and some suspicions were raised. In the meantime, dimes kept rolling in. Soon they had made more than $20,000!

Unfortunately (at least for the cousins) one visitor happened to be Galusha Parsons, a lawyer from Fort Dodge. And he must have known his gypsum because he recognized in the form of the giant the huge rock that had been shipped out of his hometown a year earlier. The jig was up and Hull, at last, revealed the true origins of the colossal man. But you will have to go to New York to see this sleeping giant lie. He is at rest in the Farmers' Museum in Cooperstown. Or perhaps, the "real" giant is on display at the Fort Museum. Who knows?

admission is charged. For more information call (515) 573-4231 or see www
.fortmuseum.com.

Also in Fort Dodge is the ***Blanden Memorial Art Museum,*** the first permanent art facility in the state of Iowa. You're likely to be surprised by the diversity and quality of its collection, which includes such treasures as Chagall's *The Fantastic Horsecart* (one of the painter's personal favorites), Miró's *The Cry of the Gazelle at Dawn,* and Maurice Prendergast's *Central Park,* plus bronzes by Henry Moore, an Alexander Calder mobile, and a collection of non-western art highlighted by Asian works from the seventeenth through nineteenth centuries, pre-Columbian art, and tribal objects from North America and Africa. The museum also sponsors traveling exhibits and art classes for both adults and children.

The museum was founded in 1930, a gift to the community from former Fort Dodge mayor Charles Granger Blanden in memory of his wife. Since then other benefactors have donated money and works of art to the museum, including the Philadelphia art collector Albert Barnes.

The Blanden Memorial Art Museum is located at 920 Third Ave. South. It is open Tues through Sat from 11 a.m. to 5 p.m. Admission is free. For more information call (515) 573-2316 or see www.blanden.org.

Visit **Dolliver Memorial State Park,** south of Fort Dodge, for a picturesque view of this part of the state. The Des Moines River and Prairie Creek flow through the park, embellished by canyons, bluffs, and Indian mounds. Cabins, campsites, and picnic shelters are available.

In **Dows,** visit the **Dows Depot Welcome Center,** an 1896 Northern/Rock Island Railroad Depot. It is furnished with period railroad memorabilia and serves as a handy place to gather information on the area. You'll find the depot at 1896 Railroad St., and it is open daily. Call (515) 852-3595 for information.

Just across the street is the **Quasdorf Museum,** housed in a building built in 1899. The museum has displays relating to the days when blacksmith, wagon, and machine shops were an indispensable part of small-town life. It is open daily; call (515) 852-3595 for more information.

Next pay a visit to the **Dows Mercantile** at 122 E. Ellsworth St. Built in 1894 after a disastrous fire had all but destroyed Main Street, it is now run by the Dows Historical Society and sells gift items and antiques. The store is open from 9 a.m. to 4:30 p.m., Mon through Sat and from 1 to 4:30 p.m. on Sun. Call (515) 852-3533 for more information.

A good time to visit Dows is during **Corn Days,** which is held on the first weekend in August. Enjoy a parade, rodeo, and other live entertainment.

From Dows head north to the town of **Clarion,** home to the **4-H Schoolhouse Museum.** The museum, located in the town's Gazebo Park, is housed

## An Apple a Day

If an apple a day keeps the doctor away, then one of the healthiest places in the state to visit is the **Community Orchard** at the northwest corner of the airport in Fort Dodge. Owned by Greg and Bev Baedke, with help from their children (son Jon graduated from Iowa State with a degree in horticulture), the orchard is a great place to visit between August 1 and Christmas. I can't quite figure out exactly what the Baedkes won't do. There is a cafe serving delicious desserts and lunches, a well-stocked gift shop , family and individual photos taken by a professional photographer (in the orchard, of course), an AppleFest in early October, and much, much more. And you just can't leave without taking home one of their frozen apple pies as a souvenir. I can't think of anything better than a perfect fall afternoon spent at Community Orchard. I'd start with apple pie, move on to lunch, maybe an apple dumpling next, some more apple pie . . . you get the idea! Call (888) 573-8212 or see www.communityorchards .com for more information.

in the early twentieth-century schoolhouse where O. H. Benson, superinten-
dent of Inside the museum you'll see various displays on 4-H memorabilia and
history, including 4-H uniform style changes through the years. Other displays
take you back in time to the days of the one-room country schoolhouse. The
museum is open by appointment; call (515) 532-2256 to arrange a visit.

North of Clarion lies the town of *Britt,* which each August plays host
to one of the state's most unusual events, the *National Hobo Convention.*
Hoboes have been traveling to the convention since 1900, though their numbers have dwindled, and by now most of them are well past middle age.
Each year they return to Britt to swap stories, meet old friends, and enjoy the
hospitality of the town.

Britt hosted its first hobo convention in 1900, eager to gain some publicity for the town and show the rest of the world that "Britt was a lively little
town capable of doing anything larger cities could do." The national media did
indeed report on the convention, not realizing that the town was serious in its
intentions until hundreds of hoboes began arriving for the event. The travelers
were treated to games and sports competitions, musical performances, and a
clean place to stay, and the newspapers around the state gave Britt the publicity it had hoped for.

Though the 1900 convention was declared a rousing success, it wasn't
until 1933 that Britt once again hosted the convention. Some townspeople
were reluctant to sponsor the event again, but they were won over by those
who pointed out that the convention was for hoboes, not tramps or bums. A
hobo is defined as a migratory worker who is willing to work to pay his way;
a tramp is a traveler who begs for food rather than works for it; and a bum

## Two Fun Car Games

*Count Ks.* Iowans like to spell words that begin with Cs with Ks. You score a point
for each one you find. Bonus points are awarded for double and triple Ks. For example: Kolleen's Kountry Kabinet. Look around, have fun, patronize these businesses.
After all, they just might put you in the winner's circle. (Prizes should be named in
advance, to avoid disagreements.)

*License Plate Game.* For the most part, Iowa license plates have three letters of the
alphabet in them. Following the order they come in, make words out of them. For
example, BND could be bind, bend, bandanna, abundant, abandon, etc. In some
counties this will be more difficult than others, and you may have to make adjust-
ments to the rules, like making phrases, proper names, or even sentences out of the
letters. For example: SRO could be "standing room only" or "Sally Roberta Olson" or,
if you're paying attention to the road, "see rigid opossum."

# What Is the Proper Way to Eat Sweet Corn?

Once, when I was in high school, a friend of mine had an exchange student from France staying with her family for the summer. I was invited there for dinner one evening and, as we all crowded around the large dining table, I was happy to see sweet corn was on the menu. We all sat down to eat and as we "dug in," as the saying goes, I saw Pierette's face fill with shock, then amazement, followed quickly by horror. "Why, Pierette, whatever is the matter?" someone asked. She replied, barely able to get out the words, "You eat za corn like . . . like zee peegs!" We all shifted uneasily in our chairs for a few seconds, looked furtively at one another (wondering to whom she could possibly be referring), and then simply resumed eating our corn like "zee peegs."

There are, as far as I know, only three alternatives:

1. Hold the large end in your left hand (in your right if you're left-handed), the small end in the other. Pick the best spot at the large end and start to chew to the small end in an orderly fashion, remembering to surface occasionally for air. When you get to the tip, stop! Do not bite your fingers! Return calmly to the large end just under the place where you started the first row. Proceed in this manner, being orderly and neat. (This, of course, is the right way!)

2. Begin as in 1 but eat vertically, i.e., the small way around instead of the long way down, making wasteful circular motions with your wrists.

3. Eat at random, taking a bite here, a bite there, using no method whatsoever.

(I have actually seen people eat sweet corn this way! I am happy to say I didn't know them very well.)

—T. S.

is too lazy either to work or to roam around. At a time when many people were out of work and homeless, a hobo was seen as an honorable—even romantic—character.

The town agreed to host the convention again and renewed a tradition that continues to this day. Through the years the event has grown to include more activities, from the crowning of a hobo king and queen to the serving of free mulligan stew. Hoboes like Mountain Dew, Hardrock Kid, and Fry Pan Jack have become legendary in Britt, though today fewer and fewer of their brethren come to the event each year. A new breed is taking their place, however: "weekend hoboes," who love the open road but still have stable jobs. Both groups gather in Britt once a year to renew their ties to each other and the traveling life.

You don't have to be a hobo to attend the convention, however. Visitors are welcomed, and the town offers a full slate of activities for their amusement: a flea market, a parade, an antique- and classic-car show, musical entertainment, an art show, a carnival, and a fireworks display. Visitors are welcome to stop by the "hobo jungle" (the area where the hoboes camp) to listen to storytelling and singing and learn more about life on the road. The National Hobo Convention is held each year on the second weekend in August. For more information call (641) 843-3867.

If you can't make it to Britt for the convention, you can still learn more about the hobo life at the town's **Hobo Museum,** 51 Main Ave. Located in the former Chief Theatre in downtown Britt, the museum celebrates hobo history through photographs, printed materials, musical instruments, and other artifacts. It is open May through Aug, Mon through Fri, from 9 a.m. to 5 p.m. For information call (641) 843-9104.

# newdealmurals

During the Depression, the Works Progress Adminstration commissioned artists to paint murals across the state. You can see these WPA murals in towns that include:

**Ames:** Post Office and the Iowa State University Library

**Forest City:** Post Office

**Algona:** Post Office

**Clarion:** Post Office

**Jefferson:** Post Office

Plan a visit—especially during spring and fall migration seasons—to the **Union Slough National Wildlife Refuge.** Take CR B35 north from Britt to CR A42 and head east to **Bancroft.** This area was established in 1938 by the Department of the Interior to help maintain the waterfowl population of the Midwest Flyway, including ducks, geese, whistling swans, and a wide variety of shorebirds. The slough is all that remains of a pre-glacial riverbed. Now 3300 acres, it once covered more than 8,000. It marks the confluence, or union, of two watersheds: the Blue Earth River and the East Fork of the Des Moines. There is a picnic area and nature trail at the southern end of the refuge. More information is available from the Refuge Manager at (515) 928-2523. The refuge office is located off CR A42, 6 miles east of Bancroft, and is open from 7:30 a.m. to 4 p.m. Mon through Fri.

Drive west to the town of **West Bend,** the site of the **Grotto of the Redemption.** The grotto was the lifetime work of Father Paul Dobberstein, who started its construction in 1912. As a young seminary student he suffered a serious illness and vowed that if he recovered, he would erect a shrine to Mary. For forty two years he labored to build the grotto in West Bend, setting into concrete ornamental rocks and gems from around the world. After his death in 1954, his work was continued by Father Louis Greving.

## The Remarkable Gift of the Prison on the Prairie

During World War II a German prisoner-of-war camp was established just outside the town of Algona. One of the 3,200 prisoners, an architect and noncommissioned officer named Eduard Kaib, enlisted the help of some of his fellow prisoners, and together they went to work to fashion a nativity scene. It was a way, Kaib thought, for them to fight their loneliness and their longing for their families and the festivities of Christmas in their native land. They pooled their money in order to purchase the materials they needed and built the figures to a one-half life-size scale, using concrete over wire frames. They finished the detailing with hand carving in plaster. The project took more than a year to complete, and it was displayed at the edge of the camp for the first time in December 1945.

When the camp was being dismantled after the war, the citizens of Algona asked that the nativity scene be left behind for the community to enjoy. Kaib and his helpers agreed, with the stipulation that no admission fee ever be charged. They helped the townspeople assemble the display in a newly repaired building. It remains open to the public during the Christmas season, and several of the prisoners have returned here to visit. One of them, freelance photographer Werner Meinel, stopped in Algona in 1963 while returning to his home in Massachusetts from a shoot in Alaska. Surprised that the nativity scene was still being displayed and touched by the friendliness of the Algona residents, he sent one of his prize-winning photographs—a pair of white swans flying side by side, titled *Correlation*—to be hung in the nativity building as a symbol of peace.

During December you can see the nativity in a building at the Kossuth County Fairgrounds. Call the Algona Methodist Church at (515) 295-7241 to see it at any other time of the year. It is open Memorial Day through Labor Day, Mon through Fri, from 10 a.m. to 5 p.m. For information call (641) 843-9104.

Today the Grotto of the Redemption covers an area the size of a city block. Contained within its twisting walls and encrusted caverns are nine separate grottoes, each portraying a scene from the life of Christ. Highlights include a replica of Michelangelo's *Pietà* and a life-size statue made of Carrara marble portraying Joseph of Arimathea and Nicodemus laying Jesus into the tomb. Adjacent to the grotto is St. Peter and Paul's Church, which includes a Christmas Chapel that is considered to be Father Dobberstein's finest work. It contains a Brazilian amethyst that weighs more than 300 pounds. The church's main altar (a first-place winner at the Chicago World's Fair in 1893) is of hand-carved bird's-eye maple.

The grotto is financed by the freewill donations of visitors, and forty-five-minute tours are given from 10 a.m. to 5 p.m. daily from May to Oct (though the grotto is open for viewing year-round). The Grotto Cafe serves inexpensive home-cooked meals during the summer months. Camping and motel facilities are also available. The grotto is located 2 blocks off IA 15 at the north end of town at 300 N. Broadway Ave. For more information call (515) 887-2371 or see www.westbendgrotto.com.

Also of interest in West Bend is the *Sod House* (201 First Ave. Southeast; 515-200-9234), a home built of earth and managed by the West Bend Historical Society to help preserve part of the pioneer heritage of the area. At one time sod houses could be found throughout the prairie states, for in a land of few trees they were a quick and inexpensive answer to the housing needs of new settlers. A sod home cost between $15 and $30 to construct, and its thick walls and roof were good insulation against the heat of summer and cold of winter.

The sod-house era in Iowa lasted only thirty years, from the 1850s to the 1880s. It ended when the expansion of the railroad made lumber cheap enough to be used as a common building material. The historical society also operates a country schoolhouse and a historical museum. Tours are by appointment, and a small admission is charged.

## don'trun hogwild

The first Kossuth County law (1856) was known as the hog law because it prohibited hogs and cattle from running around at large. Watch out for escapees!

The town of *Emmetsburg,* which lies northwest of West Bend, is also worth a visit, particularly if you have a bit of Irish in your background. The town was settled by Irish immigrants and named in honor of Robert Emmet, the Irish patriot who was executed by the English in 1803. The customs and heritage of the old country remain strong in Emmetsburg, especially during its annual St. Patrick's Day celebration. This three-day festival includes a Miss Shamrock Pageant, parade, a musical performances, and various Irish-themed entertainments. For more information call (712) 852-4326 or log onto www .emmetsburgirishgifts.com.

## Clear Lake Region

The region that surrounds beautiful Clear Lake is dominated by two towns, Mason City and Clear Lake. *Mason City* is perhaps best known as the birthplace of Meredith Willson, who wrote the book, lyrics, and music for the award-winning musical *The Music Man*. Begin your 76-Trombones-Tour at the *Meredith Willson Boyhood Home,* 314 S. Pennsylvania Ave. Willson grew up right here in Mason City and based his smash hit on his boyhood experiences. The house is chock-full of Willson family memorabilia and musical treasures. It is open Tues through Sun, from 1 to 4 p.m. Call (641) 424-2852 or (866) 228-6262 for more information.

Anyone who loves Willson's best-loved musical will feel right at home in **Music Man Square** at 308 South Pennsylvania Ave. The square features storefronts based on the sets used in the Warner Brothers 1962 film version of the musical, from Mrs. Paroo's front porch (a gift shop) to the Pleez-All pool hall. The streetscape is open from 1 to 5 p.m. Tuesday through Sunday, with no admission charge.

While you're on the square, be sure to visit the **Meredith Willson Museum,** where you can hear your favorite Willson songs and learn more about his life in music. The museum also includes exhibits about the importance of music in American culture, with displays on topics ranging from Civil War bands and Victorian parlor music to swing bands. There's even an interactive radio sing-along booth where "adoring fans" will applaud your warbling. The museum is open Tues through Sun from 1 to 5 p.m., and admission is $5. For more information call (866) 228-6262.

Mason City has another claim to fame as well: Architecture buffs regard Mason City as a mecca for Prairie School architecture. The city is credited with having one of the finest collections of Frank Lloyd Wright–inspired architecture to be found anywhere, a style known for its open, flowing designs, low roofs, and skillful use of natural materials. The **Rock Glenn-Rock Crest National Historic District** includes eight houses that were designed by Walter Burley Griffin and Barry Byrne of the Chicago office of Frank Lloyd Wright and built between 1912 and 1917.

Adjacent to the district is the **Frank Lloyd Wright Stockman House,** a Prairie School house designed by the famous architect himself. Constructed in 1908, the home was one of very few houses built by Wright in this period to address middle-class housing needs. It features such details as an open floor plan, ribbon windows, overhanging eaves, and exterior wood banding that emphasizes its horizontal lines. The Stockman House (530 First St. Northeast; 641-421-3666) is open for tours from May through Oct. Call for hours or visit www.stockmanhouse.org. Admission is $5 for adults and $1 for children.

A good way to see all of these architectural treasures is on a **Mason City Walking Tour.** The Mason City Convention and Visitors Bureau puts out a detailed booklet that will guide you on your walk, with photographs of the significant landmarks and explanations of their architecture. Thirty-seven

didyouknow?

Meredith Willson also wrote the popular holiday song "It's Beginning to Look a Lot Like Christmas."

## 76 Trombones and More

Meredith Willson was born in Mason City on May 18, 1902. He loved music from an early age, and when he was seventeen he left Mason City for New York, soon earning a place in the legendary John Philip Sousa Band and then the New York Philharmonic. At age twenty-seven he launched his career as a composer and lyricist. Hundreds of songs later, Willson began writing a musical comedy about his state and hometown. The effort took more than five years.

*The Music Man* opened on Broadway in 1957 and became a smash hit. A few years later a movie version was filmed, with its premiere taking place at the Palace Theater in Mason City.

Willson's seventy-five-year musical career won him many awards. The most prestigious came in 1988, four years after his death, when he was awarded the Presidential Medal of Freedom, the highest honor bestowed on an American citizen.

buildings are described, as well as the Music Man Footbridge over Willow Creek. Copies of the guide are available at the Convention and Visitors Bureau at 25 W. State St., Mason City. For more information call (800) 423-5724.

On your tour of the city, you should also plan a visit to the *MacNider Art Museum.* Housed in a handsome Tudor-style building, the museum has a permanent collection focusing on American art and boasts works by such well-known artists as Thomas Hart Benton, Grant Wood, Alexander Calder, Moses Soyer, and Adolph Gottlieb. Another highlight of the museum is its collection of Bil Baird puppets and memorabilia. Baird, a native of Mason City, was a famous puppeteer whose creations appeared in the theater, in films, and on television for more than fifty years. His puppets starred in the Ziegfeld Follies, appeared in the movie *The Sound of Music,* and performed on television for Ed Sullivan, Jack Paar, and Sid Caesar. In 1980 Baird donated a major collection of his work to the MacNider Museum, including some 400 puppets and marionettes.

The Charles H. MacNider Museum is located at 303 Second St. Southeast. It is open Tues through Sat, and admission is free. For more information call (641) 421-3666 or see www.macniderart.org.

More insights into the region's past can be found at another Mason City attraction. The *Kinney Pioneer Museum* off US 18 West, located on the airport grounds, includes a pioneer village with a one-room schoolhouse, log cabin, and blacksmith shops. The museum is open May through Sept, and a small admission fee is charged. Call (641) 423-1258 for hours.

Lovers of the outdoors will enjoy the *Lime Creek Nature Center,* which sits atop the limestone bluffs of the Winnebago River. The center includes both live and static displays of a variety of animals, plus an outdoor amphitheater and more than 9 miles of trails through prairie, forest, and wetlands. The center is at 3501 Lime Creek Rd.; it is open daily. For more information call (641) 423-5309 or visit www.limecreeknature.org.

Another Mason City institution is the ***Northwestern Steakhouse,*** purveyor of tender steaks and several Greek specialties. Its founder, Tony Papouchis, the son of a Greek Orthodox priest, came to the United States in 1912 and opened the restaurant in 1920.

Today, Tony's son Bill and his wife, Ann, run the business. Northwestern Steakhouse is located at 304 Sixteenth St. Northwest. Hours are from 5 to 10 p.m. daily, and prices are moderate. Call (641) 423-5075 or see www.north westernsteakhouse.com for more information.

Just west of Mason City on US 18 is ***Clear Lake,*** one of the state's most popular recreation areas. The lake itself is one of the few spring-fed lakes in Iowa, a lovely 3,600-acre expanse of water that draws boating and fishing enthusiasts, water-skiers, swimmers, and confirmed beach bums all summer. Even in winter the area is a popular tourist spot, with cross-country skiing, snowmobiling, and ice fishing for those who don't mind the cold.

The water is not the only attraction in Clear Lake. In the downtown area you'll find a number of antiques stores and specialty shops, and during the summer months many special events are scheduled, from fishing tournaments to band concerts in the park.

One way to see the area is on board the **Lady of the Lake,** a sternwheeler ferryboat that takes passengers on a scenic cruise around Clear Lake. Cruises are offered May through Sept. Tickets are $12 for adults and $6 for children. Call (641) 357-2243 for information.

Don't miss the ***Surf Ballroom*** on your tour of Clear Lake. The ballroom is best known as the site of the last performances given by rock 'n' roll legends Buddy Holly, Ritchie Valens, and J. P. "The Big Bopper" Richardson. Following their concert, the three were killed nearby in the crash of their small plane in the early morning hours of February 3, 1959—an event that became the basis for Don McLean's hit song "American Pie." In 1988 a monument was erected in their memory outside the Surf, and their music lives on in an annual memorial concert. For devoted rock 'n' roll fans, the Surf has become a landmark on the same order as The Cavern in Liverpool, where the Beatles got their start. People from around the country make pilgrimages here to relive the memories.

Even without the Buddy Holly connection, the Surf is worth a visit on its own. At a time when most ballrooms have gone the way of the horse and buggy, the Surf is a living reminder of the big-band era, when swing was king. Today it books a variety of music and dance bands, from country to big band to fifties and sixties classics. The Surf Ballroom is located at 460 N. Shore Dr. For more information call (641) 357-6151 or visit www.surfballroom.com.

Clear Lake is also home to the *Clear Lake Fire Museum.* The facility opened in 1986 and depicts a fire station from the early twentieth century. Inside you can see some of Clear Lake's earliest firefighting equipment, along with other antique firefighting memorabilia. Highlights of the museum include the town's 1924 Ahrens-Fox fire truck, an 1883 hand-pulled hose cart, a fire bell, antique fire extinguishers, photographs, and brass poles.

The Clear Lake Fire Museum is located at 112 N. Sixth St. It is half a block north of the fire station. It is open Memorial Day through Labor Day on Sat and Sun from 1 to 4 p.m. Admission is free. Donations are welcomed. For more information call (641) 357-2613.

Next head to the *Fort Custer Maze.* This is a fun place to test your sense of direction, for inside the western-style "fort" is a 2-mile-long maze that changes weekly during the summer season. The maze was designed by Adrienne Fisher of Portsmouth, England, author of several maze books and the designer of more than 200 mazes worldwide. It was constructed with more than 250,000 board feet of lumber, enough to construct ten large homes. At Halloween, there's a special haunted maze, and there are weekly prizes in the summer. The object of the maze competition is to find the eight stamps scattered throughout the structure in the shortest time. For the directionally challenged, there are guides who can offer helpful hints if asked. The Fort Custer Maze is at exit 193 off I-35. Admission is $6 for adults and $4 for children. Call (641) 357-6102 or see www.fortcuster maze.com for more information.

## didyouknow?

Iowa is one of the top-ten states in the country as far as wind resources go—or blow. Cerro Gordo County, averaging winds of 17 mph, is one of the windiest spots in the state. Now, wasn't that a breeze?

Before you leave the Clear Lake area, plan a visit to the viewing area of the *Cerro Gordo Wind Farm,* 6 miles south of Ventura on CR S14. The wind farm produces free, renewable, and clean energy and covers more than 10 square miles—the giant windmills are really quite impressive. Even though the wind farm covers a significant amount of land, only eighteen acres of it are actually used by the wind farm because the rotors are more than 100 feet off the ground; therefore, the land beneath them can be used for grazing or crop production. The wind farm is open daily from daylight to dusk. Admission is free.

Continue your tour of north central Iowa with a visit to *Charles City,* which lies east of Mason City. The town boasts one of the largest county museums in Iowa, the *Floyd County Historical Museum.* The museum is housed in the former Salsbury Laboratory Building, constructed in 1933, and contains more than forty rooms of exhibits. Its best-known display is a complete original drugstore that operated on Charles City's main street from 1873 to 1961. The store was founded by German immigrant Edward Berg and was later owned by John Legel Jr., who donated it to the historical society in 1961. Tour the store today and it's like stepping back a generation or more. The shelves are filled with patent medicines designed to cure every ailment known, plus items like cigar molds, chimneys for kerosene lamps, and ink bottles and cosmetics such as 7 Sutherland Sisters Hair & Scalp Cleaner.

Elsewhere in the museum you can see a restored 1853 log cabin, displays of old-time vehicles and tools, and materials relating to the history of the county. The museum also contains the nation's most complete collection of information relating to the founders of the gasoline-tractor industry, the Hart-Parr Company. The business was founded in Charles City and produced the first successful gasoline tractor in 1901. Another display contains information about Carrie Chapman Catt, a Charles City native and early leader in the women's suffrage movement.

The Floyd County Historical Museum is located at 500 Gilbert St. It is open year-round Mon through Fri from 9 a.m. to 4:30 p.m. During the months of

## Who Was Carrie Lane Chapman Catt?

Born in 1859 in Wisconsin, Carrie Lane moved with her family to Charles City, Iowa, in 1866 and graduated from Iowa State University in 1880 as valedictorian and the only woman in her graduating class. Because her father opposed her ambition to receive a higher education, she worked for a year at a country school and then as a dishwasher and library aide for nine cents an hour to pay her way through college. During her college years, she fought for the right of women to participate on the university debating team and in military exercise. Nationally, she led the women's suffrage movement until the ratification of the Nineteenth Amendment in 1920. (When she married her second husband, George Catt, in 1890, they both signed a contract allowing her to work on suffrage issues for four months a year.) She founded the League of Women Voters, worked ardently for international peace, and remained a powerful and well-respected advocate for women's rights issues until her death at the age of eighty-eight in 1947.

When visiting the Charles City area, plan a visit to the *Carrie Lane Chapman Catt Childhood Home.* Go south on US 218, turn right on 220th Street, then left on Timber Avenue and it will be about 2 miles down the road on the right side. Call (641) 228-3336 to arrange a tour. See www.catt.org for more information.

May through Labor Day, the museum is also open on Sat and Sun from 1 to 4 p.m. Admission is $4 for adults and $2 for ages twelve to eighteen. For more information call (641) 228-1099 or log onto www.floydcountymuseum.org.

At the Charles City Public Library, tour the ***Mooney Art Collection,*** which features prints, engravings, and etchings by artists that include Rembrandt, Picasso, Cezanne, and Manet. The works were donated in 1941 by a Eastman Kodak Company executive who grew up in Charles City. They are an extraordinary treasure for a public library to have, particularly one in a small town. The library is at 106 Milwaukee Mall and is open daily. Call (641) 257-6319 for information.

If you've brought your fly rod along, you may want to take a trip up to ***Otronto,*** just south of the Minnesota border, to the catch-and-release zone of the ***Big Red Cedar.*** The "no kill" zone, established in 1993, runs from there to Halverson Park south of St. Ansgar. This is a beautiful spot to fish for smallmouth bass, but please remember the first rule of anglers' etiquette: Do not encroach on another angler's spot! Usually this is not a problem at this particular location, but you should always be on the lookout for other established anglers and avoid them. Remember, this is not a group activity. Look for large rocks that break the current or fallen trees or logs where there is shade and you may be rewarded.

Amateur geologists will love paying a visit to the ***Fossil & Prairie Park Preserve,*** a 400-acre nature area along the Winnebago River, 1 mile west of Rockford on CR B47. It is one of only a handful of public fossil-collecting sites in the nation, with Devonian-era fossils in its quarry that can be easily collected by visitors of any age. The site also has historic beehive kilns, more than sixty acres of native prairie, a re-created sod house, hiking trails, and a visitor center.

The Fossil & Prairie Center Foundation hosts a fascinating celebration, its annual ***Prairie Heritage Day,*** on the second weekend in September. The event celebrates the region's pioneer heritage with live demonstrations of various crafts, military life, and pioneer days. To add to the fun, a 5K walk/run takes participants through its fossil quarry and out onto the prairie trails for a true cross-country race.

The park is open year-round from sunrise to sunset. Its visitor center is open from 1 to 4 p.m. daily, Memorial Day through Labor Day, and on weekends in May, Sept, and Oct. For more information call (641) 756-3490 or see www.fossilcenter.com.

# Places to Stay in Fertile Plains

## AMES

**Iowa House Historic Inn**
405 Hayward Ave.
(515) 292-2474
www.iowahouseames.com
inexpensive to moderate

## CHARLES CITY

**Sherman House
Bed & Breakfast**
800 Gilbert St.
(888) 528-3826
expensive

## CLEAR LAKE

**Norsk Hus By-the-Shore**
3611 N. Shore Dr.
(641) 357-8368
expensive

**Dickson's Landing**
1401 Main Ave.
(641) 357-8015
www.dicksonslanding.com
moderate

## FOREST CITY

**Elderberry Inn B&B**
19024 345th St.
(641) 581-2012
www.elderberryinn.com
moderate

## IOWA FALLS

**Rivers Bend Bed
& Breakfast**
635 Park Ave.
(641) 648-2828
www.iafalls.com/rivers
bendbandb
moderate

## MARSHALLTOWN

**Tremont Inn on Main**
24 W. Main St.
(641) 752-1234
www.tremontonmain.com
moderate

## MASON CITY

**The Decker House
Bed & Breakfast**
119 Second St. Southeast
(888) 363-4700
www.masoncityia.com/
deckerhouse
moderate to expensive

## ST. ANSGAR

**The Blue Belle Inn**
513 W. Fourth St.
(877) 713-3113
www.bluebelleinn.com
inexpensive to expensive

# Places to Eat in Fertile Plains

## BOONE

**Tic Toc Restaurant**
716 Keeler St.
(515) 432-5979
inexpensive

## CLEAR LAKE

**Cabin Coffee Company**
303 Main Ave.
(641) 357-6500
www.cabincoffeecompany
.com
inexpensive

## FORT DODGE

**Marvin Gardens**
809 Central Ave.
(515) 955-5333
moderate

## IOWA FALLS

**Porter's on Main**
205 Main St.
(641) 648-4067
moderate

## MARSHALLTOWN

**Cecil's Café**
13 Iowa Ave. East
(641) 753-9796
inexpensive

**Tremont on Main**
22 W. Main St.
(641) 752-1234
www.tremontonmain.com
moderate

## MASON CITY

**Whiskey Creek Wood
Fire Grill**
1519 Fourth St. Southwest
(641) 426-4000
www.whiskeycreek.com
moderate

## MONTOUR

**Rube's Steakhouse**
118 Elm St.
(641) 492-6222
moderate to expensive

# PRAIRIE BORDERLAND

Western Iowa has a rich array of attractions to tempt travelers, including the Loess Hills, a rare and beautiful geologic formation that borders the Missouri River between Sioux City and Council Bluffs. Here you'll also find the scenic beauties of Iowa's Great Lakes region, plus the cultural treasures of the Council Bluffs area.

## Spirit Lake Region

Tucked into the far northwestern corner of the state, the **Gitchie Manitou State Preserve** will interest travelers who love outdoor adventures. Located about 10 miles northwest of the town of **Larchwood** (follow CR A18), this beautifully preserved site contains the oldest rock bed (Precambrian) left exposed in Iowa. The outcroppings of Sioux quartzite that you see here, battered and polished by the winds for more than a billion years, are composed of sand compacted by silica. A century ago this lovely rock was quarried, and the resulting depression is called Jasper's Pool. The surrounding prairie and woodlands are also worthy of notice and have been attracting Iowa botanists for decades.

# PRAIRIE BORDERLAND

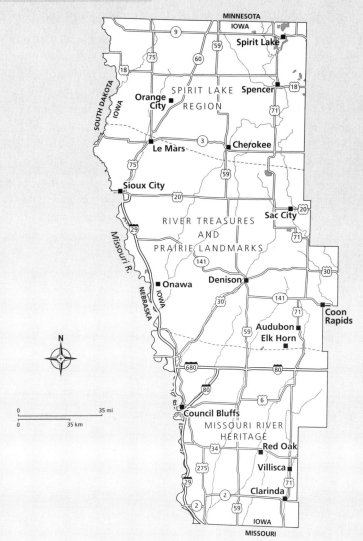

Continue your tour of western Iowa by exploring the *Iowa Great Lakes.* The region has been one of the state's most popular recreation areas ever since the railroad first came here in the early 1880s. Thirteen lakes are located here, the largest being *Big Spirit Lake* and *West Lake Okoboji.* You'll find some of the best swimming, boating, fishing, camping, and golfing in the state, in a beautiful setting surrounded by sparkling water. Once you visit you'll realize why midwesterners have been flocking to the area for more than a hundred years.

Many of the charms of Dickinson County are best discovered on your own—antiques stores, lovely parks and nature areas, fine restaurants, and quiet walks by the water. On your tour be sure to schedule time for a visit to *Arnolds Park,* which has been attracting visitors to the area since 1915 and is one of the longest-operating amusement parks in the world.

A highlight of any visit to Arnolds Park is a ride on one of the country's few remaining wooden roller coasters, the Legend. The ride made its debut in the park in 1929 and has thrilled thousands of children (and adults) with its clickety-clack ride and stomach-churning maneuvers. When Arnolds Park was being restored a number of years ago, a top priority was saving the local landmark. The Legend was completely dismantled, cleaned, repainted, and refurbished, and new side rails, bearings, cars, and brakes were installed. Today it is once again the park's featured attraction, drawing roller-coaster connoisseurs from across the country.

The Legend isn't the park's only asset. Thirty rides and attractions, gift shops, restaurants, picnic areas, and sandy beaches will tempt you into relaxing. The park's Preservation Plaza upholds another lake tradition, that of dancing and musical performances by local and touring artists.

Arnolds Park is located on the south side of West Lake Okoboji off US 71. A full-day pass is $25 for adults; $17 for children. The park is open daily (with

## AUTHORS' FAVORITES

| | |
|---|---|
| Arnolds Park | Orange City Tulip Festival |
| Gitchie Manitou State Preserve | Sergeant Floyd Monument |
| Ice Cream Capital of the World Visitor Center | Prairie Pedlar |
| | DeSoto National Wildlife Refuge |
| Loess Hills Scenic Byway | Danish Immigrant Museum |

# The Most Famous Mythical University in Iowa

No description of the Iowa Great Lakes region would be complete without mention of the **University of Okoboji.** Its campus is one of the largest in the world, stretching from the northern tip of Big Spirit Lake to south of Milford. As you walk through its campus, you'll see many signs of a strong school spirit: thousands of bumper stickers, sweatshirts, and pennants proudly bearing the university's name and hundreds of trash barrels that read HELP KEEP YOUR CAMPUS CLEAN. Prospective students will be relieved to learn, however, that the administration of the University of Okoboji believes that standard academic pursuits like books and lectures are unnecessary to true learning. Instead, its students major in roller-coaster engineering at Arnolds Park, culinary arts at local restaurants, and human anatomy at local beaches.

The school was founded in the early 1970s, when Herman Richter (director of student affairs), his brother Emil (administrative dean), and Roger Stolley (director of admissions) ordered T-shirts emblazoned with the university's logo to wear at local sporting events. Before long, the joke had spawned a local—and then a national— phenomenon. Today there are U of O alumni chapters all over the country, made up of former visitors to the Great Lakes region. The school has its own radio station, KUOO, and even established an endowment fund that is used to support community projects. Each year many local events are sponsored by the school, including a homecoming weekend, winter games, and golf tournaments. Its football team, the Phantoms, is undefeated despite one of the most grueling schedules in college football.

It's not unusual for the Phantoms to play the University of Iowa at 1 p.m., Nebraska at 4 p.m., and Notre Dame at 8 p.m. At each game, all the tickets sold are for Row A, Seats 1 and 2 on the 50-yard line, with proceeds going for a dome over West Lake Okoboji. University officials concede that the school's amazing record is helped by the fact that no other teams ever show up to play but contend that their team's excellence is so intimidating that other schools know they could never win. Even if you can't get tickets for the U of O football games, you'll still enjoy your time as a student at the University of Okoboji. The tuition is low, the classes easy, and each year everyone graduates at the top of the class.

some exceptions made for the local school year) from mid-May to mid-Sept. If you want more information call (712) 332-2183 or visit www.arnoldspark.com.

Arnolds Park is also home to a the **Queen II,** a faithful reproduction of the 1884 *Queen* that plied the waters of the Iowa Great Lakes for eighty-nine years. Local volunteers are responsible for her existence, working both to help raise money for the boat and to help with her construction. More than half of the boat's $350,000 cost was raised through auctions, bake sales, and door-to-door solicitations. In 1986 the *Queen II* was officially launched, with

Iowa governor Terry Branstad commissioning her as the Flagship of the Iowa Navy.

Today the *Queen II* offers multiple cruises daily throughout the summer on West Lake Okoboji . The cruises last for seventy-five minutes, with the captain providing a narrative of the history and attractions of that region. The fare is $15. Call (712) 332-2183 for more information.

After your cruise, don't miss paying a visit to the nearby *Iowa Great Lakes Maritime Museum.* There you can see nautical exhibits, old wooden boats, and historical photos and artifacts and also view a video of Iowa Great Lakes history. The Iowa Great Lakes Maritime Museum is located in the Okoboji Spirit Center in Arnolds Park. It is open year-round, with extended hours June through Aug. Call (712) 332-2183 for information.

History buffs will want to further explore the area's colorful past. The Dakotah first settled near the lakes after being pushed westward by settlers, but by the mid-nineteenth century the area was attracting more and more white people. The tension between the two groups eventually led to the Spirit Lake Massacre in 1857, in which forty settlers were killed by a band of warriors led by the Dakotah Sioux chief Inkpaduta. The murders sparked an uprising of the Dakotah that echoed through Minnesota and the Dakota Territory.

You can learn more about the history of the area at several sites in Dickinson County. The *Abbie Gardner Sharp Cabin* in the town of Arnolds Park was the only dwelling left standing after the massacre and is now a museum as well as the last resting place for the victims of the tragedy. The cabin is also the site of the *Spirit Lake Massacre Monument,* erected by the state in 1895 in memory of those who had lost their lives. The cabin is open daily from Memorial Day through Labor Day, and on weekends in Sept, and admission is free. It is located at 34 Monument Dr., Arnolds Park. It is 1 block west of the amusement park.

Another Great Lakes region attraction is *Cayler Prairie State Preserve,* a 160-acre tract of prairie located west of Big Spirit Lake. The site is one of the largest remaining areas of virgin prairie in the state. It is both a State Botanical Preserve and a National Historic Landmark, and it will give you a chance to see a little of Iowa's once-vast grasslands as they appeared more than a century ago. As you walk through its waist-high grasses, it's easy to imagine how it must have seemed to the early pioneers. Here you will find more than 250 types of grasses and wildflowers. Blooming begins in April with delicate pasqueflowers and ends in October with brilliant blue gentians. Other wildflowers can be found in bloom throughout the summer, with the height of color to be seen in early August. The prairie is also home to badgers, foxes, jackrabbits, meadowlarks, partridge, and the rare upland sandpiper.

## TOP ANNUAL EVENTS

**JANUARY**

**University of Okoboji Winter Games**
Okoboji, end of Jan
(800) 839-9987

**MARCH**

**St. Patrick's Celebration**
Emmetsburg, weekend before
Mar 17
(712) 852-4326

**MAY**

**Tulip Festival**
Orange City, third weekend in May
(712) 707-4510
www.octulipfestival.com

**Tivoli Fest**
Elk Horn/Kimballton
Memorial Day weekend
(800) 451-7960

**JUNE**

**Glenn Miller Festival**
Clarinda, second weekend in June
(712) 542-2461
www.glennmiller.org

**Lewis & Clark Festival**
Onawa, second weekend in June
(712) 423-9099

**AUGUST**

**Sidney Iowa Rodeo**
Sidney, first weekend in Aug
(712) 374-2695
www.sidneyrodeo.us

Cayler Prairie is located 6 miles west of Big Spirit Lake off IA 9. A parking lot is provided along the country road on the southwest side of the prairie. Visitors are welcome during daylight hours but are urged to read the regulation signs before entering the prairie. The picking or digging of plants is forbidden because of the rarity of many of the prairie's species.

From the Great Lakes region, head south to *Hannah Marie Country Inn* (4070 US 71 in Spencer), a "country Victorian" farmhouse that offers overnight accommodations for visitors as well as elegant afternoon teas and luncheons. Its owner is Mary Nichols, a retired home-economics teacher who named the place Hannah Marie after her mother. Mary's warm touch is evident throughout the house, as well as in the individually themed rooms. "People feel at home here, but still pampered," says Mary.

The two-story frame farmhouse offers a comfortable place to relax and unwind. In the morning you'll be served a hearty breakfast or you can have a basket delivered to your room. There are six guest rooms, all with queen-size featherbeds and down comforters.

The Hannah Marie Country Inn is located 4 miles south of *Spencer* on US 71. It is open year-round, and room rates are moderate. For reservations, call (712) 262-1286 or visit www.hannahmarieinn.com.

Another attraction that begins in Spencer is the ***Inkpaduta Canoe Trail*** on the Little Sioux River. The trail winds for 134 miles from Spencer south to the town of Smithland in Woodbury County. The Little Sioux is the largest interior stream of the Missouri River watershed in Iowa and has a sand, mud, and gravel bottom and high banks along most of its scenic course. The river current is quite slow, which makes for excellent fishing as well as canoeing.

The trail is named for the Dakotah Sioux chief who led the Spirit Lake Massacre. Inkpaduta and his followers were never caught after the raids.

As you travel the canoe trail, keep your eyes on the lookout for river otters. Once the most prevalent mammal in North America, unregulated hunting and trapping and habitat destruction decreased its numbers to the point of extinction in Iowa. In 1985 a program was started to reintroduce the river otter to the state. Iowa's native wild turkeys were trapped and traded for Louisiana otters. If you're lucky enough to see one of these graceful creatures, you're asked to report the information to the Wildlife Diversity Program of the Iowa Department of Natural Resources (515-432-2823). Many other animals can be seen along the river as well, including great blue herons, raccoons, beavers, muskrats, turtles, and white-tailed deer.

The Inkpaduta Canoe Trail can be entered at various sites. For a brochure and map, write to the Clay County Conservation Board, 420 Tenth Ave. Southeast, Spencer 51301; or call (712) 262-2187. (Don't plan on using the trail in winter.)

West of Spencer lies the town of ***Orange City,*** which takes great pride in its ethnic heritage and offers a number of attractions. Here you can see a variety of Dutch architecture (including a drive-in bank housed in a windmill), hundreds of beautiful flower beds full of tulips in season, and stores selling traditional Dutch dolls, pottery, lace, baked goods, wooden shoes, and meats.

A good place to begin your tour is at the ***Dutch Windmill Visitors Center*** on IA 10 East. The windmill stands more than 70 feet tall, with a dome that weighs five tons and vanes weighing more than seven tons. The center (712-707-4510) is open from 9 a.m. to 4 p.m. Mon through Fri.

Each spring during the third weekend in May, Orange City becomes even more of a Little Holland during its annual ***Tulip Festival.*** One of its most popular attractions is the Volksparade, when hundreds of people take to the streets with their buckets and scrub brushes to make the way clean for the festival's queen. Then board the Wilhelmina or the Juliana, the town's two horse-drawn streetcars, to see the rest of the sights in town. The Dutch street organ will likely catch your attention—one of only two in the United States, the organ was built in Holland and plays melodies for the enjoyment of passersby. The Dutch Dozen is a musical and dance group that will also entertain you, and in the evening you can kick up your own heels in a street dance or attend a theater performance.

At any time of year, you can visit the **Century Home,** a house built in 1900 by Orange City's first mayor and decorated with furnishings that might have belonged to a typical Orange City family at the beginning of the twentieth century. Included within are a pump organ handmade in 1903, a silver tea service that belonged to the home's original owner, and a clock brought from the Netherlands by the founder of Orange City. One of the upstairs rooms is filled with memorabilia from former Tulip Festival queens. The home is located at Albany Avenue and Fourth Street Northeast. It is open during the Tulip Festival and by appointment. Call (712) 707-4510 for more information.

At the **Old Mill** (102 Albany Place Southeast), at the entrance to the Vogel Paint and Wax Company, you can learn more about the Dutch influence in Orange City. The site contains three different types of windmills and an office building designed after a Dutch *stadshuis* (city hall). The Old Mill itself has displays on how wind power can be used for a variety of purposes, and the living quarters show life as it was generations ago. Some of the furnishings were brought from Holland, and others came from local pioneers. The Old Mill is open Mon through Fri. Call (712) 737-4993 for more information.

didyouknow?

The Kneirim Bank in Kneirim (now a private residence) was robbed of $272 in 1934 by Clyde Barrow and Bonnie Parker.

Before you leave Orange City, stop by the **Dutch Bakery** at 221 Central Ave. Northeast. There you can buy such treats as almond patties, St. Nick cookies, Dutch rusks, apple rolls, and Wilhelmina Peppermints imported from Holland.

For more information on attractions in the Orange City area, call the town's chamber of commerce at (712) 707-4510 or log onto www.orangecity iowa.com.

Southeast of Orange City lies the town of **Cherokee.** There you'll find the **Sanford Museum and Planetarium.** The facility was donated to the town by a local couple in memory of their son, Tiel Sanford, and opened in 1951.

Permanent exhibits at the Sanford deal with a variety of subjects relating to this region of the country and its past. Rocks, minerals, and fossil and animal specimens help explain the natural environment of the region. There are also displays about the Native American tribes who once lived in the area.

The Sanford Museum and Planetarium is located at 117 E. Willow St. It is open daily and admission is free. Planetarium shows are given on the last

Sunday of each month at 2 p.m. For more information call (712) 225-3922 or see www.sanfordmuseum.org.

Before you leave the area, you might want to pay a visit to a natural landmark located about 2 miles south of Cherokee on US 59. Pilot Rock is an enormous boulder of red Sioux quartzite about 160 feet in circumference and 20 feet high. It was left behind when the last continental glacier receded and offers a panoramic view of the surrounding landscape. During pioneer days, Pilot Rock served as an important landmark for travelers.

# newdealmurals

During the Depression, the Works Progress Adminstration commissioned artists to paint murals across the state. You can see these WPA murals in towns that include:

**Emmetsburg:** Post Office

**Hawarden:** Post Office

**Storm Lake:** Public Library

**Sioux City:** East Junior High and Castle on the Hill

**Ida Grove:** Post Office

**Rockwell City:** Post Office

**Onawa:** Post Office

**Audubon:** Post Office

**Harlan:** Post Office

**Missouri Valley:** Post Office

**Corning:** Post Office

Southeast of Cherokee lies **Storm Lake,** a lovely town of about 10,000 people on the shore of the 3,200-acre natural lake of the same name. Home to Buena Vista University, the town also boasts a beautiful network of parks that follows the shoreline, each park connected by a biking and walking trail that winds for about 5 miles.

In Sunset Park on West Lakeshore Drive, visit the **Living Heritage Tree Museum,** where you can see a unique collection of trees with illustrious histories. The Village Blacksmith Chestnut, for example, is a descendant of the tree that inspired the poet Longfellow to write "Under the Spreading Chestnut Tree." Another tree nearby was grown from a seed carried to the moon and back. Also in the museum is a tulip poplar descended from a tree planted by George Washington at Mount Vernon, as well as an apple tree traced back to the famed Johnny Appleseed. Dozens of historically significant trees are interspersed amid serene landscaping near the lake. The park is open to the public at no charge, twenty-four hours a day. Call (888) 752-4692 for more information.

A couple of historical attractions in Storm Lake are worth a visit. One is the Victorian-era **Harker House** at 328 Lake Ave. It was built in 1875 by a local banker in the French mansard-cottage style. The home, which contains many of the original furnishings, is open for afternoon tours from June through Aug on Sat and Sun. Call (712) 732-3267 for information. Admission is $3 for adults and $1.50 for children. The Buena Vista Historical Society also operates a history museum at 214 West Fifth St. It is open from noon to 4 p.m. year-round. Call (712) 732-4955 for more information.

**Santa's Castle** is a fascinating place to visit if you're in Storm Lake between Thanksgiving and Christmas (or any other time of the year if you make an appointment). Begun in 1962 with the purchase of four animated elves, the castle now houses what may be the largest collection of antique, animated Christmas figures in the world. These are real classics from old department store displays. They make their home in an original Carnegie Library building at 200 E. Fifth St. A small admission fee is charged. For more information or to arrange a tour, call (712) 749-9247.

Northeast of Storm Lake lies the town of **Albert City** and a rather unusual historical museum. Don't miss the depot where a shoot-out following a bank robbery claimed the lives of three. You can still see the bullet holes in the walls and look at the gun used by one of the robbers. There are many vintage cars as well. Check out the funeral parlor where you can view old memorial wreaths and candlesticks, as well as a picture of the first motorized hearse. The museum is located at 212 N. Second St. It is open on Sun from 2 to 5 p.m., from Memorial Day to Labor Day. Call (712) 843-5684 for more information.

# River Treasures and Prairie Landmarks

From Albert City head west to **Le Mars,** home to one of the nation's top steak houses (according to celebrity chef Rachel Ray). **Archie's Waeside** has been serving tender aged steaks for more than sixty years. The third-generation restaurant was one of 200 steak joints nominated by readers of Ray's magazine in 2009, and after food writers secretly visited the restaurant and sampled its offerings, Archie's made it into the top-four ranking. Owner Bob Rand and his staff serve about 2,000 hand-cut steaks a week, feeding customers who come from three states and beyond. You'll find the restaurant at 224 Fourth Ave. For information call (712) 546-7011 or see www.waeside.com.

Next head to Iowa's western border. At the junction of Iowa, South Dakota, and Nebraska lies **Sioux City.** Ever since the Lewis and Clark expedition passed through here in 1804, Sioux City has been a focal point for travelers and settlers heading west. Located on the bank of the Missouri River, the city became a major nineteenth-century river port and the center of a booming stockyard and meatpacking industry. The Missouri River is still important to the city, though today it's prized primarily for its recreational attractions. Sioux

## It's a Scoop!

It is a commonly known fact that we all scream for ice cream—and if there is one place where such screaming is more appropriate than others, that place is Le Mars, the Ice Cream Capital of the World! Here, in northwestern Iowa, more ice cream is made in one location than anywhere else in the world—this is the home of Wells' Dairy Inc., makers of Blue Bunny ice cream and other popular frozen treats.

This dairy is one of the few remaining family-owned dairy processors in the country. In May of 2000 they opened the *Ice Cream Capital of the World Visitor Center.* Located at the intersection of IA 3 and US 75 in Le Mars, the visitor center is causing people to scream their heads off for more and more ice cream. At the center you will find everything you wanted to know about the history of ice cream—there are also interactive exhibits and you can take a peek inside the ice-cream plant. If all of this has churned up a hankering for your favorite food, satisfaction is only a few steps away. Next door is the ice-cream parlor, where you can order all kinds of ice-cream delights at the antique marble bar—including shakes, sodas, and phosphates.

The visitor center is located on US 75 North at 24 Fifth Ave. Northwest. Summer hours, May through Sept, are Mon through Sat from 10 a.m. to 4 p.m. and on Sun from 1 to 4 p.m. Call (712) 546-4090 for winter hours or to schedule a tour. Admission to the visitor center is $3 for adults, $1 for children ages five to twelve, and free for age four and under. All paid admissions receive a coupon for use at the ice-cream parlor. So go ahead—indulge yourself!

City has developed its riverfront into an extensive park-and-trail system, with a number of historical points of interest along the way.

Several of these attractions focus on Sergeant Charles Floyd, a member of the Lewis and Clark expedition who died here on August 20, 1804—the only casualty of the entire two-year expedition. His death is memorialized at the *Sergeant Floyd Monument,* a 100-foot-high white stone obelisk that is located on a high bluff overlooking the Missouri River. The monument became the country's first National Historic Landmark in 1960 and is located on US 75 near Glenn Avenue. It is ½ mile east and 1 mile north of exit 143 of I-29.

The *Lewis & Clark Interpretive Center* explores the dramatic story of the expedition in more detail. Interactive exhibits bring to life the hardships and challenges of this epic journey. At the entrance visitors sign on as members of the Corps of Discovery and then explore a day in the life of the expedition as it travels near Sioux City. You'll learn more about the military discipline that helped the team weather hardships, as well as the men's daily routines of cooking, standing guard, and setting up camp. The exhibits include animatronic mannequins, mapmaking tools, computers, hand-painted murals, brass-rubbing stations, and replicas of military equipment and Indian artifacts. A video presentation, produced exclusively for the interpretive center, is shown every fifteen minutes in the Keelboat Theatre. And don't miss the sculpture of Lewis, Clark, and their fearless Newfoundland dog, Seaman.

The Lewis & Clark Interpretive Center is at exit 149 off I-29. It is open daily from Memorial Day weekend through Sept (it is closed on Mon the rest of the year). Admission is free. For more information call (712) 224-5242 or log onto www.siouxcitylcic.com.

The young soldier who died near this spot is also remembered at the *Sergeant Floyd Welcome Center and Museum.* The center is housed aboard an original 1932 Army Corps of Engineers vessel, named in honor of Sergeant Floyd. From 1933 to 1975 the boat did towing, survey, and inspection work on the Missouri River, and in 1983 it was permanently dry-docked to serve as a combined welcome center and river museum. On the main deck you'll find tourist information and on the second deck an Upper Missouri River history museum. The displays include the largest collection of scale-model Missouri River steamboats in the Midwest.

The Sergeant Floyd Welcome Center and Museum is located off I-29 at exit 149. It is open daily from 9 a.m. to 6 p.m. and admission is free. Call (712) 279-0198 for information.

Another riverfront site recalls a more recent part of Sioux City history. The *Flight 232 Memorial* commemorates the heroic rescue efforts made by the Sioux City community after the crash of United Flight 232 in 1989. The monument includes a statue of Colonel Dennis Nielsen carrying a young child to safety. Nearby is the *Anderson Dance Pavilion,* a lovely public space that is

## With All the Honors of War

*Regarding the death of Sergeant Floyd, the journals of Lewis and Clark read thus:*

"20th August, 1804—I am Dull & heavy been up the greater Part of last night with Sgt. Floyd who is as bad as he can be to live. . . We set out under a jentle Breeze from the southeast. . . We came to make a bath for Sgt. Floyd hoping it would brace him a little, before we get him into his bath he expired with a great deal of composure . . . having Said to me before his death that he was going away and wished me to write a letter . . . . We buried him to the top of a high round hill overlooking the river & Country for a great distance situated just below a small river without a name to which we name & call Floyd's river, the Bluffs, Sergt. Floyd's Bluff. . . we buried him with all the honors of War, and fixed a Ceeder post at his head with his name title and day of the month & year . . . we returned to the Boat & proceeded to the Mouth of the little river 30 yd wide & camped a butiful evening. . . ."

used for festivals that include Labor Day weekend's ARTSPLASH. You'll find the memorial and pavilion on the riverfront in Gateway Park.

Sioux City is also proud of the renovation of its historic **Orpheum Theatre.** The Orpheum first opened in 1927 and was once one of the most magnificent movie palaces in America. During 2000-01, hundreds of builders and artisans labored to restore the structure, using a mixture of antique and reproduction furnishings. Today the opulent 2,588-seat theater offers a full schedule of top-name performances, including touring Broadway shows. The Orpheum is at Sixth and Pierce Streets; for a schedule of events, call (712) 279-4850 or visit www.orpheumlive.com.

You can learn more about area history at the **Sioux City Public Museum,** housed in one of the most spectacular homes ever built in the city. Its original owner was John Pierce, an early Sioux City real estate agent and developer who lost his fortune soon after building the house in the early 1890s. The house is a Romanesque mansion of Sioux quartzite with twenty-three rooms filled with stylish paneling and ornately carved woodwork.

On the first floor of the museum, you'll find exhibits on Sioux City history, the Civil War, and life on the frontier. The second floor has displays on natural history, fossils, and minerals, while the third floor is devoted to an extensive Native American collection. On display are various Native American artifacts, including articles of clothing and beautiful quill- and beadwork. Most items are from the Plains and Woodland tribes that once inhabited this area.

The Sioux City Public Museum is located at 2901 Jackson St. Its hours are Tues through Sat from 9 a.m. to 5 p.m. and Sun from 1 to 5 p.m. Admission is free. For more information call (712) 279-6174.

A fun and interesting place to visit while you're in Sioux City is the **Historic Fourth Street** area downtown. This area's early twentieth-century architecture now houses numerous pubs, restaurants, and antiques and specialty shops. The buildings along this street, noted for their Richardsonian Romanesque style, popular in the late 1800s, line a 2-block-long area from Virginia Street to Iowa Street. Two of the buildings, the Evan's Block and the Boston Block, are included on the National Register of Historic Places.

There are several paces to eat on Historic Fourth Street. You can customize a pizza (more than thirty different ingredients!) and sample a beer from more than 115 different varieties at **Buffalo Alice.** Owner Mike Salviola has been in business for over twenty-five years and has got his pizza down pat. The restaurant is located at 1022 Fourth St. Call (712) 255-4822 or see www .buffaloalice.com for more information. If you don't think you can cope with all those decisions, try **Luciano's** at 1019 Fourth St., which serves authentic

Italian foods and homemade breads. Call (712) 258-5174 or see www.lucianos restaurantiowa.com for information.

After all that eating, it's time to venture out-of-doors. Take IA 12 north of town to CR K18, where you'll find *Five Ridge Prairie.* The ridges that give the 790-acre park its name include eight miles of trails that wind through tall grass prairie and woodlands. Call the Plymouth County Conservation Bureau at (712) 947-4270 for more information.

And if you spot a dragon along the way, don't say I didn't warn you! (Hint: Look carefully near the junction of IA 12 and the county road.)

No description of western Iowa would be complete without mention of the *Loess Hills* (of which Five Ridge Prairie is a part). The hills begin just north of Sioux City and stretch in a narrow band south to the Missouri state line. They are formed from deposits of windblown silt—a unique geological phenomenon found only in Iowa and in the Kansu Province of northern China. In places they look like a miniature mountain range rising out of the Iowa plains, soft hills covered with a mixture of prairie and woodland plants. They were formed after the retreat of the last glaciers and since then have been eroded by wind and rain into the beautiful ridges and valleys visible today.

An excellent place to learn more about this unique and diverse ecosystem is at the *Dorothy Pecaut Nature Center* (4500 Sioux River Rd., Sioux City), which is located by Stone State Park on the northeast edge of Sioux City. The nature center includes a variety of interactive exhibits, including a model of the underground life of the Loess Hills, displays on the wildlife and plants of the region, and exhibits on the geologic forces that formed the hills. A network of hiking trails outside the center lets visitors explore the hills on their own. The Dorothy Pecaut Nature Center (712-258-0838) is open from 9 a.m. to 5 p.m. Tues through Sat and from 1 to 5 p.m. on Sun.

As part of your tour of western Iowa, you may want to explore part or all of the *Loess Hills Scenic Byway,* which flanks Iowa's western border. This 220-mile route stretches from Plymouth County in the north to Fremont County in the south and roughly parallels I-29. It is anchored by the town of Akron in the north and Hamburg in the south. Make sure you take advantage of the numerous "loops" off the main byway; they offer a unique opportunity to experience the Loess Hills more intimately. Some of these roads are gravel, however, so drive carefully. Some particularly nice loops are the Ridge Road Loop near Westfield, the Preparation Loop just south of Turin (home of the Turin Man, an assemblage of human bones 5,500 years old, discovered here in 1955 by a young girl), and the Spring Valley Loop near Sidney.

For more information, contact the Loess Hills Hospitality Association at (712) 886-5441 or see www.loesshillstours.com. Another good resource is

## The Barn Quilts of Sac County

Throughout rural Iowa you're likely to see the occasional barn that sports on its front a brightly colored hanging designed like a quilt square. These are "barn quilts," and there's no better place to view them than Sac County.

The county's barn quilts began as a 4-H project in 2005 led by Kevin Peyton of Sac City. Area quilters chose the patterns, volunteers painted the designs, and soon the brilliant hangings were found throughout the area.

Sac County has the largest concentration of barn quilts in the country, fifty-five at last count. Almost all of them are within a few miles of each other, making for a pleasant driving tour. You can find detailed maps at local convenience stores as well as at www.barnquilts.com.

The names of the quilts reflect the interests of the women who worked the original quilts with their richly abstract designs. Here are some of the designs you'll see that are identified by roadside signs: Hole in Barn Door, Flock of Geese, Bear's Paw, Double Aster, Railroad Crossing, Indian Puzzle, Hen and Chicks, Arrowheads, and Harvest Star. These, truly, are the glowing stars of Sac County: they illuminate the past and serve as a shining testament to the homely, yet startlingly beautiful work of pioneer women across the country.

Cornelia F. Mutel's book *Fragile Giants,* which explores the Loess Hills and their delicate ecology.

From Sioux City travel east on US 20 for 60 miles and then head south on CR M43 to the ***Prairie Pedlar*** at 1609 270th St. in ***Odebolt.*** Here you can stroll through seven acres of perennial and annual theme gardens filled with hundreds of varieties of flowers and herbs. This family-owned business also includes a gift shop and a greenhouse with hundreds of hard-to-find perennials and annuals. Special events include a Mother's Day Tea Party and Moonlight Garden Party in midsummer.

Owner Jane Hogue began the business more than twenty years ago and since then has seen her hard work blossom into an enterprise that draws visitors from across the state. Assisted by family members, Jane raises the flowers in the gardens and harvests, dries, and arranges them in delightful combinations.

The Prairie Pedlar gardens and gift shop are open Apr through mid-Oct, Mon through Sat from 11 a.m. to 4 p.m. and on Sun from 1 to 4 p.m. Free garden walks convene at 2 p.m. each Sunday afternoon in July and Aug, weather permitting. Call (712) 668-4840 or see www.prairiepedlar.com for more information.

***Onawa*** (located midway between Sioux City and Council Bluffs) is home to a most unusual business: ***L & C Replicas,*** which creates replicas of the boats that plied America's rivers and lakes in the eighteenth and nineteenth centuries. Using an extensive library of research materials, owner Butch Bouvier and his team make both full-scale and model replicas of vessels such as the keelboats used by the Lewis and Clark expedition. You can see one of their boats at the **Lewis and Clark State Park** north of Onawa. Butch also welcomes visitors to his business at 613 Fifth St., Onawa. For information call (712) 420-3180 or see www.keelboat.com.

You can also visit the **Monona County Historical Museum** in Onawa while you're in this area, at 47 Twelfth St. You simply can't miss the Eskimo Pie display (the treat was invented in Onawa in 1920) and the barbed-wire collection. Call (712) 433-1661 for more information.

Next head south to **Denison,** birthplace of one of America's favorite moms, actress Donna Reed. Reed was raised on a farm near Denison and completed her schooling here. After graduation she left Iowa to become an actress, starring in *The Donna Reed Show* and more than thirty movies. Reed returned often to Denison, remaining in contact with her family and friends in the area until her death in 1986.

The **Donna Reed Performing Arts Center** celebrates Denison's most famous daughter. The center is located in the former German Opera House, which first opened its doors in 1914. The Opera House was later converted into the Ritz Movie Theater, where Donna Reed fell in love with motion pictures. In 1988 the Donna Reed Foundation, with financial support from the community, corporate grants, and thousands of volunteer hours, saved the building.

Today the center houses the Donna Reed Foundation headquarters, a charming old-fashioned soda fountain, and the 550-seat Donna Reed Theater. A miniature replica of Bedford Falls, the town from the movie *It's a Wonderful Life,* is on permanent display, as are photos, personal items, and movie mementos from Donna Reed's life.

The Donna Reed Center for the Performing Arts is at Broadway and Main Street in Denison.

In honor of the famous actress, each June Denison hosts the **Donna Reed Festival for the Performing Arts**. The festival draws an impressive list of professionals. In years past, participants have included Debbie Reynolds, Shelley Fabares, Nanette Fabray, and Bonnie Franklin, plus nationally known writers, directors, and producers. Workshops are held on various topics relating to musical theater, television, writing, acting, and directing.

The Donna Reed Festival for the Performing Arts is held each year in Denison on the third weekend in June. For more information call (712) 263-3334 or see www.donnareed.org.

Denison is also the site of the **W. A. McHenry House.** This beautiful Victorian home was built in 1885 by Denison pioneer William A. McHenry. With six fireplaces and fourteen rooms (including a ballroom), the home was for many years a showplace for the area. Today it has been restored and contains a variety of historical artifacts, including the Academy Award won by Donna Reed for her role in *From Here to Eternity.*

The W. A. McHenry House is located at 1428 First Ave. North. It is open Thurs and Sun from 1 to 4 p.m., Memorial Day through Labor Day. For more information call (712) 263-3806.

Southwest of Denison lies **Dow City,** site of the **Simon E. Dow House.** The historic home sits high on a hill with a commanding view of the surrounding countryside. Its builder, Simon Dow, was traveling through Iowa on his way west in 1855 when he decided to cut his journey short and remain here because he liked the area so much. Later he became a prominent cattleman, and in 1874 he built a substantial redbrick house that became the nucleus of a settlement called Dow City. At a time when the average home cost $2,000, Dow spent a princely $11,000 for his home.

The Dow House is unusual in that its floor plan is the same on all three floors. All the walls are three bricks wide to keep the home warm in the winter and cool in the summer, and ornamented keystones and carved roses are centered over the first- and second-floor doors. Today the home has been restored to its original appearance and will give you an interesting introduction to the lifestyle of a prominent, upper-middle-class citizen of the nineteenth century.

## Al Capone's Favorite Whiskey

If you were traveling through this part of Iowa during Prohibition Days—and you didn't mind breaking the law—you would have made a beeline to the little town of Templeton (population 350) just east of Manning. There, a number of the town's citizens performed a valuable public service by making Templeton Rye whiskey. The drink commanded top dollar—the equivalent of $70 a gallon in today's dollars—and so impressed Al Capone that he started bootlegging it across the country. After Prohibition ended, the whiskey continued to be made in small batches for select patrons, but was not commercially available.

In 2006 Templeton Rye was reborn as a legal brand that still uses the original Prohibition-era recipe. Since then it has quickly attained a national reputation (while its flavor is superb, its association with Al Capone doesn't hurt its marketing efforts). Tours of the distillery are given several times each month. For dates, call (712) 669-8793 or see www.templetonrye.com. Tell 'em Al sent you.

The Simon E. Dow House (712-263-2748) is located south of US 30 at the end of Prince Street in Dow City. It is open May through Sept from 1 to 5 p.m. on Sat and Sun.

Before you leave this neck of the woods, plan a visit to the community of **Manning** on IA 141. Here you'll find what is probably the oldest building in Iowa, the **Hausbarn,** a combination house and barn built in the middle of the seventeenth century in the German region of Schleswig-Holstein and dismantled and shipped over to Manning, where it was reconstructed piece by piece. The Hausbarn is part of Manning Heritage Park, a complex of sites celebrating the town's history and German roots. It is located at 12196 311th St., and is open year-round, with extended summer hours. For more information call (712) 655-3131 or see www.germanhausbarn.com.

A quite lovely place to tour in this area of the state is the community of **Woodbine.** Once a stop on the old Lincoln Highway, the town has relaid all of its downtown sidewalks with brick to match the oldest remaining brick segment of the first highway to span the country. Several stately Victorian houses still overlook this section of the road. Don't miss the old Lincoln Highway marker near the Harrison County Genealogical Center, or Eby's Drug Store (423 Walker St.), an old-fashioned soda fountain in business since 1916. Then take a stroll through the White Floral Gardens at Eleventh and Park Streets, a lovely park filled with peonies, shrubs, and trees.

Plan a visit to the community of **Gray** at the end of May or June. "Gray" may be its name but gray is not its nature, especially during the summer months, when the **Heritage Rose Garden,** located on the first block of Main Street, comes alive with the fragrance and color of roses. This garden has been planted with old garden roses known for their hardiness, durability, fragrance, and beauty. Here you'll find rugosas, climbers, gallicas, albas, and lovely big-headed cabbage roses. Don't miss the angel garden and the other old-fashioned flowers. Call (712) 563-2742 for more information.

Traveling south on US 71, you may think your eyes are deceiving you but look again—it's **Albert the Bull** of **Audubon.** The world's largest anatomically correct bull stands as a monument to the beef industry and weighs in at forty-five tons. Erected in 1963 and made of concrete and steel, he is a mere 30 feet tall with a horn span of 15 feet.

While you're in Audubon don't miss the wonderful mural in the post office of John James Audubon, artist and naturalist, for whom both the town and the county were named. Commissioned by the Works Progress Administration (WPA) in the 1930s, it was painted by Virginia Snedecher of Brooklyn, New York. The town also celebrates the famous artist with a series of mosaics in the downtown's Bird Walk and the John James Audubon Festival on the last Saturday in April.

Farther south toward **Hamlin** and easily seen from US 71 are the eighteen antique windmills that were donated by local farmers and are used now to show the way to **Nathaniel Hamlin Park.** This unusual park, part of the old Audubon County Home, includes a bluebird house trail, a preserved prairie, and an elk couple—not to mention what may well be the world's largest nail collection! The park is open on weekends June through Sept from 1 to 4 p.m. Call (712) 563-3984 for more information.

Southeast of Dow City you'll find the charming villages of **Elk Horn** and **Kimballton,** which are home to the largest rural Danish settlement in the United States. Danish immigrants settled the area in the late nineteenth century, and their descendants have worked hard to preserve their unique heritage.

Your first stop on a visit to the area should be the **Danish Immigrant Museum,** which tells the story of the Danish settlement of North America and the Danish-American ethnic heritage that lives on today. Located in Elk Horn, the three-story structure has a pitched roof and a half-timber, half-stucco finish that suggests a Danish farmhouse. Inside are exhibits that describe the immigrant experience both in the Old Country and the New World. Elk Horn was chosen as the site of the museum after a nationwide search because of its strong town spirit and commitment to the project. The Danish Immigrant Museum (800-759-9192) is located at 2212 Washington St. It is open daily. Admission is $5 for adults and $2 for children.

Next pay a visit to Elk Horn's **Danish Windmill.** The landmark brings to mind the bumper sticker that says, YOU CAN TELL A DANE, BUT YOU CAN'T TELL HIM MUCH. If that weren't the case, it's doubtful the historic mill would ever have left its home in Norre Snede, in the Danish province of Jutland. It was during the worst days of the farm crisis in the mid-1970s that local resident Harvey Sornson came up with the idea of finding a Danish windmill to bring to the area. Many people thought the idea was crazy, but their skepticism gradually gave way to

## twotalltales

Two famous trees are located not far from each other in Audubon County between Exira and the Cass County line.

The Plow-in-the-Oak is located 1 mile south of Exira on US 71. Legend has it that a farmer left his plow leaning against a sapling when he went off to the Civil War and that the tree has been growing around it ever since. Set in a five-acre park, you'd better hurry to see the plow, for less and less of it is visible every year.

The Landmark Tree, a cottonwood that separates Audubon County from Cass County, is said to have taken root when a surveyor stuck a stick into the ground to mark the county line. Local legend has it that the stick grew into the tall tree you see today. Sorry, you have to ask for directions—that's half the fun of getting there!

Sornson's persistence. A mill was located in Denmark, and an emergency town meeting in Elk Horn resulted in $30,000 being pledged to the project in just a few days. The 1848 structure was then laboriously dismantled and brought over piece by piece to Iowa. When it arrived it still had ocean salt on its timbers, and eighty-seven-year-old Peder K. Pedersen, who had left Denmark at the age of twenty-one and never returned, tasted the salt of a distant sea and cried.

Many of Elk Horn's townspeople worked together to reassemble the jigsaw puzzle of the dismantled mill, which was rebuilt in 1976. The total cost of the project eventually came to $100,000, a hefty amount raised through fund-raising projects and contributions from all over the country. Today the windmill stands some 60 feet high, with four 30-foot wings that catch the wind, turn the gears, and grind locally grown grain. The base of the mill houses a welcome center with extensive tourist information, and the adjacent Danish Mill Gift Shop offers stone-ground flour and a wide selection of Scandinavian gifts and foods.

The Danish Windmill is located at 4038 Main St. It is open daily. For more information call (712) 764-7472 or see www.danishwindmill.com.

Another Elk Horn attraction that owes its existence to the town's volunteer spirit is **Bedstemor's House,** meaning "grandmother's house." More than a hundred volunteers have donated time, materials, and furnishings to restore the 1908 home. Inside you'll find a glimpse of the life of a Danish immigrant family from the early twentieth century. (To furnish the home, volunteers used a 1908 Sears Roebuck catalog as their guide).

Bedstemor's House is located 3 blocks north and 1 block west of the Danish Windmill at 2015 College St. It is open daily from May 15 to Sept 15. For more information call (800) 759-9192. Two miles north of Elk Horn you'll find its sister village of Kimballton, also an enclave of Danish-American culture. The town's pride and joy is the **Little Mermaid,** a statue modeled after the famous landmark in Copenhagen's harbor (the Little Mermaid, of course, is the immortal character from the fairy tale by Hans Christian Andersen). Kimballton's little mermaid is the focal point of the town's Little Mermaid Park on Main Street. Nearby is the Mermaid Gift Shop, featuring many imported gift items.

While touring Kimballton you may also want to visit the **General Store Museum** (112 N. Main St.), where you can see antique toys, vintage machinery, and examples of the skill of the Danish immigrant mason Nels Bennedsen. The building was constructed in 1910 and was used as a barbershop until 1940. Its hours are from 1 to 4 p.m. Mon through Sat, June through Aug. Call (712) 773-2430 for more information.

# Whiterock Resort

Perhaps you want to spend a weekend in the country or are planning a family reunion. Perhaps you just want to kick back and do some fishing during the day and some stargazing at night. Maybe you'd rather mountain bike or launch a canoe or take a trail ride. Then again, it might be fun to learn something new—like tatting or dried-flower arranging. Maybe you'd like to learn more about alternative agriculture methods or beekeeping or how to start a prairie. Whatever your interests, whatever your energy level, you are sure to find something you like at Whiterock Resort. The list is practically endless.

Whiterock Resort is located on the farm once owned by Roswell Garst, hybrid corn promoter and diplomat, bought in 1916 (originally 200 acres) and developed and extended over the years until his death in 1977. It was here that Mr. Garst entertained Nikita Krushchev and his family in 1959 during the height of the cold war. In the same progressive and entrepreneurial spirit, this working farm of 4,500 acres offers the visitor a unique and rewarding visit.

The resort is still owned by the Garst family, and Garst's daughter Liz is the manager. The "headquarters" of this fascinating place is the family home, which is now a five-bedroom bed-and-breakfast. Additional lodging is available (with optional breakfast) at the Hollyhock Cottage, which began its life as a chicken coop and then became Mrs. Garst's garden shed; or the Oak Ridge Farm House, which can accommodate up to thirty people; or the woodland campsites. In other words, something for everyone.

The resort is part of the Whiterock Conservancy, a nonprofit organization that is a national leader in the areas of sustainable agriculture, low-impact recreation, and ecological restoration. The Garst family, it's clear, continues the family tradition of public service. To make reservations or to get more information, call (712) 684-2964 or log on to http://whiterockconservancy.org/accomodations.aspx. The resort, ½ mile east of Coon Rapids, is located at 1390 IA 141.

A good time to visit this area is during its two annual Danish festivals. *Tivoli Fest* is held each year on Memorial Day weekend. *Julefest* (the town's Christmas festival) is held the weekend after Thanksgiving and celebrates the season in true Danish style. Whenever you visit, you're likely to leave these friendly communities with an appreciation for their Danish heritage and with plans to return again. For more information on attractions in Elk Horn and Kimballton, call the Danish Windmill at (712) 764-7472.

From the Danish villages head south to the small town of *Walnut*, which is known as *Iowa's Antique City*. More than a dozen antiques stores make Walnut one of the best havens for nostalgia buffs in the state. From antique brass beds to ice-cream parlor stools and vintage dollhouses, you're likely to find an eclectic mixture of treasures on a visit to Walnut.

The town's old-fashioned downtown is graced by a beautiful collection of hand-painted murals. In 2001, twenty-seven artists converged on Walnut to enhance the ambience of Iowa's Antique City by creating these nostalgic recreations of the past. Some of the murals have direct ties to the Walnut area (for example, a picture of the stagecoach that once ran here), while others show popular commercial icons from the early twentieth century. For more information on Walnut, see www.iowasantiquecity.com.

# Missouri River Heritage

From Walnut head west to *Harrison County,* which borders the Missouri River and contains some of the most varied and beautiful scenery in the state of Iowa: lush farmland, gently rolling foothills, and the fragile loveliness of the Loess Hills. The county is also known as an apple-producing area. The fruit was first planted here before 1880, and today Harrison County has more acreage in apples than any other county in Iowa. These beautiful orchards, many of which line the county roads, are located near the towns of *Missouri Valley, Mondamin, Pisgah,* and *Woodbine.* Several orchards have facilities for picking your own apples, and orchard tours are also available. Apples are available for sale from mid-August to the end of the season. For more information call the Harrison County Historical Village and Welcome Center at (712) 642-2114.

Near the town of Missouri Valley in Harrison County, you'll find one of the state's major wildlife areas, the *DeSoto National Wildlife Refuge,* located 5 miles west of I-29. The refuge lies on the wide plain formed by prehistoric flooding and shifting of the Missouri River. Each spring and fall since the end of the last ice age, spectacular flights of ducks and geese have marked the changing seasons along this traditional waterfowl flyway. During a typical year some 200,000 snow and blue geese use the refuge as a resting and feeding area during their fall migration from their arctic nesting grounds to their Gulf Coast wintering areas. Peak populations of 125,000 or more ducks, mostly mallards, are common in the refuge during the fall migration. Other birds commonly seen in the area include bald eagles, warblers, gulls, pheasants, and various shorebirds.

Bird life is not the only attraction at the refuge. Deer, raccoon, coyote, opossum, beaver, muskrat, and mink make their homes here and can often be seen by patient observers. During the spring and summer, the refuge is open for fishing, picnicking, mushroom and berry picking, hiking, and boating. Twelve miles of all-weather roads meander through the refuge, and during the fall a special interpretive brochure is available to guide visitors and explain the annual migration.

# The Great Morel Hunt

If *you* spend much time with Iowans, you may, if you're wily enough, discover one of their private passions that amounts almost to an addiction: morel mushrooms. I don't know if it's their general elusiveness (I mean the mushrooms, not Iowans!), their wonderful woodsy flavor, or just the thrill of the chase that makes people go to such lengths to keep their private morel locations to themselves. These secret places are guarded possessively and guarded well. The best places to find morels are often passed along only within families. If someone sidles up to you with a confidential wink and a knowing smile and promises that they'll head you in the right direction, you should be immediately on your guard. You have been taken for a greenhorn.

I notice with interest that the DeSoto Wildlife Refuge lets people wander into "usually closed" areas of the park April 15 through May 31 during daylight hours. This is the time when, as their brochure hints, "a profusion of morels *usually* emerges" (emphasis mine). I have a sneaking suspicion that the profusion is probably somewhere else, unmarked and unknown, except by a few initiates. But maybe refuge guidelines are more stringent, and misdirection is not permitted. My father assures me (and he is a champion morel hunter) that the best place to look is on the north side of dead elm trees, but I have noticed through the years that he always, always, finds more than I do. Would a father mislead his own daughter? Nothing, I've found, is impossible when morels are involved. Here's what you do when (or if) you find them:

Soak the morels overnight in saltwater. Like leeks or spinach they harbor a lot of grit. This bath removes the grit and any lingering wildlife. Take a frying pan, get it hot, and melt a lot of butter in it. (If you're conscientious you may substitute olive oil, but there are some instances when I think a lot of butter is, if not okay, at least good.) Slice the mushrooms—or the mushroom if, like me, you've only found one—and fry them (sauté, if you prefer). Purists eat them straight out of the pan; martyrs fold them into crepes, omelets, or quiches because they like to wait for the good things to come. Enjoy!

—T. S.

The visitor center at the refuge should definitely be part of your visit to Harrison County. In addition to its natural-history displays, viewing galleries, wildlife films, and special programs, the refuge center is also the site of the **Bertrand *Museum,*** a facility housing some 200,000 artifacts recovered from the steamboat *Bertrand,* a vessel that sank with all its cargo in the treacherous Missouri River in 1865.

The wreck of the *Bertrand* mirrors that of many steamers, 400 of which sank in the Missouri during the nineteenth century. The boat was a mountain-packet stern-wheeler designed for the shallow, narrow rivers of the West. She was built to carry supplies that would eventually find their way to the gold miners of the Montana Territory and was said to be loaded with 35,000 pounds of mercury, $4,000 in gold, and 5,000 gallons of whiskey—a fortune worth $300,000 or more back then. Luck was not with the steamer, however, for on her first trip upriver she hit a snag and sank in 12 feet of water. The passengers and crew escaped unharmed, but the bulk of the cargo had to be abandoned. By the time a full-scale salvage operation could be mounted, the boat was irretrievable.

Over the years many treasure hunters searched unsuccessfully for the *Bertrand* and her costly cargo. With time, the Missouri changed its course, leaving the boat in a low-lying field under 25 to 30 feet of silt and clay. It wasn't until 1967 that the wreck was located after an extensive search by treasure hunters Sam Corbino and Jesse Pursell. Unfortunately for them, the cargo didn't contain the rumored riches, though it did contain bounty of another sort: some 10,000 cubic feet of hand tools, clothes, foodstuffs, furnishings, munitions, and personal effects, a virtual time capsule of nineteenth-century life. What was even more remarkable was that most of the cargo was in an excellent state of preservation, though the boat itself had to be returned to its resting spot once the artifacts were removed.

Visit the *Bertrand* Museum today and you can view many of those items, a collection that provides a fascinating look at a vanished time. More than the story of the *Bertrand* is revealed here: The saga of the western expansion unfolds through the boat's artifacts and other exhibits depicting the history and wildlife of the Missouri River basin.

The *Bertrand* Museum, located in the DeSoto National Wildlife Refuge Visitor Center, is open from 9 a.m. to 4:30 p.m. daily, except for holidays. Additional interpretive displays can be seen at the Bertrand excavation site 3 miles south of the visitor center. For more information call (712) 642-4121.

More of the history of the area can be viewed at the **Harrison County Museum and Welcome Center,** located 3 miles northeast of Missouri Valley on US 30. Included in the museum are ten buildings, including an 1853 log cabin, an 1868 school, a mill, a harness shop, a fur museum, a broom factory, and a chapel. The museum also serves as one of Iowa's official welcome centers and offers a large selection of brochures and other visitor information. The museum is open daily from mid-Apr through Nov, from 9 a.m. to 5 p.m. Mon through Sat and from noon to 5 p.m. on Sun. The Welcome Center is open daily. Call (712) 642-2114 for information.

Next head south to the **Council Bluffs** area. The city is named for the council meeting that took place near here in 1804 between the explorers Lewis and Clark and the chiefs of the Otoe and Missouri tribes. Council Bluffs later became a major stopover point on the Mormon Trail, and it was here that Brigham Young was elected president of the Mormon Church in 1847. By the mid-nineteenth century Council Bluffs had become a wild and lawless town, a place where "gambling and sin of almost every description flourished," to quote one observer of the day. The Ocean Wave Saloon was one of the most notorious sporting houses in the entire West until it burned to the ground during a violent thunderstorm (some held that it had been struck by lightning, while others believed it was the wrathful hand of God). Henry DeLong, a former regular customer of the establishment who had mended his ways, bought the property and gave it to the Methodist Church with the provision that it be used forever after as a church site. The Broadway Methodist Church now stands on the property, and it's most likely the only church in the country with a plaque on the front commemorating a saloon.

You can learn more about the history of the area at the ***Western Historic Trails Center*** at exit 1B off I-80/29. The site tells the stories behind the four trails that once passed through Council Bluffs: the route followed by Lewis and Clark, the journey of the Mormons west to Utah, and the California and Oregon Trails taken by the pioneers. The challenges and hardships of the trails are explored through exhibits and a film by award-winning filmmaker John Allen.

The site also includes 400 acres of hiking and biking trails that wind amid wildflowers and prairie grasses along the Missouri River. A fun time to visit the center is for Jam and Bread on Thursday afternoon from 1 to 4 p.m., when acoustic musicians jam, and free samples of homemade bread are served. Admission to the center (712-366-4900) is free. It is open daily from 9 a.m. to 5 p.m. (closed Mon during the winter months).

Council Bluffs' most famous and influential citizen was General Grenville M. Dodge, a man who has been called the greatest railroad builder of all time. Born in the East, Dodge first saw Council Bluffs while making a railroad survey and was so captivated that he made the city his home in 1853. In 1859 he met Abraham Lincoln, and the two developed a strong friendship. After Lincoln became president, he appointed Dodge as the chief engineer of the first transcontinental railroad. During the Civil War, Dodge served with distinction in a number of positions and was responsible for creating the first military spy system. After the war he was elected to Congress without campaigning and later became an adviser to Presidents Grant, McKinley, Roosevelt, and Taft, as well as a business leader in Council Bluffs and the East.

Today you can visit the ***General Dodge House*** to learn more about the life and times of this remarkable man. The home was built in 1869 and was designed by the architect responsible for Terrace Hill in Des Moines. The Second Empire–style mansion stands on a high hillside overlooking the Missouri Valley and contains lavish furnishings; parquet floors; cherry, walnut, and butternut woodwork; and a number of "modern" conveniences quite unusual for the period. Today it has been restored to the opulence of the general's day and is open for tours.

The General Dodge House is located at 605 Third St. It is open from 10 a.m. to 5 p.m. Tues through Sat and from 1 to 5 p.m. on Sun. It is closed during the month of Jan, and the last tour begins each day at 4 p.m. Admission is $7 for adults; $3 for children. For more information call (712) 322-2406 or see www.dodgehouse.org.

General Dodge's wife, Ruth Anne, is commemorated by the ***Ruth Anne Dodge Memorial.*** On the three nights preceding her death in 1916, Mrs. Dodge had a dream of being on a rocky shore and, through a mist, seeing a boat approach. In the prow was a beautiful young woman who Mrs. Dodge thought to be an angel. The woman carried a small bowl under one arm and extended the other arm to Mrs. Dodge in an invitation to drink of the water flowing from the vessel. Twice Mrs. Dodge refused the angel, but on the third night she accepted the invitation to drink—and died the next day.

Dodge's two daughters later commissioned Daniel Chester French, who also sculpted the Lincoln Memorial in Washington, to construct a statue of the angel in memory of their mother. Though the daughters were reportedly disappointed with the finished work, the monument is now considered to be one of French's finest works. Today you can see the graceful angel, cast in solid bronze, in Fairview Cemetery. As in Mrs. Dodge's dream, the heroic-size statue holds a vessel of water and beckons with her hand.

The Ruth Anne Dodge Memorial, locally known as the ***Black Angel,*** is located in Fairview Cemetery at Lafayette Avenue and North Second Street. (Also buried in the cemetery is Amelia Bloomer, the inventor of bloomers, the first trousers for women.)

Another historic monument in Council Bluffs is the ***Squirrel Cage Jail,*** once considered the ultimate in prison facilities. The unique design was patented in 1881 by two Indiana men with the idea of providing "maximum security with minimum jailer attention." Also called a "lazy-Susan" jail, the cell block consists of a three-story drum surrounded by a metal cage. Each of the three decks contains ten pie-shaped cells, with only one opening on each level of the drum. To enter a cell, the jailer would turn the central drum so that a cell doorway was lined up with the cage opening—like a squirrel cage. It may seem dehumanizing today, but in 1885, when it was opened, the jail was considered an improvement over the damp, unsanitary quarters prisoners had been kept in previously.

Though it remained in use up until the 1960s, the jail was declared a fire trap in 1969 because only three prisoners could be released at one time during an emergency. It was later in danger of being destroyed until the

# A Mormon Refuge

The original name of Council Bluffs was Kanesville, a tribute to a man who was sympathetic to the plight of the more than 30,000 Mormon refugees who flooded into the area beginning in 1846. The pioneers were escaping religious persecution in Nauvoo, Illinois, where their leader Joseph Smith had been killed. By the time the Mormons left the area for Utah in 1854, they had established more than eighty communities in southwest Iowa, organizing churches, schools, local governments, and four newspapers.

Kanesville was renamed Council Bluffs in 1853, but the Mormon history of the area lives on in a number of sites. Fairview Cemetery holds Mormon pioneer graves, and the *Kanesville Tabernacle and Visitor Center* is a reconstructed log church similar to the one in which Brigham Young was upheld in 1947 as president of the Church of Jesus Christ of Latter-day Saints. The event is one of the most significant days in the history of the church.

The Kanesville Tabernacle includes a visitor center where you can learn more about Mormon history in the area. It is located at 222 E. Broadway and is open daily. Admission is free. Call (712) 322-0500 for information.

Pottawattamie County Historical Society launched a heroic effort to save it. The jail was named to the National Register of Historic Places in 1972 and is now owned and operated as a museum by the historical society.

On a tour of the Squirrel Cage Jail, you'll also see the jailer's quarters and office and a room filled with prison memorabilia. Today the site is one of only three lazy-Susan jails still standing in this country and is unique in being the only three-story one (it also may be haunted—be sure to ask your tour guide for the stories!)

The Squirrel Cage Jail is located at 226 Pearl St. It is open Wed through Sat from 10 a.m. to 4 p.m. and on Sun from noon to 4 p.m. Call for reduced winter hours. Admission is $7 for adults; $5 for children. For more information call (712) 323-2509.

Railroad buffs won't want to miss two sites in Council Bluffs that celebrate the rich train history of the area. The first is the *Union Pacific Railroad Museum,* located in the city's historic Carnegie Library building at 200 Pearl St. The museum takes visitors on a journey through 140 years of American history, with artifacts, photographs, and documents that trace the development of the railroad and the American West. Among its treasures are the promotional materials that helped attract immigrants to make the hazardous journey west, along with a sampling of the precious possessions they brought with them. You can trace the settlement of the West on an interactive map table that highlights the towns that grew up along the railroad's route. The museum also features displays about the heyday of passenger travel and the rail industry's efforts to promote the nation's first national parks. The museum (712-329-8307) is open Tues through Sun from 10 a.m. to 4 p.m.

Council Bluffs is also home to the **Rails West Railroad Museum,** which is housed in the former Rock Island Depot that once served the city. Inside the 1898 structure are railroad memorabilia as well as a model railroad that depicts the railroad operations of the surrounding region. The museum is located at 1512 S. Main St., and is open from 10 a.m. to 4 p.m. Wed through Sat, and 1 to 4 p.m. on Sun, Apr through Oct. For more information call (712) 323-5182.

A fine place to eat is **Pizza King,** a combination steak and pizza restaurant at 1101 N. Broadway. Although the restaurant offers a full menu ranging from sandwiches to fine steaks, it is most famous for its thin-crust pizza, which is known far and wide as the best in the area. Visitors include "regulars" within a 50-mile radius as well as frequent interstate travelers who jump off at the US 6 exit. Pizza King is open seven days a week from 4 p.m. to midnight; there is plenty of seating, and prices are inexpen-

## didyouknow?

The town of Tabor (30 miles southeast of Council Bluffs) was once the headquarters of abolitionist John Brown.

sive to moderate. The phone number is (712) 323-4911. For more information about these and other attractions in the city, call the Council Bluffs Convention and Visitors Bureau at (800) 228-6878 or see www.councilbluffsiowa.com.

From Council Bluffs you can also explore the **Wabash Trace Nature Trail,** which is one of southwest Iowa's premier attractions. The 63-mile trail stretches between Council Bluffs and the small town of **Blanchard** on the Iowa-Missouri border, following an old railroad bed through the Loess Hills and rolling farm country. The trail's gentle inclines are perfect for walking and biking, winding through many small towns where travelers can quench their thirst and grab a bite to eat. The Council Bluffs trailhead is located on US 275, near Lewis Central School. The trail's user fee is $1 per day, $10 per year. For information see www.wabashtrace.org.

Twenty-five miles east of Council Bluffs on US 6 you'll find the **Nishna Heritage Museum** in the town of **Oakland.** Housed originally in a 1905 drygoods and grocery store, the museum now comprises four lots. Don't miss the bathtub in the barbershop, the scooter-bike, the collection of bride's dresses and children's clothes, and especially the Buster Brown display! The museum is located at 118–123 N. Main St. It is open from 10 a.m. to 3 p.m. Mon through Fri. Call (712) 482-6814 for more information.

## here'sjohnny!

Johnny Carson, former host of the *Tonight* television show, was born in Corning, Iowa, when his father was area manager of the Iowa-Nebraska Power & Light Company. His birthplace at the corner of Thirteenth Street and Davis Avenue is being restored and will eventually be open to the public.

About 25 miles east of Oakland is the small town of **Lewis,** home of the **Hitchcock House** (63788 567th Lane), one of the few remaining stations left in Iowa that were once stops on the Underground Railroad. Located on the route designated by the famous abolitionist John Brown, this brownstone house built in 1856 and inhabited by a sympathetic circuit preacher, his wife, and eight children, served as a shelter for escaping slaves en route to Canada

before the onset of the Civil War. The house is open from May to Sept, from 1 to 5 p.m. Tues through Sun. A small donation is charged. Call (712) 769-2323 for more information or to schedule a guided tour.

From the town of Lewis, travel south to the town of **Villisca** on US 71. There you'll find a museum located at the site of one of the state's most notorious crimes. In 1912 an ax murderer killed eight people in a home in this small town, a crime that remains unsolved to this day. The murders have been the subject of a play and a documentary and are still the subject of some speculation. Paranormal investigators continue to flock here. The **Ax Murder House,** where the killings took place, has been restored to its 1912 appearance and is

## Is It a Bird? Is It a Plane?

Okay, you're standing around in Stanton. You've admired the church, the town, the view. Why are you suddenly, unaccountably overtaken by a powerful and relentless thirst? Not just any thirst, but a craving, an overwhelming desire, a passionate and undeniable urge for a cup of coffee. And not just for any coffee, but for "a cup of the richest kind."

You may, if you cast your eyes skyward, discover the cause, for looming on the skyline is the world's largest Swedish coffeepot! Stantonites claim it holds 125,000 cups, but it's really just a water tower in disguise. However, if you pay attention to the sign at the base of the water tower, you'll find that Stanton was the birthplace of Virginia Christine, who played Mrs. Olson of Folger's Coffee fame. Did she grow up in the shadow of the famous coffeepot and so go on to pursue her career, or was the coffeepot put there to commemorate her? I would prefer to believe the former. Please don't tell me if I'm wrong, and I just might buy you a cup of coffee.

—T. S.

operated in conjunction with the Olson-Linn Museum, which contains dozens of antique cars, trucks, and tractors along with other historic artifacts. Begin your tour at the **Olson-Linn Museum** at 323 E. Fourth St. There you can learn about the crime and its aftermath before you visit the Ax Murder House. The museums are open daily from Apr to Oct (the truly brave can even schedule an overnight visit to the house). For information, see www.villiscaiowa.com.

Northwest of Villisca, on CR M63, lies the lovely community of **Stanton,** "the little white city," home of a predominantly Swedish population where almost all of the houses are painted white. Crowning the top of the hill around which the town is built is the beautiful gray-stoned Mamrelund Lutheran Church with its Gothic architecture and soaring steeple. You may also want to visit the Swedish Heritage and Cultural Center, located at 410 Hilltop Ave. Call (712) 829-2840 for more information.

For your final stop in western Iowa, visit **Clarinda,** about 20 miles south of Villisca on US 71. Glenn Miller, the famous big-band conductor, trombonist, and founder of the Glenn Miller Orchestra, was born here in 1904, and his birthplace, purchased by his daughter in 1989, has been restored by the **Glenn Miller Birthplace Society** and is open for tours May through Oct, from 1 to 5 p.m. Tues through Sun (a new, expanded museum is under construction). A great time to visit Clarinda is during the Glenn Miller Festival, held the second weekend in June. Highlights of the festival are informational talks and panels, musical performances, and dances. It is capped off by the society's own big band, which uses Miller's original Café Rouge bandstands. The address is 601 S. Glenn Miller Dr. Call (712) 542-2461 for more information or visit www .glennmiller.org.

## Places to Stay in Prairie Borderland

**ATLANTIC**

**Chestnut Charm Bed & Breakfast**
1409 Chestnut St.
(712) 243-5652
www.chestnutcharm.org
moderate to expensive

**CARROLL**

**Adams Street Bed & Breakfast**
726 N. Adams St.
(866) 792-0726
www.adamsstreetbandb
.com
inexpensive to moderate

**CHEROKEE**

**Prairie Path Lodge**
5148 "S" Ave.
(888) 299-4940
www.nwiowabb.com/
prairie.htm
inexpensive to moderate

### CLARINDA

**Colonial White House
Bed and Breakfast**
400 N. Sixteenth St.
(712) 542-5006
www.colonialwhitehouse
.com
moderate to expensive

### COUNCIL BLUFFS

**Historic Wickham House
Bed & Breakfast**
616 S. Seventh St.
(712) 328-1872
www.cbbedandbreakfast
.com
moderate

### DENISON

**Conner's Corner Bed
& Breakfast**
104 S. Fifteenth St.
(712) 263-8826
www.connerscorner.com
moderate

### ESSEX

**Railroad Inn**
508 Railroad St.
(712) 379-3267
www.homeinnstead.com
moderate to expensive

### OKOBOJI

**Wild Rose Inn**
2329 170th St.
(800) 855-7673
www.wildroseresort.com
expensive

## Places to Eat in Prairie Borderland

### ARNOLDS PARK

**Smokin' Jakes**
117 W. Broadway
(712) 332-5152
moderate

**Yesterdays**
131 W. Broadway
(712) 332-2353
moderate

### COUNCIL BLUFFS

**Tish's Restaurant**
1207 S. Thirty-fifth St.
I-29 exit 53A
(712) 323-5456
www.tishs.com
moderate

### RED OAK

**Kate and Lainie's Coffee
House**
322 E. Coolbaugh St.
(712) 623-2218
inexpensive

### SERGEANT BLUFF

**Aggie's**
107 Sergeant Square Dr.
(712) 943-8888
inexpensive

### SIOUX CITY

**Green Gables**
1800 Pierce St.
(712) 258-4246
moderate

**Luciano's**
1019 Historic St.
(712) 258-5174
www.lucianosrestaurant
iowa.com
moderate

### SPIRIT LAKE

**Garden View Cafe**
2213 33rd St.
(712) 336-449
inexpensive

### STANTON

**Susie's Kitchen**
404 Broad Ave.
(712) 829-2947
inexpensive

# Index